P9-DIG-860

LINCOLN CHRISTIAN COLLEGE AND SEMINARY

CANNOT BE CHECKED OUT

BILL MANLEY

THE PENGUIN
HISTORICAL ATLAS
OF ANCIENT EGYPT

PENGUIN BOOKS

Published by the Penguin Group
Penguin Books Ltd, 27 Wrights Lane, London W8 5TZ, England
Penguin Putnam Inc., 375 Hudson Street, New York, New York 10014, USA
Penguin Books Australia Ltd, Ringwood, Victoria, Australia
Penguin Books Canada Ltd, 10 Alcorn Avenue, Toronto, Ontario, Canada M4V 3B2
Penguin Books (NZ) Ltd, Private Bag 102902, NSMC, Auckland, New Zealand

Penguin Books Ltd, Registered Offices: Harmondsworth, Middlesex, England

First published 1996
06

Text copyright © Bill Manley, 1996
Design and maps copyright © Swanston Publishing Limited, 1996
All rights reserved

The moral right of the author has been asserted

Printed and bound in Great Britain by The Bath Press, Avon

Except in the United States of America, this book is sold subject
to the condition that it shall not, by way of trade or otherwise, be lent,
re-sold, hired out, or otherwise circulated without the publisher's
prior consent in any form of binding or cover other than that in
which it is published and without a similar condition including this
condition being imposed on the subsequent purchaser

ISBN 0–14–0–51331–0

Foreword

The history of pharaonic Egypt is not a subject which lends itself easily to presentation in map-form: the ancient world-view was rather like a mediaeval *mappa mundi,* with pharaoh taking the place of Jerusalem at the centre of the earth. Not surprisingly, therefore, the Ancient Egyptians left no maps of their own, apart from a few workmen's sketches, and their written descriptions of lands and events generally offer little information which can be translated onto a map straight-forwardly. Nevertheless, the present volume offers a continuous series of maps detailing the political and economic development of Ancient Egypt, and so stands as a tribute to the skill, ingenuity and hard work of the production team. Many aspects of the subject have never been presented in this way before.

On the maps, the names of sites in Egypt are often given in duplicate forms. The classical names in grey type are widely used, and it would serve no purpose to omit forms like Heliopolis and Thebes; but the ancient names are given in black type where they are known, e.g. Wast (for Thebes). If the classical/modern name of a place is obviously derived from the ancient name, then the former is given instead of the latter. This is because ancient names were not vocalised in writing and so their pronunciations are conjectural; for example, the classical form Memphis is used for ancient *mnnfr.*

I must acknowledge an enormous debt to the work of others, only some of which could be noted in the following suggestions for further reading. However, this is also a very personal interpretation of the history of Egypt reflecting in particular my own unease about the traditional "imperialist" view of Egypt's relations with Palestine. Some readers may find my emphasis on commerce and political pragmatism overstated, but it should at least serve to highlight some interesting topics and unresolved controversies. I would also like to thank sincerely the many people who have helped me. Within the production team, I am especially grateful to Malcolm Swanston, Stephen Haddelsey and Andrea Fairbrass—above all, for their patience! In various ways also: Dr José Pérez-Accino; Dr Mark Collier; Dr Aidan Dodson; Louise Lambe; Dr Robert Morkot; David Rohl; Dr Ian Shaw; Dr Louise Steel; Richard Stops; Richie Turnbull; Mr & Mrs Darouger. The hardest work was accomplished smilingly by my wife, Kathy McFall. Dr Morkot and David Rohl kindly provided photographs from their own research, and Dr Collier kindly provided the quote on page 46 from his unpublished collaborative work on the Kahun papyri. All other translations from extra-Biblical sources were prepared by myself, and so responsibility for any errors in the text and translations rests entirely with the author.

Bill Manley
Edinburgh, April 1996

for Kathy, and all the family

108877

Contents

Timeline: 5000 BC to 1490 BC

EGYPT	NUBIA	LANDS OF THE BIBLE	EUROPE & THE NEAR EAST
c. 5000 Earliest Egyptian settlements	c. 4500 trade between southern Egypt and Nubia	c. 5000 trade between northern Egypt and Palestine	c. 5000 Late Neolithic culture in Mesopotamia; organised irrigation farming
c. 4000 Nagada I artefacts apparent throughout south			
c. 3500 Nagada II artefacts apparent throughout Egypt	c. 3500 semi-nomadic A-group living and trading in southern Egypt and Nubia		c. 3500 urban settlement in Mesopotamia
c. 3000 major towns in south, associated with élite burials			c. 3000 early historic dynasties in Mesopotamia; cultural ascendancy of Sumer
c. 2950 earliest written texts from élite burials at Abydos			
c. 2900 Narmer or Aha first king of all Egypt; royal burial at Abydos	c. 2900 Aha attacks Nubia	c. 2900 Egyptian royal trade with Palestine	c. 2800 Gilgamesh, king of Uruk (?)
c. 2770 2nd Dynasty			
c. 2650 3rd Dynasty	c. 2700 Egyptians work Wadi Allaqi gold mines	c. 2700 Egyptian artefacts at Byblos	
c. 2630 Step Pyramid of Netjerykhet (Djoser) at Sakkara	c. 2600 depopulation of Wawat apparent		
c. 2575 4th Dynasty			
c. 2550 Great Pyramid of Khufu	c. 2500 Egyptian town founded at Buhen		
c. 2465 5th Dynasty; sun temples at Abu Gurob			
c. 2323 6th Dynasty	c.2400 repopulation of Wawat by C-group		c. 2325 Sargon, king of Agade, builds an empire in Babylonia and Assyria
c. 2150 death of Pepy II marks end of Old Kingdom	c. 2250–2240 Harkhuf's expeditions to Nubia		c. 2090 Utukhegal reasserts historic independence of Sumer c. 2080 Ur-Nammu establishes pre-eminence in Babylonia of 3rd Dynasty of Ur
c. 2050 war between Thebes and Asyut			
c. 1994–1986 civil war; Montjuhotep II king of reunified Egypt	c. 1993 tribute levied from Wawat; southern oases occupied by Egyptian troops		c. 1995 regional authority of Ur dwindles during reign of Ibbi-Sin
c. 1937 12th Dynasty; Amenemhat I establishes royal residence at Itjtawy	c. 1913–1903 armies of Senusret I reduce Wawat to Egyptian control; first series of forts built	c. 1920 border with Egypt fortified and policed	
c. 1842 workmen's town founded at Kahun	c. 1840 Red Sea port founded at Sawu		
	c. 1829–1818 Senusret III pushes Egyptian control beyond second cataract: second series of forts built	c. 1830 campaign of Senusret III in southern Palestine	c. 1790 Shamshi-Adad I, king of Assyria builds an empire in Mesopotamia
c. 1759 end of 12th Dynasty	c. 1750–1650 Egyptian garrisons gradually assimilated into local population		c. 1765 Hammurabi, king of Babylon c. 1730 Hammurabi attacks Mari
c. 1639 Hyksos kingdom at Avaris		c. 1730 Yantin, governor of Byblos, buried according to Egyptian funerary cult.	c. 1650 early Kassite kings at Babylon c. 1640 earthquake destruction affects Minoan Crete
	c. 1560 unified kingdom of Kush		c. 1550 early shaft-graves at Mycenae
c. 1540 Kamose attacks city of Avaris	c. 1540 Kamose captures Buhen; Viceroy of Nubia appointed		
c. 1539 18th Dynasty			
c.1520 Ahmose defeats kingdom of Avaris		c. 1520–1518 Sharuhen beseiged by Egyptian army	c. 1520 volcanic event affects Minoan Crete
c. 1493 Valley of the Kings and workmen's village at Deir el-Medina founded by Thutmose I	c. 1490 Wawat divided into five provinces under Egyptian control		c. 1490 army of Thutmose I marches to Mittani

Timeline: 1489 BC to 841 BC

EGYPT	NUBIA	LANDS OF THE BIBLE	EUROPE & THE NEAR EAST
c. 1473 Hatshepsut becomes coregent with Thutmose III	c. 1460 Hatshepsut's expedition to Punt	c. 1457 Thutmose III captures Joppa, and triumphs at the Battle of Megiddo c. 1453 Thutmose III attacks Kadesh	
			c. 1447 army of Thutmose III marches to Mittani
	c. 1430 unconquered Kush becomes a trading partner of Egypt	c. 1441 Thutmose III campaigns in Southern Palestine c. 1425–1418 Amenhotep II campaigns in Takhsy, Galilee and Palestine	c. 1425 end of Minoan palace culture in Crete
	c. 1400 Egyptian town and fortress founded at Napata		c. 1400 floruit of palace culture in Mycenaean Greece
	c. 1385 Egyptian expansion into the gold mines of Ikuyta and Ibhet	c. 1350 Byblos threatened by Amurru	
c. 1341 new royal residence and cemetery founded at el-Amarna	c. 1334 Amenhotep IV orders suppression of rebellion in Ikuyta	c. 1331 Aziru of Amurru switches allegiance to Hatti; Labayu killed by Egyptian–sponsored coalition	c. 1333 campaign of Hittite king Suppululiuma I reaches Ugarit, Qatna and Kadesh; Assuruballit asserts Assyrian independence from Babylon
			c. 1318 Carchemish conquered by Hittites c. 1304 Carchemish threatened by Assyria
c. 1295 19th Dynasty		c. 1290 Seti I engages Hittite army at Kadesh	
		c. 1275 Ramesses II fights to stalemate at Battle of Kadesh c. 1258 peace treaty between Egypt and Hatti divides influence in Syria and Canaan	c. 1260 Shalmaneser I initiates Assyrian expansion
c. 1209 incursions by Libyan tribes and others repulsed by Merenptah	c. 1249 temple of Ramesses II at Abu Simbel		c. 1210 Tukulti-Ninurta I of Assyria conquers Babylon
c. 1186 20th Dynasty			
c. 1180–1174 Libyan incursions repulsed by Ramesses III			c. 1185 demise of Hittite empire
c. 1177 incursion by "Sea Peoples" driven back in the delta		c. 1150 appearance in Palestine of locally-made "Philistine" ware	c. 1150 beginning of Greek Dark Age
c. 1111 major investigation into tomb-robbery in the Valley of the Kings	c. 1087 Panehsy invades Egypt and occupies Thebes c. 1080 Panehsy's regime secedes from Egypt		
c. 1080 Herihor appointed high priest and king of Thebes		c. 1080 Wenamun's voyage to Byblos	
c. 1069 Smendes becomes king at Tanis			
		c. 1030 Saul, first king of Israel	
		c. 970 Solomon, king of Israel	
c. 945 22nd Dynasty; Shoshenk I becomes king at Tanis		c. 950 Hiram I, king of Tyre	
		c. 930 division of Solomon's kingdom into Judah and Israel	
		c. 925 Shoshenk I invades Israel	
			c. 900 earliest Phoenician settlement in Cyprus
		c. 879 stela from Moab, recording revolt against Israeli rule: earliest historical record of Biblical events c. 853 coalition of rulers, including Ahab of Israel, defeated by Assyria at the Battle of Karkar	859 Shalmaneser III, king of Assyria 841 Jehu of Israel pays homage to Shalmaneser III

Timeline: 840 BC to 521 BC

EGYPT	NUBIA	LANDS OF THE BIBLE	EUROPE & THE NEAR EAST
c. 836–825 civil disturbances at Thebes follow the appointment of king's son Osorkon as high priest			
c. 818 23rd Dynasty; Pedubast I becomes king at Leontopolis			c. 800 foundation of Carthage c. 776 foundation of Olympic Games c. 750 earliest Greek colonisation of Italy
	c. 760 Kashta becomes king at Napata		
c. 728 expansionism of chief of Ma Tefnakht halted by Piy	c. 728 Piy invades Egypt		c. 745 Tiglath-Pileser III, king of Assyria, initiates period of expansion 717 Carchemish captured by Assyrians
		722 Samaria, capital of Israel, captured by Assyria	
		701 Hezekiah of Judah allied with Egypt against Assyria; Egyptian-Nubian army defeated at Battle of Elteka	701 Sennacherib king of Assyria
		700 Byblos captured by Assyria	
	c. 690 Taharka initiates anti-Assyrian policy		c. 680 Esarhaddon, king of Assyria
c. 674 Assyrian invasion defeated			
c. 671 Assyrian army reaches Memphis		671 Tyre captured by Assyria	c. 669 Assurbanipal, king of Assyria
664 Assyrian army sacks Thebes	664 Taharka flees Egypt and dies at Napata		
656 Psamtek I, king of all Egypt			c. 650 Gyges of Lydia allied with Egypt against Assyria
		c. 630 Psamtek I occupies Ashdod	c. 616 Psamtek I campaigns against Babylon, in alliance with Assyria
			c. 605 Egyptian armies defeated by Babylon at Carchemish and Hamath
601 Babylonian invasion repulsed			
c. 600 Red Sea canal initiated by Neko II	c. 600 Anlamani assembles army in Wawat	c. 597 early deportations from Judah to Babylon 592 Psamtek II tours Philistia	
	593 Psamtek II attacks Napata		
		589 Apries relieves Jerusalem in support of anti-Babylonian revolt	
570 Defeat of Egyptian army at Kyrene leads to removal of Apries in favour of Amasis; Naukratis established as centre of Graeco-Egyptian trade		587 Nebuchadrezzar of Babylon captures Jerusalem; Judaean population transported to Babylon	570 Apries received in Babylon; given support of Nebuchadrezzar
567 Babylonian army defeated, and Apries killed in battle			
			560 Cyprus occupied by Amasis
			c. 559 Cyrus, king of Persia
			546 Cyrus conquers Lydia
			545 Cambyses leads Persian occupation of Cyprus
		539 Judaean exiles begin to return after fall of Babylon	538 Cyrus captures Babylon
526 Egyptian army defeated by Persia at Battle of Pelusium			530 Cambyses, king of Persia
525 Psamtek III deposed, and later executed by Cambyses		515 reconsecration of temple in Jerusalem	521 Darius I, king of Persia

Timeline: 520 BC to 305 BC

EGYPT	NUBIA	LANDS OF THE BIBLE	EUROPE & THE NEAR EAST
			490 Persia defeated by Greek forces at Marathon
			485 Xerxes, king of Persia
			475 eruption of Etna in Sicily
c. 459 Athenian ships from Cyprus sail into the Nile in support of anti-Persian revolt			
c. 455 anti-Persian rebellion of Inaros brutally suppressed			c. 449 Peace of Callias agreed between Athens and Persia
c. 440 Herodotos visits Egypt			447 construction of the Parthenon begun in Athens
c. 414 anti-Persian rebellion of Sais	c. 431 Amunnetyerike first king known to rule at Meroë		
c. 404 Amyrtaeus, king of Sais			409 Hannibal's first expedition to Sicily
c. 397 Nepherites I, king at Mendes			
c. 374 Persian invasion repulsed by Nectanebo I			
c. 358 Takos deposed			359 Philip II, king of Macedon
c. 351 Persian invasion repulsed by Nectanebo II			356 birth of Alexander of Macedon
343 Egypt conquered by Artaxerxes III	c. 335 military campaign of Nastasen		336 Philip of Macedon murdered; Alexander emerges as successor
332 Egypt conquered by Alexander of Macedon			323 death of Alexander at Babylon
323–311 Ptolemy, son of Lagos, regent for Philip Arrhidaeus and Alexander II		319 Egypt invades Phoenicia	312 Seleucid Dynasty established in Babylonia with Egyptian support
305 Ptolemy becomes king	c. 310 Nastasen last king buried at Nuri		

I: The Origins of Ancient Egypt

Egypt is a diverse, cosmopolitan land, in which agriculture nevertheless requires communities to work together for economic success. Ease of travel on the River Nile promoted close contacts in prehistoric times so that constantly increasing economic and cultural cohesion was obvious centuries ahead of any administrative union.

"I am one loved by his father, praised by his mother, who loves his brothers and sisters. I buried my father, Djau, more splendidly and more correctly than any of his peers in this Nile valley. I begged as a favour from the person of my lord, the dual king Neferkara (Pepy II), that a coffin, cloth, and festal perfume should be issued for this Djau. His person caused a coffin made of Lebanese wood to be brought, with perfume, oil, and two-hundred strips of finest linen... The same was never done for any of his peers."
Tomb inscription of the governor Djau

Until the advent of Egyptology, the principal sources for the study of Ancient Egypt were classical authors. The most influential has been the Greek Herodotos, whose *Histories* examined the relationship between Europe and the vast kingdoms of Asia and Africa. Of the former, the greatest in his time was Persia; of the latter, the greatest for many centuries had been Egypt. In the mid-5th century BC, Herodotos visited Egypt to see for himself a land and people whose customs and beliefs, he maintained, were the exact opposite of those found anywhere else. Even the wildlife—including sacred cats and bulls, crocodiles, hippopotamuses, the sacred ibis and the phoenix—was a unique mix of the exotic and fantastical. Another influential source was the Egyptian priest Manetho, who wrote a history of his country in Greek in the 3rd century BC in order to establish that his nation was the oldest on earth. It was Manetho who first divided the kings of Egypt into thirty dynasties, although it is not always easy to reconcile his arrangement with the evidence of earlier sources. His work has not survived, but excerpts—and possibly quotes—were preserved by later authors.

Influenced by these and other authors, Europe has long seen Egypt as a source of wisdom and power, and Egyptian images have been adopted by Europeans since the cult of Isis flourished in Imperial Rome; a continuous thread of influence can be traced from the obelisks of the emperor Hadrian to the pharaonic bee-motif used by the Bonaparte family. It is not so surprising, therefore, that the modern study of Ancient Egypt was born out of colonial warfare following Napoleon Bonaparte's invasion of Egypt in1798. The latter-day warlord was accompanied by a gang of *savants* charged with the task of recording and interpreting the wonders of the pharaohs—a task which they undertook with admirable vigour and success. Their presence was not the glint of enlightenment but witness to the fact that Bonaparte was the latest ruler to be seduced by the myth of Egypt, in which he wished to clothe himself. Nevertheless, the efforts of the *savants* allowed copies of ancient monuments to circulate in Europe, using which a group of scholars—including Jean François Champollion, Thomas Young and later Karl Richard Lepsius—were able once more to translate Egyptian texts.

Nowadays texts are supplemented by insights gained from archaeology and scientific analysis. A picture has emerged of a country whose political and economic integrity was a constant source of strength, but whose geographic and cultural diversity has been obscured by an incomplete material record. In the past, for example, excavation has tended to concentrate on the well-preserved temples and tombs of the Nile valley, in preference to settlement sites which lie awkwardly buried beneath modern towns. The wet, often waterlogged, Nile delta is a difficult archaeological challenge and has less often been studied, although excavations there confirm Herodotos' observation that it was a region distinct from the valley in many ways. Another distortion in the record arises from the ancient understanding of the earth as "twin lands"—a balance of opposites expressed in many forms: the lands of the rising and setting suns; the fertile fields and sterile desert; the lands of the living and the deadand so on. To express this awareness, two styles of

Above: Ivory label from the Sakkara tomb of a 1st Dynasty official named Sekhemkasedj. The label originally indicated the contents of a jar which was part of his burial equipment, and is typical of the very earliest hieroglyphic texts. At the top left, the "Horus-name" of king Djet has been written in a rectangular enclosure (representing the palace), surmounted by a hawk (the symbol of the sun-god Horus).

Below: A view of the 4th Dynasty pyramid at Meidum, probably built for king Snofru. The shape of the pyramid has been distorted by the deliberate pulverizing of its original stone casing in order to produce agricultural lime in Roman and Arab times. The king emerged as the spiritual leader of his nation during the early dynastic period, and his tomb became the most important construction project; during the Old Kingdom, royal pyramids dominated the skyline, symbolizing the belief that the death of the king was the spiritual link between earth and heaven.

architecture, art and writing were devised: one lively, creative and temporary; the other formal, traditional and enduring. For example, the largest of royal palaces were built mainly of mud-brick—eventually to crumble—whereas even the smallest religious shrine was built of stone. As a result our received images of Egypt are funerary and religious, and—since the ability to write was an indication of power—a typical Egyptian as transmitted into modern perception is likely to have been an élite male corpse!

Prehistoric Egypt

The earliest Egyptians were farmers who settled near the Nile *c.* 5000 BC. Agriculture is by no means an inevitable way of life beside the Nile—there are many Nilotic peoples in equatorial Sudan with pastoral economies—but it has been the foundation of Egyptian society since its beginning. Exploiting the inundation effectively demanded that communities work together to fashion the basins, irrigation canals and terracing which held the flood-water over the fields until it deposited its full weight of silt (*see page 18*). The farmers could then cultivate a wide variety of crops including emmer and barley, flax, lentils and chickpeas, lettuce, onions, figs and pomegranates. The infrastructure required was massive and labour-intensive, but still vulnerable to neglect or chance: a year's crops could be lost to a community following the failure of any single component. The inundation itself, though generally reliable, was another source of anxiety: too large an inundation could burst dykes and flood villages; too little flood-water would reduce the land available for planting.

The demands of agriculture in Egypt have obvious implications for social organization because it was beyond the capacity of an individual working alone to exploit the inundation effectively, and so success was based on large-scale co-ordination of work. It was perhaps this fundamental feature of life which promoted increasing uniformity in the material culture of prehistoric Egypt, as administrative and commercial structures emerged which encompassed large areas of the country. The Nile itself was the tie which binds—allowing the easy transport of workers, administrators and resources between far-flung communities and work-sites rarely located more than a few kilometres from the river. By *c.* 4000 BC the loose assemblage of artefacts indicative of the Nagada I cultural phase was in use throughout much of the Nile valley; by the development phase known as Nagada II, about 600 years before the pharaonic period, a range of typical objects was in use throughout the whole

country, including parts of the delta. The greatest uniformity is apparent in the grave-goods of an emergent social élite, which controlled the commercial networks and so grew rich enough to be buried with gold and silver jewellery. However, this élite—greater in number and culturally more diverse than in pharaonic times—did not form a coherent ruling class, so there is no reason to maintain the belief of some earlier scholars that the unification of Egypt was imposed by force of arms from the top of society.

The Early Dynastic Period

It used to be possible to argue that the formation of the unified state coincided with the accession of the 1st Dynasty, and with the earliest written texts from Egypt. This belief was based on a native tradition that two kingdoms—the kingdom of Lower Egypt and the kingdom of Upper Egypt—were brought together by the first king, Menes. It was widely believed that the most celebrated early hieroglyphic monument—the palette of King Narmer from Hierakonpolis—commemorated this very event. Unfortunately, the progress of research has tended to undermine such a convenient equation. Texts recently discovered in the oldest royal cemetery at Abydos confirm that writing began at least three decades before the 1st Dynasty, and archaeology has tended to suggest that the prehistoric kingdom of Lower Egypt owes more to mythology than history. Menes, indeed, has become a kind of King Arthur figure—partly historical perhaps, but largely legendary, and not too much credence can be lent to the traditions surrounding him in later times.

It seems more realistic to recognize that Egypt became a unified cultural and economic domain long before her first king ascended the throne. Political unification followed gradually as local districts created integrated trading networks, and the administrators of the regions were able to organize agriculture and labour on an ever-larger scale. As much as a century before the 1st Dynasty, well-planned and fortified towns existed in southern Upper Egypt at Nagada, Hierakonpolis and Elephantine; at the first two of these sites, a ruling class was buried in elaborate tombs. The kings of the 1st Dynasty, however, were buried at Abydos. It has been suggested that the tombs of Nagada and Hierakonpolis are those of predynastic kings, in which case kingship may have developed in more than one region, and the 1st Dynasty should be seen as the victors in a struggle for supremacy in the Nile valley involving at least three powerful proto-kingdoms. The scenario is distorted by lack of evidence concerning the north of the country at this time—so giving undue prominence to the southern towns—but it can be compared to the Second Intermediate Period, when the Theban administration grew to dominate the Nile valley, before annexing a relatively impotent delta region divided into several smaller kingdoms. Nevertheless, it is not even clear that the ruling élites of the main towns were different people, rather than different members of the same ruling group. Abydos was later the cult site of Osiris—king of the dead—and a pilgrimage site of national importance from the Old Kingdom onwards; this may be precisely because the earliest kings were buried there, but it may also follow that the site was deliberately created for royal burial, and that kings buried there were not necessarily from the surrounding region—they may have originated in Hierakonpolis, Nagada or somewhere else.

The early royal titulary was developed around the "Horus-name", which identified the king in his palace as the legitimate heir to a divine throne, and was used by virtually every later pharaoh. During the 2nd Dynasty, Peribsen adopted instead a "Seth-name"—thereby identifying himself

View of the royal cemetery at Abusir showing the tomb of Ptahshepses, a 5th Dynasty vizîr and son-in-law of king Nyuserra. It had been normal during the 3rd–4th Dynasties, for men who held high office to be closely related to the king, but it became increasingly unusual after Ptahshepses' time. His tomb is an exceptionally large example of the mastaba type, consisting of a subterranean burial chamber covered by a series of partly-decorated rooms for the burial equipment, which even included a pair of funerary boats—a feature otherwise unknown in a non-royal tomb.

with Horus' irreconcilable enemy in later mythology; his successor, Khasekhemwy, used a conciliatory "Horus-and-Seth-name". This observation has been mooted as evidence of a continuing civil war between rival factions for whom the two gods were emblems, but there is no compelling evidence to support this. Probably the variation in the two names simply indicates that royal conventions, strictly adhered to in later periods, such as the "Horus-name" were still being formulated at this early date. Likewise, the formal styles of art and the iconography of kingship were not established in their definitive forms until the 3rd Dynasty.

It is not possible to make definite statements about the kingship and government of the early dynastic period except insofar as they anticipate the Old Kingdom. The kings buried at Abydos were surrounded in death by their courtiers—in the case of king Djer by nearly six hundred—but not usually by members of the royal family, high officials or local administrators as was to become the custom in the Old Kingdom. The tombs of officials were built throughout the country from Nagada to Sakkara, some of the latter being so massive they were originally identified as royal tombs. However, the locations of burials provide no definite clues about the composition of the highest levels of society, nor about the shape of the administration. Nevertheless, the tombs at Abydos—which were only one part of much larger funerary complexes—are the major monuments of the period, and for this reason alone the cultural pre-eminence of the king is obvious. Officials were also identified by titles which typically suggest that the source of their authority was a relationship with the king or palace, rather than any hereditary right to hold high office. This was to be a fundamental feature of pharaonic government in later periods.

The Old Kingdom

Conventionally, the Old Kingdom is defined as the 3rd–6th Dynasties, although the division from the formative early dynastic period is an arbitrary one. A single line of kings probably occupied the throne from the 2nd Dynasty until the end of the 4th Dynasty. Many stylistic traditions associated with the late predynastic period still flourished during the 3rd Dynasty, and the burial practices of the mass of the population changed very little throughout the intervening years. However, by the 4th Dynasty traditional items of high status such as ceremonial knives, mace heads and palettes were no longer produced, since the right to work materials like stone or ivory could only be granted as an exceptional royal privilege. Images and prayers in the tombs of the ruling élite in the 3rd Dynasty had assumed the recognizable forms of pharaonic Egypt, and were dominated by the presence of the king as the source and guarantor of authority and justice, so that even regional officials operated essentially as royal agents. In fact, many of the highest offices of the land were occupied by members of the royal family itself—including most of the vizîrs of the 3rd–4th Dynasties.

If there is a convenient marker for the beginning of the Old Kingdom, then it is surely the Step Pyramid of Netjerykhet (Djoser) at Sakkara, the earliest of the vast pyramid complexes of the god-kings. Thereafter, the preparation of the royal burial became the major industry of Old Kingdom Egypt, requiring not only the stone pyramid itself—complete with an enormous hard-stone sarcophagus for the royal corpse—but also a series of connected temples and causeways for the king's funeral ceremonies, smaller pyramids for the royal women, and avenues of tombs in which the officials could accompany their lord into eternity. The complex was also the country's major temple, devoted principally to the mortuary cult of the king himself. The perfectly formed pyramids—over shadowing the settlements of the living from on high—are still, as they were intended to be, the most enduring image of the confidence of a great nation at the dawn of history.

The reasons for the apparent decline in the authority of the king after the 6th Dynasty are as obscure as those which first promoted it. The curtain can conveniently be said to fall with the death of Pepy II after a 96 year reign. Pepy was buried in a major pyramid complex at Sakkara, but his courtiers were laid to rest in an undistinguished cemetery reminiscent of those of the early dynastic period. This was a clear indication that the palace had lost the ability to organize major royal building projects on the scale of the previous 500 years. Whether the cause of this was political weakness or a change in the ideology of kingship is a moot point, because the following era—the First Intermediate Period—is the most obscure of the whole pharaonic period. It is widely assumed that the long reign of Pepy II was itself a cause, he had become king as a mere infant, and later ruled for decades as an old man; either of these periods may have resulted in weak government. On the other hand, the end of the Old Kingdom may have resulted from the administration reasserting the less restrained position it had held in relation to the king during the early dynastic period; such a development may have helped to diminish the emphasis placed on royal pyramid-complexes in a society which would not—or could not—support such elaborate schemes any longer. Although there was no challenge to the king's authority, his central presence was tempered by the power of local officials, as the balance of reponsibility for government shifted from the palace to the provinces.

Foreign Contact

The traditional borders of Egypt are determined by passage on the Nile: east and west, Egypt is bordered by desert, to the north by the Mediterranean, and to the south by the granite rocks of the first cataract. None of these borders is impassable, but they clearly defined a territory within which the early state of Egypt could emerge with a sense of common identity. However, even the earliest settlers had an extensive network of direct and indirect commercial contacts with foreign populations, which regularly moved commerce in and out of the country. Communities in the north of Egypt were able to trade by land with Palestine and Sinai, (which supported a settled population until the early 3rd millennium BC); other countries along the Mediterranean coast were probably contacted indirectly, although foreign traders may have reached Egypt by sea even at this early stage. Traders certainly reached Egypt via the Red Sea from Palestine, Sinai or even Mesopotamia during the late predynastic period, to judge from images of ships sketched in the desert wadis of Upper Egypt, and a variety of foreign motifs current in the grave-goods and religious art of the social élite. During the early dynastic period and the Old Kingdom, expeditions to the mines of Wadi Maghara and Serabit el-Khadim were accompanied by troops conscripted by the king, and the movement of commercial goods in and out of the country became a royal monopoly.

The foreign land which had the most crucial part to play in the history of Ancient Egypt was Nubia. Traders in Upper Egypt were in contact with their Nubian counterparts from the mid-5th millennium BC, thereby establishing an economic and cultural link that would thrive throughout the pharaonic period. In later prehistoric times, Nubia was settled by a semi-nomadic population known collectively as the A-group, some of whom also traded and settled in southern Egypt. Nubia was rich in valuable minerals, and its chiefs transported incense, oils, ebony, ivory and animal skins from the African hinterland. The emergence of a unified state allowed Egypt to assert its relative strength in Nubia, at the expense of the less settled A-group. An Egyptian army invaded Nubia as early as the reign of Aha, and the regular appearance of Egyptian merchants and soldiers at the second cataract coincided with a long-lasting decline in the population of Lower Nubia. It was in this period that Egyptians first began working the Nubian gold-mines, which would later be the basis for Egypt's commercial superiority in the Ancient Near East. During the 5th Dynasty a new population, identified as the C-group, began to settle Lower Nubia, leading to fears for the security of Egyptian caravans, and perhaps even for the safety of communities in the south of the country. A social élite amongst this group began to establish their own chiefdoms, and to challenge the commercial hegemony of Egypt in the region. As a result the governors of Elephantine—the southern-most town of Egypt—became *de facto* ambassadors to Nubia, entrusted to maintain alliances of goodwill with the local chiefs, but also required to dominate the caravan routes running between Egypt and Nubia through commercial wit, or force of arms if necessary.

The boat of king Khufu (4th Dynasty) has been reconstructed using mostly original fragments. Boats were the principal means of transport in Ancient Egypt, and this example was built, using imported timber, in order to carry the king in procession; the royal cabin is located in the centre of the boat, behind the pilot's canopy. According to one ancient belief, the dead king ascended to heaven to travel in his boat alongside the sun-god, and so it was dismantled and buried with companions in five boat-shaped pits alongside the Great Pyramid at Giza.

The Egyptian Environment

The source of life in Egypt is the river Nile, and the cycle of the seasons, in ancient times, was dictated by the rise and fall of its waters; but the wealth of the nation arose from commerce.

"Not only is the Egyptian climate peculiar to that country, and the Nile different in the way it behaves from rivers elsewhere, but the manners and customs of the Egyptians themselves seem to be the opposite of the typical practices of mankind." Herodotos, *The Histories".*

The river Nile cuts a course through the Sahara desert in north east Africa. For much of its length it is fringed by a thin strip of cultivable land, before sweeping out across a low-lying, marshy delta. Near Cusae, a single branch of the river feeds the broad, wet Faiyum region. Elsewhere the land is arid and hostile, with only a string of oases in the western desert able to support a settled community. Rainfall is rare, and occasionally destructive—reducing homes and granaries to mud and unleashing flash-floods from the desert. Nevertheless, because of the river, Egypt is an exceptionally fertile country, where agriculture has been the basis of society since the beginning of history.

The Nile is formed by the confluence of the White Nile, the Blue Nile and the Atbara. The Blue Nile and Atbara are filled with water, silt and vegetation by summer rains in Ethiopia and Sudan. Consequently—until the building of major dams in our own century—the Nile in Egypt began to rise and by August had burst its banks and inundated the flood-plain. When the water receded, it left a silty soil, which was the literal basis for Herodotos' celebrated remark that Egypt is given as a gift of the river. The crumbly silt also gave the Egyptians a name for their country: *kemet*, "black land"; anywhere not touched by the inundation was *desert*, "red land". The seasons of the year were the phases of the river: *akhet* ("inundation"), *peret* ("emergence"), and *shemu* ("dry time"). The Nile was also a calm and undemanding highway, conveying traffic north with the stream, or south with the prevailing winds. Only in certain areas, known as cataracts, has the river not cut a true course; the first cataract, at Elephantine, marks the traditional boundary between Egypt and Nubia, her closest relation geographically and culturally.

Most ancient Egyptians lived at a subsistence level, but not usually in hardship. The constancy of agriculture afforded the nation a self-sufficiency which was enhanced by the region's mineral wealth. The Nile valley is formed of sandstone and limestone, and both were used in building; granite, diorite, quartzite, alabaster and many other stones were available within easy reach of the river, and could be transported by barge over great distances. In the eastern desert and Sinai, copper and semi-precious stones—including turquoise and amethyst—were available, along with ores such as malachite used for cosmetics and paints; natron from the western desert was used for hygiene and purification. And, of course, there was gold: one covetous foreign ruler remarked that gold was in Egypt like the sands of the desert! Such wealth allowed Egypt to exploit her location as the tie which binds Africa and the Near East. Constant commercial traffic brought the one commodity Egypt conspicuously lacked—straight, true timber—and a dazzling array of incenses, spices and luxury goods: Asian lapis-lazuli, Assyrian silver, East African ebony and ivory, and Cretan olive oil.

The Egyptian landscape exhibits a stark contrast between the Nile flood plain and the surrounding desert. Without the soil brought by the inundation of the river, human settlement would be difficult in this part of Africa; because of it, however, Egypt is an exceptionally fertile land, enriched still further by the mineral wealth of the desert.

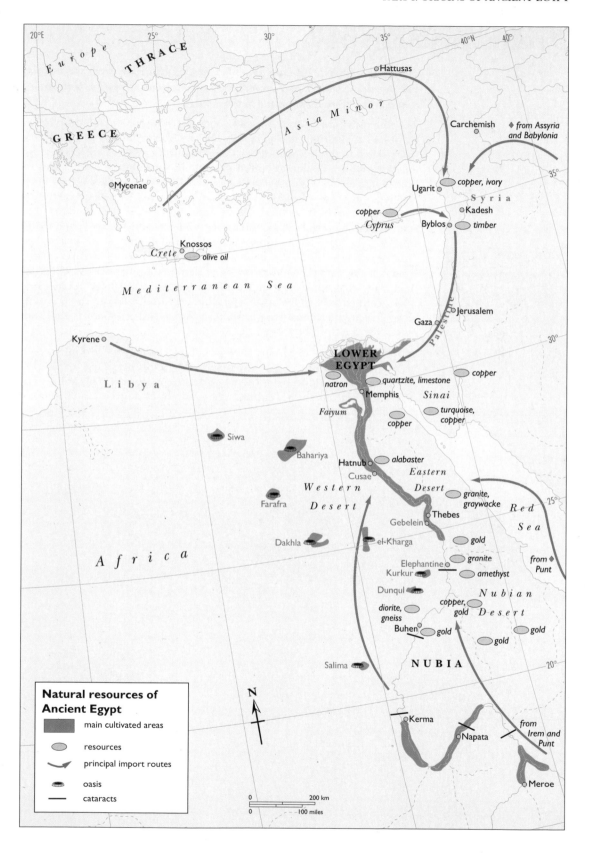

Natural resources of Ancient Egypt

- main cultivated areas
- resources
- principal import routes
- oasis
- cataracts

Europe

THRACE

GREECE

Asia Minor

Hattusas

Carchemish

♦ from Assyria and Babylonia

Mycenae

Ugarit ○ copper, ivory

Syria

copper

Cyprus

Kadesh

Byblos ○ timber

Knossos

Crete ○ olive oil

Mediterranean Sea

Jerusalem

Gaza ○

Palestine

LOWER EGYPT

natron ○ copper

Kyrene ○

Libya

quartzite, limestone

Memphis

Sinai

Faiyum

copper

turquoise, copper

Siwa

Bahariya

Hatnub ○ alabaster

Cusae ○

Eastern Desert

Western Desert

Farafra

granite, graywacke

Red Sea

Gebelein ○

Thebes ○

Dakhla

el-Kharga

gold

Africa

Elephantine ○ granite

from Punt

Kurkur

amethyst

Dunqul

Nubian

diorite, gneiss

copper, gold

Desert

Buhen ○ gold

gold gold

Salima

NUBIA

N

Kerma

from Irem and Punt

Napata

Meroe

0   200 km

0   100 miles

Prehistoric Egypt

Agriculture became the basis of settled life in Egypt many centuries before the pharaonic period, and promoted close economic interaction between communities from Elephantine to the delta.

"We see that the beginning of Egypt is the oldest of all kingdoms, so let us record its beginning...I will put first the reigns of the gods which are recorded by the Egyptians themselves."

Africanus' Chronicle (AD 220)

The River Nile was by no means always naturally hospitable to human settlement and civilization. It is generally believed that around 700 BC climatic changes made the Egyptian deserts hotter and the river valley less marshy, encouraging the human adoption of agriculture along the latter's peripheries. The Faiyum region became larger and more temperate at this time, and it is here that the earliest Egyptian settlements have been identified dating from at least 5000 BC. Other early sites include Merimda on the southern fringe of the delta, and Omari, Matmar and Badari in the valley. Interestingly, these communities already cultivated emmer and barley, the crops which were to be the staples of agriculture in the pharaonic period. Although the material cultures of the different communities are quite distinct from each other, they show clear evidence of widespread trading networks: communities in the north typically traded with Palestine and the lands along the Mediterranean coast, whereas people further south traded with Nubia and the lands bordering the Red Sea.

By *c.* 4000 BC a more expansive material culture can be observed in cemeteries from Elephantine to Asyut, characterized by a distinctive type of red pottery with a polished black rim (hence "black-topped ware"). This pottery has been used to distinguish a cultural phase known as Nagada I, after the site

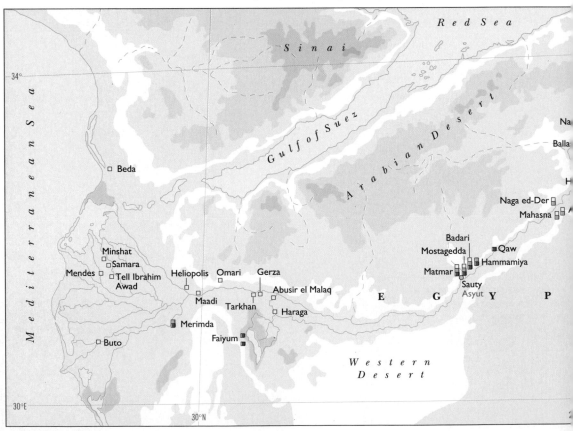

A detail of the "Hunter's Palette" from Hierakonpolis; such objects, based on palettes used for grinding cosmetics, were typical temple-offerings in the late predynastic-early dynastic period. Various wild animals, notably a lion, are shown defying a group of hunters, and the scene may be symbolically associated with an early ruler or king. Typically for the period, the pictorial elements are arranged with a dynamic freedom that was usually moderated in later royal art.

where it was first identified; it is important to remember that such labels refer to a group of typical objects and not to a people as such, and most archaeologists stress the obvious continuity linking Egypt in the Nagada I phase with the earlier cultures. The major industry of Nagada culture was the production of stone vessels and ceremonial items such as mace-heads and animal-shaped cosmetic palettes. Many of these were worked in very hard stones, such as basalt and granite, and the craftsmen attained a level of skill never matched in pharaonic Egypt.

By the phase of development known as Nagada II, beginning about 600 years before the pharaonic period, Nagada-type artefacts were in use as far north as Buto. It is likely that this diffusion of objects and ideas was the result of trade and the increasing cohesion of Egypt as a cultural and economic system, rather than evidence of the spread of a dominant group of people. The wide-ranging character of trade in Nagada II is evident in the appearance *c.* 4300 BC of so-called "wavy-handled pots", which were obviously inspired by vessels imported from Palestine and Syria. The decoration of these pots emphasizes hunting, athletics, warfare, boating and dancing—activities. which in historical times were associated with the rule of kings, but which at this time may illustrate a growing sense of community. Nagada culture was most uniform in the grave-goods of a social élite, which had grown rich from trading and presumably maintained close personal links with one another. However, the largest northern communities, at Buto, Merimda, Omari and Maadi, maintained practices which were still distinct from those of the south, and some of which (such as the burial of the dead beneath the house) continued in parts of the delta into the pharaonic period.

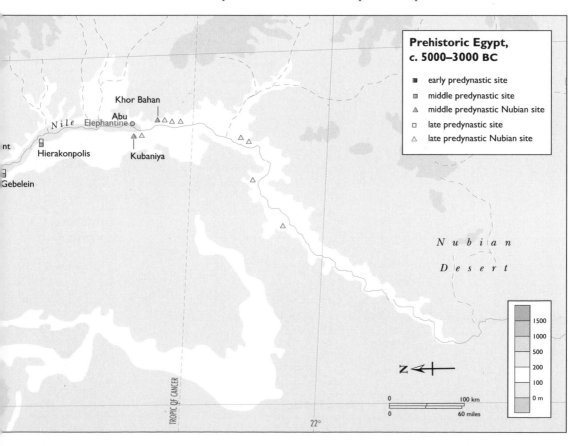

Prehistoric Egypt,
c. 5000–3000 BC

■ early predynastic site
▨ middle predynastic site
▲ middle predynastic Nubian site
□ late predynastic site
△ late predynastic Nubian site

The Emergence of Egypt

The increasing cohesion of society in late prehistoric Egypt and the expansion of district administrations fostered a ruling class, and eventually a belief in divine kingship.

"After the spirits and demigods, the 1st Dynasty is reckoned to be eight kings. The first of theses was Menes, who won great renown for his government of the kingdom."
Manetho's
Aegyptiaka

In the late predynastic period, the so-called Nagada III phase, the burials of many people in Egypt included stone jars and other sophisticated goods, such as elegant flint knives and jewellery decorated with gold, silver and turquoise. Although reflecting a marked élitism, such expensive items were more widely distributed amongst the population than would later be the case in dynastic times. Also by this time, large brick-built towns had appeared at sites such as Elephantine, Hierakonpolis and Nagada, which were well planned and boasted regular street plans, fortified walls, and monumental cult buildings. Art of the period frequently used warfare as a theme, although this may rather emphasize the defence of the community than reflect a culture of aggression.

Traditionally, the state of Egypt was created when the legendary king Menes led the armies of Upper Egypt to defeat the kingdom of Lower Egypt, and then founded his new capital at Memphis. The story of Menes, however,

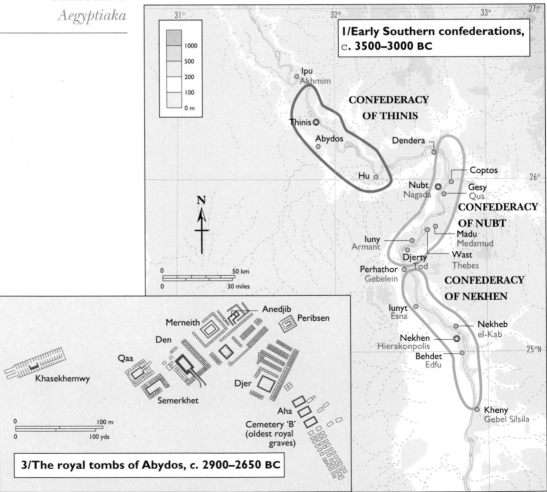

1/Early Southern confederations, c. 3500–3000 BC

3/The royal tombs of Abydos, c. 2900–2650 BC

belongs to mythology, as do the twin kingdoms, and it seems certain that Egypt became a unified cultural and economic domain long before her first king ascended the throne. Political unification probably also proceeded gradually, perhaps over a period of a century, as local districts established trading networks, and the ability of their governments to organize agriculture and labour on a large scale increased. Divine kingship may also have gained spiritual momentum as the cults of gods like Horus, Seth and Neith—associated with living representatives—became widespread in the country.

Evidence for the government of the Nile valley during Nagada III is dominated by three sites—Abydos, Nagada (Nubt) itself, and Hierakonpolis (Nekhen)—where enormous brick-built tombs are indicative of a powerful élite. Funerary and religious art from these sites exhibits the unmistakable iconography which was later used for kings: scenes of hunting, warfare and ceremonials, and images of the ruler as a bull, hawk or lion slaughtering rebels. However, it is not certain whether any of these people were kings as such. The earliest known kings ruled the country as a whole from *c.* 2900 BC (1st Dynasty), and were buried at Abydos; the first of their number seems to have been Aha. The existence of kings before Aha—with the names Iryhor, Ka and "Scorpion"—is not proven. The 1st Dynasty may have been the victors in a power struggle involving the three great southern towns.

The Narmer palette portrays the king as the archetypal warrior in an early example of formal royal art. The falcon-god Horus delivers captive rebels to the king who stands, backed by a courtier, ready to club a defeated chieftain.

Perhaps by *c.* 3000 BC three powerful confederacies or proto-kingdoms were competing for supremacy in southern Egypt, until a victor emerged, through political wit or force of arms, to command a confederacy so powerful it would expand to dominate the whole country. However, it is not clear that the ruling élites of the three towns were different people, particularly in the final decades before the accession of the first true king.

The only king certainly known to have reigned in Egypt before Aha was Narmer, whose monuments have been found throughout southern Egypt, and who traded with towns in the Delta and southern Palestine. Whether he was king of all Egypt or is the "missing link"—a king of Hierakonpolis—is less certain, but his celebrated slate palette from the temple at Hierakonpolis is the most enduring image of this period. Narmer is represented as a living god in a composition which utilizes three of the foundations of later pharaonic display: canonical style, hieroglyphic writing, and the support of the gods. In this sense Narmer's palette is a cultural milestone which provides a convenient marker for the beginning of pharaonic Egypt.

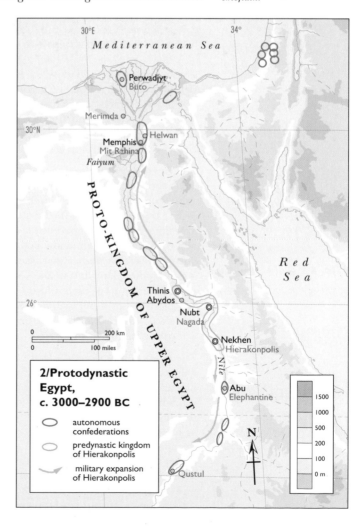

2/Protodynastic Egypt, c. 3000–2900 BC

- ⬭ autonomous confederations
- ⬭ predynastic kingdom of Hierakonpolis
- ⟿ military expansion of Hierakonpolis

The Old Kingdom Administration

The defining characteristics of pharaonic culture, including kingship, art, and the formal cults of the gods, developed their archetypal forms during the 1st–3rd Dynasties.

"Would that it were command of your spirit ... to give me a door made of stone for this tomb in the cemetery!" The king had brought from him a doubledoor made of limestone ... and it was laid in the throne-room of the palace; a chief craftsman and pyramid workmen were set to it, and the work was done in the presence of the king himself. The stone took shape daily, and what was done to it was seen in the palace in the course of each day. The king had hieroglyphs put on it, and they were painted in blue."
Tomb inscription of Nyankhsakhmet

The transition of Egypt from the formative early dynastic period to the classic grandeur of the Old Kingdom is an issue of modern perception making sense of an emerging state gradually developing the definitive characteristics of pharaonic culture. Dubious evidence of civil war in the 2nd Dynasty aside, it seems that the nation embraced the divine king and his court as its temporal and spiritual heart, which supports the view that kingship was a cohesive development and not the product of political conflict.

A crucial witness to this period is the Palermo Stone, a slab of basalt, two metres high, on which were inscribed the annals of kings from the mythical ancestors at the beginning of time to the 5th Dynasty. According to these, the life of the king was structured by the ceremonial formality of the court and the cults of the gods, and by the need to travel in order to participate in festivals as far apart as Buhen and Sais. This formality was reflected in the development of the architecture of sacred sites in towns such as Hierakonpolis, where a structured temple developed during the 2nd–3rd Dynasties upon the earlier, more informal cult site near which the Narmer palette was found. In the Old Kingdom temple was found a magnificent copper and gold statue of a hawk-deity, and valuable royal finds ranging in date from statues of Khasekhemwy (2nd Dynasty) to the beaten-copper statues of Pepy I (6th Dynasty). A schist statue of Khasekhemwy is a very early example of the fully developed elegance of pharaonic art. Formality was equally apparent in the funerary cults of the courtiers, which established the ethical norms of official conduct in pharaonic Egypt; 3rd Dynasty wooden panels from the tomb of Hesyra rank amongst the greatest masterpieces of Egyptian art.

The Palermo Stone also documents trade with lands as far afield as Syria, and court-sponsored expeditions sent with military support to mine semi-precious stones in the eastern and Sinai deserts; mining expeditions are confirmed by inscriptions in the turquoise mines at Wadi Maghara, and the need for military support apparently corresponds with evidence for the presence of a significant semi-nomadic population in Sinai during the Old Kingdom. Possibly overseas trade was already a royal monopoly, as in later periods, because power, land and wealth were increasingly concentrated in the hands of an élite group of men and their families, probably numbering less than two thousand in a population estimated at around 1.5 million. The use of stone was a restricted royal gift, and as a result the hard-stone industry, characteristic of predynastic culture, virtually died out by the 3rd Dynasty.

The heart of government was the court: authority came from regular attendance on the king, and was signified by carrying his seal. The most powerful official was the vizîr, who usually resided at the palace, unlike later periods when he toured the country. Courtiers were required to be versatile enough to wait on the king, to administer law and order in the provinces, and to act as priests on a rotating basis—even to serve as military officers if events so demanded. Other officials acted as provincial governors or mayors of individual towns, and attended court occasionally. The common factor which set these men apart from the mass of society was their ability to read and write, and so control the functions of the administration. The skill was inherited as a right, taught at court and reserved exclusively for those in power.

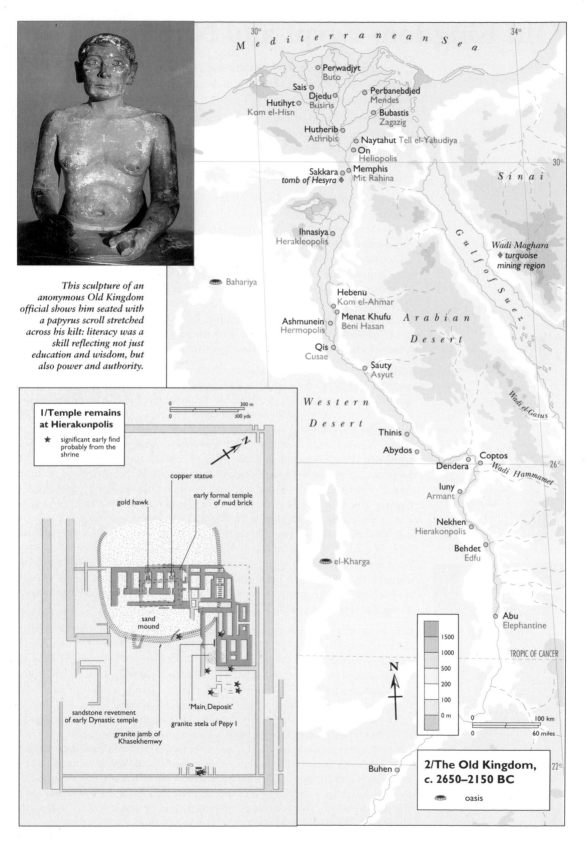

This sculpture of an anonymous Old Kingdom official shows him seated with a papyrus scroll stretched across his kilt: literacy was a skill reflecting not just education and wisdom, but also power and authority.

1/Temple remains at Hierakonpolis

★ significant early find probably from the shrine

0   300 m
0   300 yds

copper statue

early formal temple of mud brick

gold hawk

sand mound

sandstone revetment of early Dynastic temple

'Main Deposit'

granite stela of Pepy I

granite jamb of Khasekhemwy

Mediterranean Sea

Perwadjyt
Buto

Sais

Hutihyt
Kom el-Hisn

Djedu
Busiris

Perbanebdjed
Mendes

Bubastis
Zagazig

Hutherib
Athribis

Naytahut Tell el-Yahudiya

On
Heliopolis

Sakkara
tomb of Hesyra

Memphis
Mit Rahina

Sinai

Ihnasiya
Herakleopolis

Bahariya

Gulf of Suez

Wadi Maghara
♦ turquoise
mining region

Hebenu
Kom el-Ahmar

Ashmunein
Hermopolis

Menat Khufu
Beni Hasan

Arabian

Desert

Qis
Cusae

Sauty
Asyut

Western

Desert

Thinis

Abydos

Coptos

Dendera

Wadi Hammamet

Iuny
Armant

Nekhen
Hierakonpolis

Behdet
Edfu

Wadi el-Gasus

el-Kharga

N

1500
1000
500
200
100
0 m

TROPIC OF CANCER

0   100 km
0   60 miles

Abu
Elephantine

Buhen

2/The Old Kingdom, c. 2650–2150 BC

oasis

Old Kingdom Egypt and Nubia

Prehistoric links with the population of Nubia developed during the Old Kingdom into a blend of economic exchange and direct exploitation of Nubian resources by Egypt.

"King Merenra, my lord, sent me with my father, the courtier and priest Iri, to Yam, in order to open up the road to that land. I did so during seven months, brought from there every sort of beautiful and valuable gift, and was greatly praised as a result."
Tomb inscription
of Governor
Harkhuf

The inscription surrounding the doorway of Governor Harkhuf's rock-cut funerary chapel near Elephantine is the most detailed source regarding Egypt's relations with Nubia during the Old Kingdom.

The effective southern border of predynastic Egypt had been established at the island of Elephantine on the northern edge of the first cataract. The vast region stretching south from there to the confluence of the Nile and Atbara is known as Nubia, a disparate collection of lands embroiled in the affairs of their better-known neighbour.

Egyptian interest in Nubia was typically commercial: the region itself was rich in valuable minerals, and the caravans of its chiefs transported incense, oils, ebony, ivory and animal skins from lands further east and south. As early as the reign of Aha, the court had defended its commercial interests through direct intervention. By the 2nd Dynasty, Egyptian soldiers and merchants were active as far south as Buhen, beside the second cataract; their appearance coincided with a long-lasting decline in the population of Lower Nubia, although it is not known whether their interventionism was a cause or a result of this process. At the same time, Egyptians began working the gold-mines at Wadi Allaqi and the diorite-quarries at Toshka. During the reign of Khafra (4th Dynasty), Buhen was established as an Egyptian trading colony.

During the 5th Dynasty population levels in Lower Nubia began to recover and the Egyptian community at Buhen withdrew; perhaps the native chiefs were now able to resist its presence, or it may simply have become more convenient for Egypt to trade via middlemen. The new population is identified with a broad culture known as the C-group, which would be present in Lower Nubia for the next thousand years. As a result the security of Egypt's southern border became a significant issue, and the governors of Elephantine became *de facto* ambassadors to Nubia. Similarly, the western oases controlled the major caravan routes linking Egypt and Nubia: during the 6th Dynasty the office of governor of the Dakhla region was created to impose Egyptian authority on at least some of these roads (at one time the office was held by a son of King Pepy II). There is no evidence that Egypt employed a permanent army. Instead, district governors were required to muster troops as necessary, and the 6th Dynasty courtier Weni organized campaigns in Sinai and Southern Palestine employing a force in which Nubian mercenaries served alongside native conscripts. Weni also led a mining expedition to Wadi Allaqi.

The most revealing sources during the later Old Kingdom are the inscriptions of the governors of Elephantine. In the most celebrated example, Harkhuf recounts his three trading trips to Lower Nubia: on the first he accompanied his father, and then he led his own caravans to Yam and to the confederate chiefdom of Wawat and Satju; he later returned to Yam, and obtained a pygmy to dance at the court of his child-king, Pepy II. It is evident from Harkhuf's account that the Nubian chiefs could be awkward in order to underline their independence. One of his successors, Pepynakht, retaliated ith punitive raids on Wawat and Irtjet. Pepynakht later distinguished himself in Sinai by recovering the bodies of an expedition killed by nomads whilst building boats for the Red Sea trade. The success of this governor embodied the ideal of a loyal servant of his king, and after his death he was deified with the name Hekaib. Generations of governors and generals sent to Nubia worshipped at the shrine at Hekaib until the end of the Middle Kingdom.

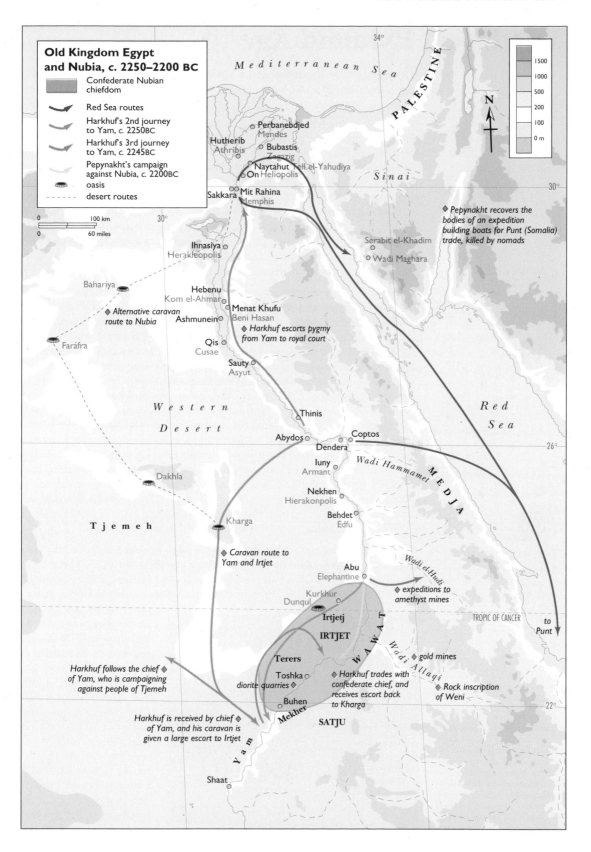

Old Kingdom Egypt and Nubia, c. 2250–2200 BC

- Confederate Nubian chiefdom
- Red Sea routes
- Harkhuf's 2nd journey to Yam, c. 2250BC
- Harkhuf's 3rd journey to Yam, c. 2245BC
- Pepynakht's campaign against Nubia, c. 2200BC
- oasis
- desert routes

0   100 km
0   60 miles

Mediterranean Sea

PALESTINE

Perbanebdjed
Mendes
Hutherib
Athribis
Bubastis
Zagazig
Naytahut Tell el-Yahudiya
On Heliopolis
Sakkara Mit Rahina
Memphis

Sinai

◆ Pepynakht recovers the bodies of an expedition building boats for Punt (Somalia) trade, killed by nomads

Serabit el-Khadim
Wadi Maghara

Ihnasiya
Herakleopolis

Bahariya

Hebenu
Kom el-Ahmar
Menat Khufu
Beni Hasan
Ashmunein
◆ Harkhuf escorts pygmy from Yam to royal court

Qis
Cusae

Sauty
Asyut

Farâfra

Western Desert

Thinis

Abydos
Coptos
Dendera
Wadi Hammamet
MEDJA

Red Sea

Iuny
Armant

Dakhla

Nekhen
Hierakonpolis

Behdet
Edfu

◆ Caravan route to Yam and Irtjet

Kharga

Tjemeh

Abu
Elephantine
Wadi el-Hudi
◆ expeditions to amethyst mines

Kurkhur
Dunqul

Irtjetj
IRTJET

WAWAT
Wadi Allaqi

TROPIC OF CANCER
to Punt

Harkhuf follows the chief of Yam, who is campaigning against people of Tjemeh

Terers
Toshka
diorite quarries

◆ gold mines

◆ Harkhuf trades with confederate chief, and receives escort back to Kharga

◆ Rock inscription of Weni

Buhen
Mekher
SATJU

Harkhuf is received by chief of Yam, and his caravan is given a large escort to Irtjet

Yam

Shaat

The Great Pyramid Age

The royal pyramid complex was a symbol of the magnificence of a nation and a statement of a shared belief in life after death.

"Now the priest Rawer in his priestly robes was following the steps of the king in order to conduct the royal costume, when the sceptre in the king's hand struck the priest Rawer's foot. The king said, "You are safe". So the king said, and then, "It is the king's wish that he be perfectly safe, since I have not struck at him. For he is more worthy before the king than any man."
Tomb inscription at Giza of the Courtier Rawer

In the royal cemetery at Abydos, the earliest kings were buried in massive mud-brick and stone *mastabas* (bench-shaped tombs); the true meaning of the king's death was symbolized by an enormous stepped tumulus over the burial chamber representing the mound of creation, the elemental soil in which he would be reborn. The king was surrounded in death by his family and members of the court, although there is no compelling evidence that they were actually slain to accompany their king into death. During the 2nd Dynasty the cemetery moved to Sakkara, the plateau occupying the horizon above Memphis. The geography of death was then organized so that the royal burial became the focus around which the tombs of courtiers and high officials were arranged in great ghostly avenues.

Netjerykhet of the 3rd Dynasty (known in later tradition as Djoser, "the special one") initiated a more ambitious project: the central tumulus was greatly enlarged and heaped above the mastaba to create the earliest "step" pyramid, and for the first time the tomb was built entirely in stone, with a gleaming white limestone casing and a granite-lined burial chamber. The pyramid itself was the centre of a complex of stone chapels which reproduced buildings associated with the ritual life of the king, surrounded by a wall giving the outward appearance of the palace. Thereafter, the building of the pyramid complex became the major industry of Old Kingdom Egypt, employing dozens of officials and thousands of craftsmen; after the king's death it continued to function as a major temple complex. Although no texts have survived to document actual construction techniques, it seems likely that much of the building took place during the inundation when many labourers had relatively little agricultural employment, and stone could be transported quite easily by floating barges on the swollen river. Foundations were laid on rocky escarpments skilfully levelled by craftsmen, and ground-plans were calculated using practical geometry and astronomical observations.

Pyramid building was so fundamental to society that Snofru of the 4th Dynasty was able to build three or even four; for these the pyramid was reinterpreted as a form of the sacred obelisk (*benben*) housed in the temple of the sun-god at Heliopolis, and so the tumulus was encased in the "true" pyramid. In fact the earliest such pyramids, at Dahshur and Meidum, are shaped like obelisks (or "bent" pyramids). Snofru's son and grandson, Khufu and Khafra, were buried in the largest of all pyramids at Giza, surrounded by a veritable city of officials' tombs. Thereafter, the king's pyramid continued as Egypt's spiritual heart until the end of the Middle Kingdom.

The pyramids at Giza. At the rear, the pyramid of Khufu is the largest of all, although that of Khafra is situated on higher ground and so appears larger. In the foreground, the pyramid of Menkaura is smaller but encased in hard granite. Around the king's pyramids are the satellite pyramids of the royal women.

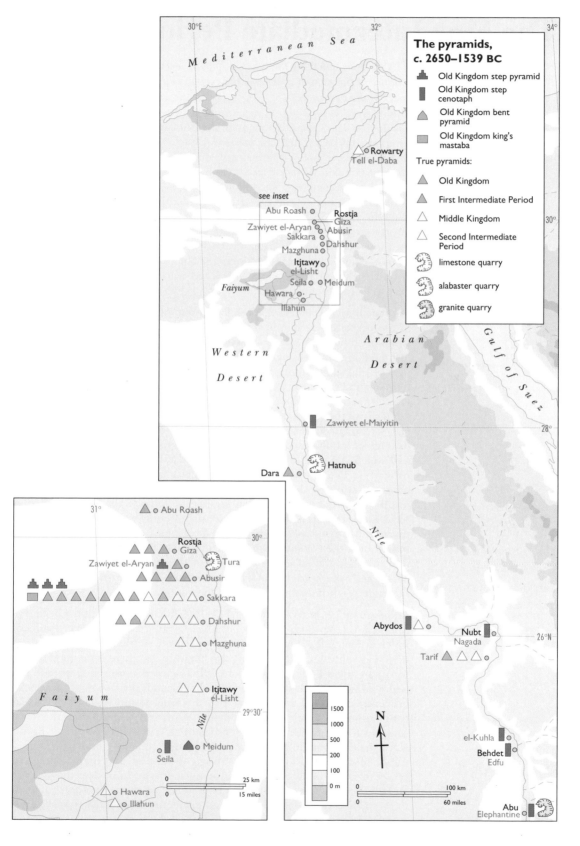

**The pyramids,
c. 2650–1539 BC**

- Old Kingdom step pyramid
- Old Kingdom step cenotaph
- Old Kingdom bent pyramid
- Old Kingdom king's mastaba

True pyramids:

- Old Kingdom
- First Intermediate Period
- Middle Kingdom
- Second Intermediate Period

- limestone quarry
- alabaster quarry
- granite quarry

Mediterranean Sea

Rowarty
Tell el-Daba

see inset

Abu Roash
Rostja
Giza
Zawiyet el-Aryan
Abusir
Sakkara
Dahshur
Mazghuna
Itjtawy
el-Lisht
Seila Meidum
Hawara
Illahun

Faiyum

*Western
Desert*

*Arabian
Desert*

Gulf of Suez

Zawiyet el-Maiyitin

Dara Hatnub

Nile

Abydos

Nubt
Nagada

Tarif

el-Kuhla

Behdet
Edfu

Abu
Elephantine

31°
Abu Roash

Rostja
Giza
Zawiyet el-Aryan Tura
Abusir
Sakkara
Dahshur
Mazghuna
Itjtawy
el-Lisht

Faiyum

Nile

Seila

Meidum

Hawara
Illahun

30°
29°30'

1500
1000
500
200
100
0 m

N

0   25 km
0   15 miles

0   100 km
0   60 miles

The First Intermediate Period

The decades following the reign of Pepy II were a period in which the balance of power and governmental responsibility had shifted from the court to the provinces.

"I am contemplating what has happened: things have happened throughout the land, changes are taking place and it is not like last year ... The ways of the gods are violated, and their offerings are neglected. The land is in distress and there is mourning everywhere. Towns and districts are sorrowful, and all alike are weighed down with iniquities."

The Laments of Khakheperrasonb

The reign of Pepy II—at 96 years probably the longest in human history—was the last act of the Old Kingdom: the old king was buried in his pyramid complex at Sakkara, the last massive royal project of the era because the ability to muster labour and materials on such a grand scale had passed out of royal control. In fact Pepy's pyramid was surrounded by an undistinguished court cemetery. The following era, the so-called First Intermediate Period, witnessed many obscure reigns, although the 7th Dynasty in Manetho's list—70 kings ruling for 70 days—is probably an invention. The direct successors of the Old Kingdom were the kings of the 8th Dynasty; at least one of their number, Ibi, was buried near Pepy II, indicating that the focus of court life remained at Memphis. They were followed by the 9th–10th Dynasty (a single group mistakenly listed twice by Manetho), whose roots were at Herakleopolis.

Scholars have speculated that the long reign of Pepy II was itself the cause of the perceived decline in royal authority: some point to his accession as an infant, others to his protracted old age—greatly respected by the ancients, it should be noted—as signs of weakness. On the other hand, it could as easily be argued that the long-lived king vigorously promoted fundamental reforms, since so little is known about the history of the period. However, what is clear is that, although there was no challenge to the authority of the king as such, the nature of that authority was very different. His charismatic presence at the heart of society was tempered by the growing prestige of locally-based officials, as more responsibility for the government and well-being of individual communities shifted from the palace to the provinces. The governors and mayors generally took sole credit for the administration of their own districts, like the governors of Asyut, who instituted an elaborate irrigation scheme to increase the land available to local farmers. The shift in emphasis from court to community echoed through the geography of death, for the highest officials now chose to be buried near their home towns rather than near their king. The king, therefore, was laid to rest in the company of the officials who maintained his palace and funerary cult, and it is not surprising that the royal pyramids were no longer so prominent in the life of the nation.

Although little is known about the First Intermediate Period, it has been represented as a period of anarchy because a group of wisdom texts—some of which are set in the 9th–10th Dynasty—portray a sterile world that has abandoned all ethical ideals, including the kingship. Yet there is no good reason to equate these literary meditations, all composed centuries later, with the reality of the time. Contemporary monuments indicate that many provincial officials were raised and educated by the king, would regularly attend at court throughout their careers, and were as anxious as any of their predecessors to defend the traditional social and religious institutions of Egypt. Nevertheless, some modern scholars obviously equate centralized administration and unified kingship with strong government, and any devolution of power to the provinces with royal impotence. It is far from clear that this was an Egyptian belief, and throughout pharaonic history local authority tended to assert itself in the face of central government—a tendency typically most assertive in the administration of the south of the country.

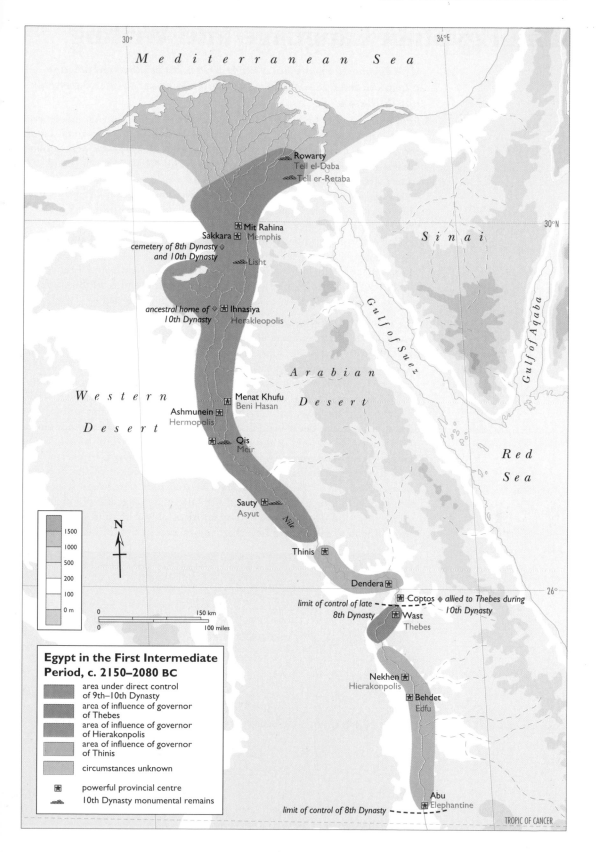

Mediterranean Sea

30°   36°E

Rowarty
Tell el-Daba
Tell er-Retaba

Sinai

30°N

Mit Rahina
Sakkara   Memphis
cemetery of 8th Dynasty
and 10th Dynasty
Lisht

ancestral home of   Ihnasiya
10th Dynasty   Herakleopolis

Gulf of Aqaba

Gulf of Suez

A r a b i a n

D e s e r t

Red

Sea

W e s t e r n

D e s e r t

Menat Khufu
Beni Hasan
Ashmunein
Hermopolis

Qis
Meir

Sauty
Asyut

Nile

Thinis

Dendera

limit of control of late   Coptos   allied to Thebes during
8th Dynasty   Wast   10th Dynasty
Thebes

26°

N

1500	
1000	
500	
200	
100	
0 m	

0   150 km

0   100 miles

Nekhen
Hierakonpolis

Behdet
Edfu

**Egypt in the First Intermediate
Period, c. 2150–2080 BC**

area under direct control
of 9th–10th Dynasty

area of influence of governor
of Thebes

area of influence of governor
of Hierakonpolis

area of influence of governor
of Thinis

circumstances unknown

⊞   powerful provincial centre

10th Dynasty monumental remains

Abu
limit of control of 8th Dynasty   Elephantine

TROPIC OF CANCER

The Egyptian Language and Writing

The Egyptian language has a longer written history than any other; in pharaonic times, it was written using two related scripts, the hieroglyphic and the cursive.

"After foreign land had given me to foreign land—after I had set off for Byblos but reached Kedem, and spent a year and a half there— Ammunenshi, who was a chief in Upper Retjenu, rescued me, saying: 'You are safe with me. You will hear the language of Egypt.' He said this because he knew my character, because he had been told of my skill, because the Egyptians who were there with him testified on my behalf."

The Story of Sinuhe

Egyptian was the principal language used in Egypt during the period covered by this book. Other languages used in the country were imposed on the administration by foreign rulers—Persian and Greek—or were spoken by settlers—such as Carian and Aramaic. The New Kingdom archive at Amarna also included letters from the palace of Amenhotep IV written in Akkadian, a language of Babylonia which was widely used in diplomacy. The languages of people from Libya, Nubia and Medja, known and perhaps spoken in parts of Egypt, are unknown to us. The Egyptian language itself is related—not surprisingly, given its geographical location—to ancient and modern languages of the Middle East (including Akkadian, Arabic and Hebrew), and still more closely to languages of North and East Africa (including Amharic, Hausa and Tuareg). Nevertheless, most of the grammar and vocabulary of Egyptian is unknown in any other language.

The earliest texts known from Egypt are hieroglyphic captions on labels and pots from the royal cemetery at Abydos, dating from the beginning of the 1st Dynasty or even a few decades earlier. Throughout the rest of the pharaonic period two scripts were regularly in use, corresponding to two cultural contexts: hieroglyphic writing was used in the monumental temples and tombs, while cursive writing was employed to record the transitory episodes of daily life. Hieroglyphic texts are weighty, spiritual, and built on the authority of tradition; most are deeply conservative in content. They were composed by priests, with the consent of the king, and generally carved in stone in order to express the permanence and gravity of their ideas. The Greek term *hieroglyph* actually means "sacred image", and is a translation of the Egyptian phrase *medu netjer*, "divine words". The hieroglyphic script represented the coming together of art and language—the two major domains of human creative expression—in order to articulate ideas about life and death which were difficult to express but nevertheless fundamental to the ancient under-

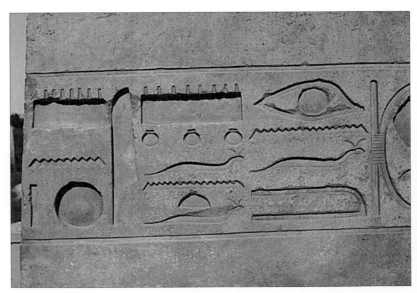

standing of the human condition. Many philosophers of classical Greece and mediaeval Europe even believed that the Egyptians had developed a perfect system capable of representing pure knowledge about the world, which offered absolute power to anybody who could interpret the signs. In fact, hieroglyphs were used to write the sounds of the language, and were not simple pictures; for example, the human eye as a hieroglyph represents, not "eye", but the sound *ir*, and the human foot as a hieroglyph represents the sound *b*.

Right: Hieratic writing from a 20th Dynasty papyrus. Following usual practice, the beginning of a new paragraph is indicated in red ink, whilst black ink is used elsewhere. This document was part of an account of the trial of members of a conspiracy against the life of Ramesses III; each of the last three lines begins with the phrase "a great enemy", and then identifies a particular conspirator.

The cursive script was used more generally by officials and scribes; texts written this way include letters, wills, stories, administrative documents, legal transcripts, doctors' prescriptions, and magical charms. The principles of cursive writing are the same as those of hieroglyphic writing, and most signs are based on hieroglyphs; however, they are adapted and simplified to be written quickly, using a reed-brush and ink, on disposable materials such as pottery, wood or limestone flakes (*ostraca*). The characteristic writing material was papyrus, a fine, very white paper made by pressing together layers of reeds. Papyrus is tough, pliable, and easy to roll up (sheets can be glued together to form scrolls); it can be stored for decades, and then reused simply by rubbing the surface smooth with a stone. During the 8th century BC, the original cursive script was replaced by another (based on the same writing principles) known to Greek visitors as *demotic*, or "common"; the original cursive script, rarely used thereafter, became known as *hieratic*, or "priestly", a name which belies its earlier, more widespread, usage.

Left: Detail from an inscription on a statue of Ramesses II in Luxor temple; it reads "a dedication he has made for his father, Amun-Ra". Since hieroglyphs were used to decorate monuments in a formal and traditional manner, pleasing visual arrangements were as important as legibility. Here the signs are placed neatly between guidelines in such a way as to fill all the available space, and there are no breaks between words.

At the end of the pharaonic period, Egyptian suffered because officials of the Ptolemaic and Roman eras were required to work with Greek; however, the Christian church in Egypt—the Coptic church—revitalized written Egyptian in order to transmit the Gospels in an idiom understandable to the masses. The Greek alphabet was adapted to writing Egyptian and then widely adopted, so that native Egyptian scripts were no longer used after the middle of the 5th century AD. Following the Arab invasion of Egypt in AD 641, even the spoken language was squeezed, and eventually displaced, by Arabic. A long poem known as *Triadon* was composed in Egyptian as late as AD 1250, and the spoken language may have survived in parts of the countryside as late as the 18th century AD, in the same way that Welsh is still widely spoken today in rural Wales, although it has generally been displaced in urban areas. In fact, Egyptian is spoken today, albeit as a dead language, in the liturgy of the Coptic church. Therefore, apart from being our principal means of understanding ancient and mediaeval Egypt, Egyptian is important because it has the longest continuously recorded history of any language—over 4000 years.

II: The Middle Kingdom

The First Intermediate Period resulted in the division of Egypt when a southern kingdom emerged in opposition to the 10th Dynasty. Eventually, Montjuhotep II exploited the political and military success of Thebes in order to reunify the country as the Middle Kingdom. At the same time he began the process of annexing parts of Nubia, a policy intensified by the kings of the 12th Dynasty. A reassertion of regional power during the 13th Dynasty led to the fragmentation of the country once more during the Second Intermediate Period.

"Accompanying a statue of 13 cubits length made from the stone of Hatnub. Now, the road upon which it came was more difficult than anything; it was especially difficult as a result in the hearts of the people who were doing the dragging...I arranged for a company of healthy youths to come in order to make a path for it, along with companies of stone-masons and quarrymen, and foremen as well who knew how to talk to hard-working men."

Tomb inscription of the governor Thuthotep

Following the shift in the balance of power between the palace and the provinces at the end of the 6th Dynasty, the beacon which illuminated the Old Kingdom—the royal pyramid complex—was dimmed. It is misleading to make a simple correlation between the size of a given pyramid and the authority of its royal owner because a decline in pyramid size only indicates a reduction in the emphasis given to royal burial within society, and this may result from any number of factors; but without the massive court cemeteries, the kings of the First Intermediate Period and their officials are often shadowy figures, and the whole era becomes anonymous to history. There is little certainity even about the duration of this enigmatic period, particularly since Manetho's lists of kings at this time, including a 7th Dynasty with impossibly short reigns, is clearly unreliable. A conventional interpretation suggests that the period ran from the end of the reign of Pepy II until the reunification of the country by the Theban armies of Montjuhotep II, conventionally *c.* 2150–1986 BC. If it could be shown, however, that key events—including the rise to power of the governing families of Herakleopolis and Thebes, which spawned the 10th Dynasty and 11th Dynasty respectively—actually took place during the reigns of Pepy II or the kings of the 8th Dynasty, then the whole period may have to be understood as much shorter.

Despite the assertiveness of the regions, the central presence of the one king of Egypt as the source of legitimate authority went unchallenged throughout the first century of the First Intermediate Period, until a new factor in the political equation challenged the ideological heart of the nation, the ruling family of the city of Thebes. Thebes was a relatively new provincial power, which previously had tended to be overshadowed by ancient power centres to its south at Hierakonpolis and to its north at Thinis. However, during the 10th Dynasty, an official named Montjuhotep brought a new family to power as governors of the city at a time when it was apparently no longer prepared to accept political or economic domination at the hands of surrounding regions. It is not clear whether the Theban governors were openly aggressive to their neighbours or merely responding to the aggression of others, but in any case their actions provoked a long period of political struggle which occasionally flared into civil war in Upper Egypt. The earliest military clash apparently took place around 2064 BC, the year in which Inyotef II became governor; perhaps the new governor was keen to make an impression on the situation, or the governor of Hierakonpolis was keen to exploit a moment of political weakness. Whatever, in that year Theban armies entered the territory of Hierakonpolis apparently intent on forcing a confrontation, and the Theban area was subsequently faced with retaliatory raids that reached the city itself and beyond. The subsequent progress of this conflict is entirely unknown except that a decade later Thebes had neutralized the power of its southern rival, and Inyotef II was able to claim dominion of Upper Egypt as far south as Elephantine.

Detail from the "White Chapel" at Karnak, showing Senusret I of the 12th Dynasty offering sweet-bread to Amun. This refined and elegant Middle Kingdom art style, balancing the use of figures with hieroglyphic captions in an uncluttered layout, became a model of royal iconography which influenced all later periods of pharaonic history.

The character of the subsequent events was fundamentally transformed when Inyotef II adopted the titles of kingship, and granted posthumous royal titles to his immediate predecessors. As a result the kings of the 10th Dynasty—the so-called "House of Khety", which originated at Herakleopolis and resided in the north—were faced with a rival kingdom, and a challenge to their royal dignity. It is impossible to determine whether Inyotef II was proclaimed king for ideological reasons arising from his political success and the patronage of his local gods—principally Amun of Thebes and Montju of Armant—or whether it was a calculated strategy designed to force the break-up of the political *status quo* in favour of Thebes. The activities of his armies continued to have clear strategic implications: *c.* 2050 BC the rival town of Thinis was annexed, bringing Theban dominion up to the borders of the territory of the governor of Asyut, who remained steadfastly loyal to Khety III as the sole ruler of Egypt. The following decades saw bitter warfare between rival Egyptian armies throughout Middle Egypt, in which many major towns were besieged, and Thinis especially suffered the depredations of war-induced poverty. The armies of governor Tefibi of Asyut temporarily wrested Thinis from Theban control in a campaign during which tombs and chapels at Abydos were vandalized and destroyed; whether this desecration stemmed from any purpose other than the venting of hatred and perhaps tomb-robbery is unknown, but it is an indication of how war had driven Egyptians to commit acts violating sacred institutions that would previously have been inconceivable.

The unresolved war dragged on sporadically until Montjuhotep II became king at Thebes around 2007 BC. The kingdom of Thebes was by then well established as the major power in the south of the country, but the inherent instability of the political situation gave the governor of Thinis the confidence to revolt against the rule of his king. Whether or not this incident was engineered by the northern king and his supporters, it provided Montjuhotep with an appropriate excuse to attack Asyut itself. The swift defeat of that town was followed within a few years by enormous territorial gains throughout Middle Egypt, and powerful towns like Hermopolis and even Herakleopolis were soon captured. These gains effectively destroyed any equilibrium which may have existed within the divided monarchy, and spelled the end of the 10th Dynasty.

The Middle Kingdom

The total success of Montjuhotep II in unifying the kingship enabled him to replace certain provincial governors—such as his principal enemy, the governor of Asyut—with Theban loyalists, but most of the incumbent ruling families were assimilated into the new regime. The king's power base, however, remained at Thebes, and the court was maintained as a basically Theban institution throughout the 11th Dynasty. The most crucial office in the post-war administration was that of vizîr, since he would have had to assume responsibility for the process of reuniting provincial administrations which had not only grown apart, but in some cases had been at war for over half a century. Montjuhotep himself lived for 30 more years, and so was able to oversee sufficient political progress to ensure that his unified state would survive him. He was buried in a magnificent tomb which transformed Old Kingdom traditions of royal funerary architecture into a strikingly original, purely Theban design. The succession stayed with his family for two more generations, after which it passed without any apparent dispute to a man who had seemingly been a Theban vizîr, and who came to the throne *c.* 1937 BC as Amenemhat I, founder of the 12th Dynasty.

Amenemhat I set about recreating the central authority of the kingship as it had existed in the Old Kingdom, but allied to this process were administrative reforms designed to establish a balance between the demands of central government and the aspirations of the governors of the provinces. He was sufficiently confident of his position to move the principal royal residence from the southern heartland to Itjtawy—near to the sacred pyramid fields of Sakkara, but also a virgin site in which to build a new palace for a new administration. The subsequent system of government was probably developed using the administration of the Old Kingdom in the 5th–6th Dynasties as its model; certainly, the king was once more the only source of legitimate authority in Egypt, and his officials were empowered by attendance at the palace to act as his agents. Members of the royal family were excluded from government, but the king's wives and daughters shared in his divinity and attended him constantly, whilst his eldest son often sat beside him on the throne as a co-regent. Amenemhat I also re-established the building of a royal pyramid complex as the central industry of the state; the scale of the mobilization of labour which the system demanded and could achieve is apparent from the records of a quarrying expedition sent by the palace to Wadi Hammamat in the reign of Senusret I, which involved 80 officials responsible for nearly 19,000 men.

The pyramid of Amenemhat III at Hawara in the Faiyum; the king also built a pyramid at the more traditional site of Dahshur. The edifice was encased in limestone, which has been stripped to leave a core of mud-bricks built around a rock outcrop. In the foreground are the shapeless ruins of the mortuary temple, known to classical writers as "the Labyrinth" and described by Herodotos as Egypt's greatest wonder of all.

The tombs of the governors of the Middle Kingdom are amongst the largest and most beautiful in pharaonic history, an observation which has been used to suggest that the reunification process had involved a political accommodation in which the independence of the provinces was left essentially unchecked; this supposition finds further support in the apparent disappearance of large tombs after the reign of Senusret III (*c.* 1836–1817 BC), a fact which has been ascribed to administration reforms which finally did break the power of the provinces. However, both suggestions are extremely dubious: the great provincial tombs were a feature of the wealth of the nation, which had been founded on absolute royal control following the reforms of Amenemhat I; moreover, their disappearance foreshadowed a decline in the size of royal tombs, suggesting that the fortunes of the king and his governors were bound together rather than opposed. Another scholarly myth, no longer tenable in the face of the evidence, is that the kings of the 13th Dynasty were impotent puppets manipulated by a powerful line of vizîrs. In the event, the 13th Dynasty succeeded the female king, Sobknefru, *c.* 1759 BC as sole rulers of Egypt without any apparent opposition, although their relationship to the preceding dynasty is not known. Life in the provinces—as witnessed, for example, at

The tombs of the governors of Menat Khufu at Beni Hasan. In the Middle Kingdom, provincial cemeteries developed "streets" in which the tombs of the governors were surrounded by those of family members and local officials. Although this arrangement is reminiscent of the royal cemeteries of the Old Kingdom, contemporary texts indicate that the will of the king retained unquestioned control over the administration of the provinces.

Kahun—continued without incident, and there is no reason to suppose that the transfer of the throne had any adverse social or political implications. The new dynasty maintained Itjtawy and Memphis as its principal royal residences, but continued to travel throughout the country. An important group of documents has survived from the reign of king Sobkhotep II (*c.* 1730 BC) giving exceptionally detailed information about the residence of the court near Thebes in order to allow the king to attend the temple at nearby Medamud. From these it can be established beyond doubt that the vizîr and other officers of the administration were regularly in attendance at the palace, along with leading military officials and agents representing the king in the provinces.

The most significant military achievement of the Middle Kingdom was the annexation of northern Nubia—Wawat and part of Kush—in order to ensure the flow of mineral wealth and trade goods into Egypt. Montjuhotep II seems to have considered the military domination of Wawat to be an integral part of a strategy for consolidating the authority of his Theban kingdom. In order to ensure the security of his southern border he invaded Wawat *c.* 1993 BC, then, having successfully concluded the reunification of Egypt, he set about securing the passage of Nubian commerce by launching a series of attacks on the southern caravan routes. Buhen was re-established as an Egyptian trade-centre, and subsequently regular payments of tribute were levied. The policies of the 12th Dynasty kings were even more militaristic and interventionist: during the decade beginning *c.*1913 BC the armies of Senusret I systematically brought the territories of Wawat under formal Egyptian control. In order to achieve this, forts were built at strategic locations which controlled both riverine and desert traffic, supported by patrols which policed the movement of caravans and potentially hostile nomads. During the reign of Senusret III, in three separate campaigns *c.*1829–1818 BC, Egyptian armies drove still further south into the territory of Kush, and a further series of forts was built in order to extend direct Egyptian control beyond the second cataract on the river.

The Second Intermediate Period

The onset of the Second Intermediate Period is enormously difficult to establish with any degree of certainty. During the early 17th century BC, a group of 13th Dynasty kings—including Neferhotep I and Ay—were still kings throughout Egypt, and are attested on monuments from Elephantine to the Nile delta. Thereafter, however, the authority of the 13th Dynasty became increasingly restricted in territory, and the kings themselves seem increasingly anonymous. So far as can reasonably be determined, three processes shaped the break up of Middle Kingdom Egypt: firstly, control of Nubia was lost during the 13th Dynasty; secondly, the delta was divided amongst several small kingdoms—presumably no bigger, in most cases, than individual towns—probably at the end of the 13th Dynasty; thirdly, a local dynasty came to power in Thebes, again at the end of the 13th Dynasty. It is not clear, however, whether these changes were causes or effects of the division of the kingdom.

In the Nubian territories controlled by Egypt, various local confederations emerged during the 13th Dynasty. There is some evidence that Buhen was abandoned and burned during this time, but a final break with the past may have been achieved with little trouble: Egyptian interest in controlling Nubia seems to have waned during the 17th century BC—perhaps as internal divisions within Egypt became apparent—and the local confederacies grew ever stronger as a result. It seems likely that many of the Nubian chiefs had collaborated with the previous administration, and may have formed alliances with the garrisons of the Egyptian forts through trading and marriage; some of their more prominent subjects during the following century were Egyptians descended from the garrisons or recruited as mercenaries. By the end of the Second Intermediate Period, c. 1560 BC, the confederate states recognized a single overlord—the king of Kush, resident at Kerma, the cultural and economic heart of northern Nubia. During the middle of the 16th century BC, Egypt was a divided land, and the unified kingdom of Kush could fulfil its own potential to be the dominant political and economic power along the Nile.

Thirteenth Dynasty rule in Egypt came to an end in the mid-17th century BC. In the south of the country, it was succeeded—apparently immediately—by the kings of the 17th Dynasty, resident at Thebes but ruling from Elephantine to Thinis, and perhaps further north. There is no evidence of any other kingdoms in the Nile valley at this time, although it is certainly possible that some of the entirely unknown kings of the 14th Dynasty ruled in Middle Egypt, the Faiyum region, or in the area of Memphis; one of the great difficulties in understanding the machinations of this period is that the circumstances of Memphis and other major towns in the valley, such as Herakleopolis and Itjtawy, are entirely unknown from the end of the 13th Dynasty until the New Kingdom. In fact, the kings in this period known from contemporary monuments are a small fraction of the number known from later king-lists; the most important source—a 19th Dynasty papyrus from Memphis known as the *Turin Royal Canon*—lists more kings for the Second Intermediate Period than for all other periods together. It may be assumed that many of these kings ruled small areas and were generally subject to a few kings wielding greater economic and military authority. In the late 16th century BC, the kings of Thebes recognized only two other royal lines as their equals, the kings of Avaris and of Kush.

The "White Chapel" at Karnak was a pavilion in which the statue of Amun would halt whilst being carried by priests during festival processions. Following the rise to prominence of the city of Thebes as a political and cultural centre under the kings of the 11th and 12th Dynasties, one of the main beneficiaries was the cult of Amun. However, this chapel is one of the few significant remains from the Middle Kingdom temple, and was itself broken up to be used as buliding material during the New Kingdom.

The temple of Qasr el-Sagha is one of the most striking Middle Kingdom monuments in the Faiyum, probably dating to the reign of Amenemhat IV. The temple has an unusual plan, composed of several small chapels, but it is largely undecorated. Alongside stood an ancient quay, although lake Moeris has since been dramatically reduced in size and the temple now stands on the edge of a desert escarpment nearly 10 kms from the water.

Developments in the north of the country are extremely difficult to track: significant archaeological material relating to this period has been discovered in the eastern delta region, but most of this relates to urban settlement at sites such as Tell el-Daba and Tell el-Yahudiyeh, and does not directly explain the contemporary political situation, least of all the relationship between the delta and the rulers of Memphis and Thebes. The discovery of the capstone from the pyramid of king Ay of the 13th Dynasty indicates that he may have been buried *c.* 1650 BC in a pyramid complex near the city of Avaris (at Tell el-Daba), rather than at Memphis alongside his predecessors. This may suggest that the power base of the ruling dynasty had shifted away from Memphis and Itjtawy, perhaps because the Nile valley was slipping out of its direct control; on the other hand, it may indicate the first appearance of a collateral dynastic line at Avaris. It certainly seems to be an unavoidable assumption that the delta was divided amongst several kings in the following decades, if only to accommodate the large number of unidentified kings; since most ruled small kingdoms in the north, it seems unlikely that they could have erected great monuments to record their presence, although greater emphasis on delta archaeology may uncover more evidence in the future. In our present state of ignorance, Manetho's 14th and 16th Dynasties are simply used to divide the names of these faceless kings into two groups, in a manner which is convenient but entirely artificial: the 14th Dynasty conventionally consists of those kings who maintained the ruling traditions of the Middle Kingdom, although politically impotent themselves; the 16th Dynasty is made up of those kings who identified themselves as "Hyksos". The former group was scattered partly in the delta and partly in the valley and Faiyum region; the latter was probably located mostly in the eastern delta and the area around Memphis, and most kings were subject to the authority of the kingdom of Avaris.

Any account of the history of the Nile delta during the Second Intermediate Period must take into consideration the thorny problem of the Hyksos. In a tradition recounted by the Jewish historian Josephus—which, he says, was derived from Manetho himself—the Hyksos were a barbarian race from the east which ravaged Egypt, before appointing a king to rule the land savagely and with contempt for its ancient traditions. Hyksos domination lasted until a Theban king called Tethmôsis destroyed their stronghold at Avaris, and hundreds of thousands of their number were expelled from the country. This version of the story—written down more than 1600 years after the events it purports to recount—is clearly based on prejudices about foreign domination which arose in the aftermath of Assyrian and Persian invasions of Egypt during the 7th–4th centuries BC, and apparently mixes other early traditions, such as stories about Thutmose III of the mid-15th century BC. Josephus recounts the story because, in his time, the word *Hyksos* was believed (though a false etymology) to mean "shepherd kings", and so had become confused with the biblical narratives of the Israelites; hence the Hyksos were also credited with a legendary exodus from Egypt. However, the main points of this late tradition are mutually contradictory and cannot be accorded any historical validity, and there is no compelling evidence in the texts or archaeology of the Second Intermediate Period to suggest that a foreign "race" invaded Egypt or subsequently left *en masse*. Wherever details in the Josephus tradition can be checked with contemporary evidence, they are found to be wrong.

However, the germ of the Hyksos tradition was the history of the six kings of the 15th Dynasty, who ruled at Avaris for 108 years from *c.* 1639 BC, along with several minor kings of the period, who, as noted above, are conventionally assigned to the 16th Dynasty. Many of these kings used as part of their royal titulary the Egyptian phrase *heka khaset*, which means "ruler of a hill country", "ruler of the desert", or even "ruler of a foreign country" (note, however, that it is never used to describe a race or population). It was first used in the Egyptian texts of the Middle Kingdom to identify the leaders of caravans travelling across the Sinai; commercial links had long existed between the populations of Palestine and the Egyptian delta, and Palestinians along with Syrians were often employed in Egypt during the Middle Kingdom, particularly as servants and labourers. Moreover, the carefully-policed border between the two regions was relaxed during the 13th Dynasty, and subsequently the material culture of towns such as Avaris developed a distinctive mix of delta-Egyptian and Palestinian traditions as newcomers settled in Egypt (albeit in a very limited area)on their own terms. The government of these towns remained firmly in Egyptian hands, but many local officials were the descendants of Palestinian settlers who maintained many of the traditions of their ancestors in their domestic lives. Following the demise of the 13th Dynasty, local potentates in the delta assumed pharaonic titles, including the men who also used the title *Hyksos*. It seems more than likely, therefore, that the Hyksos were a phenomenon comparable to the chiefs of the Third Intermediate Period, who typically became the Egyptian pharaohs of the 22nd Dynasty, although they were descended from Libyan settlers and had retained the traditional titles of their ancestral homeland.

There can be no doubt, however, that the Hyksos upheld the traditions of Egyptian kingship, art and religion, and have left no record of themselves in any language other than Egyptian; their traditional monuments and donations to the gods are apparent at various sites from Tell el-Hebua in the north east to Gebelein in the south. The only obvious departure from Middle Kingdom practice was the strong Hyksos presence in the trading towns at the Palestinian end of *The Ways of Horus*, which was based on commercial intercourse and presumably strong ties of kinship. This aspect of their government apparently caused some anxiety amongst the rulers of Thebes regarding the unity and security of Egypt. However, in the most important of these trading towns Sharuhen (probably at modern Tell el-Ajjul), there is a fairly

Detail from the sarcophagus of Kawit, a wife of Montjuhotep II, founder of the Middle Kingdom, showing the morning toilet routine during which a servant arranges the queen's hair. Hair style was an important indication of both beauty and status in Egyptian society, and high-ranking women and men devoted time to arranging their hair in elaborate styles, using perfumed oils, extensions and wigs.

generalized Hyksos archaeological presence which does not support the concept of a Hyksos "empire" centered on Avaris, stretching from Memphis to southern Palestine. Indeed, the greatest of the Hyksos kings in terms of his monumental record and his importance in later traditions was Apophis—king of Avaris *c.* 1570–1530 BC—but in the monuments of his contemporary Kamose of Thebes, he has no obvious authority beyond Avaris itself, and in a military sense was virtually impotent.

The Theban kings of the 17th Dynasty are mostly as anonymous as their northern counterparts, and are generally known only from their burials. However, at the end of the Second Intermediate Period, a group came to the throne determined to challenge the division of the kingdom, which they believed was a single, unique entity whose integrity had been compromised by the course of history. Also, on surveying the situation from their palaces in Upper Egypt, they resented having only indirect access to the trade routes of Palestine and the mineral wealth of Nubia, which should have belonged to them by right of inheritance from the Middle Kingdom. The ideology of the situation may have been more distressing than the politics, since subsequent events demonstrated that they had been able to import sufficient foreign timber, for example, to build a formidable fleet of fighting ships. The badly mutilated and decayed mummy of the first of these kings, Sekenenra Taa, indicates that he died an extremely violent death—presumably after taking to the battlefield against one of his many rivals. His son, Kamose, erected a group of stelae in the temple of Amun-Ra at Karnak, which presented his account of a raid on the kingdom of Avaris *c.* 1540 BC. According to the text, the king resolved to end the division of Egypt by force, although—following a standard Egyptian literary device—this is said to have been in defiance of the advice of his courtiers. The people of the town of Nefrusy were swiftly put to the sword for having collaborated with Avaris. Unfortunately the account is broken at the point when Memphis would have been mentioned. The text resumes with the raid on Avaris itself. The town was too well fortified to be captured in a single attack, but the Theban marines were able to ravage the surrounding estates and orchards and plunder the imported goods on board king Apophis' commercial ships. Kamose died shortly afterwards, having made little lasting impact on the kingdom of Avaris; however, references in his stelae and inscriptions at Buhen indicate that an earlier attack on the kingdom of Kush had allowed the Theban regime to take control of Wawat. At the accession of Kamose's son, the kings of Avaris and Kush clearly understood the future intentions of their Theban rivals.

The Wars of Reunification

The governors of Thebes emerged from civil war as the rulers of Upper Egypt, before challenging the 10th Dynasty for the kingship of all Egypt.

"I am one whom his lord loved, and whom he praised in the course of each day. I spent a lifetime of many years in the presence of my lord (Inyotef II); this land was under his care from Abu to Thinis, and I was truthfully his body servant and his chamberlain. He promoted me, advanced my status, and placed me in the confidence of his private chambers."
Funerary Stela of Tjeti.

The newest provincial power in Egypt during the First Intermediate Period was Wast—generally referred to by its later Greek name, Thebes. Although Thebes and its god Amun were to rank amongst the greatest names of Egyptian history, it had hitherto been relatively obscure, squeezed between ancient power centres at Hierakonpolis and Thinis; even within its own administrative district or nome, Thebes had probably played a secondary role as an administrative and religious centre to Coptos. However, during the 6th Dynasty the city had grown sufficiently in importance to be granted its own governor, and, following the accession to that office of the Inyotef family, its destiny was transformed.

The activities of Theban governors during the 10th Dynasty were typically aggressive, although it is not clear whether they were themselves intent upon expansion or whether they were forced to react to the ambitions of more powerful neighbours. Nevertheless, they became a major force in a political struggle which often flared into civil war in Upper Egypt; model-soldiers are common amongst the funeral goods of contemporary officials, and tomb scenes offer glimpses of assaults on towns by armies of fellow Egyptians. By *c.* 2064 BC Thebes was on the offensive, challenging the might of the governor of Hierakonpolis, whose armies in turn ravaged land and villages throughout the Theban area. Within a few years Thebes prevailed and became the dominant power in the south, assuming direct control as far as Elephantine. The Theban ruling family asserted its pre-eminence in defiance of the accepted order when Inyotef II adopted the titles of kingship and his immediate predecessors were granted posthumous royalty. As a result the struggle for power assumed a new dimension: the governors of Asyut set themselves in defence of the dignity of the 10th Dynasty as kings of all Egypt. The focus of dispute switched to Thinis, which may have fallen into 56 years of war-induced poverty: *c.* 2050 BC the loyalist armies of king Khety III, led by Tefibi of Asyut, wrested Thinis from Theban control in a campaign marred by the desecration of Abydos. Inyotef's armies were well able to respond, and drove Theban control as far north as Akhmim.

The decisive reign was that of Inyotef's grandson, Montjuhotep II. In his 14th Year (*c.* 1994 BC) an anti-Theban rebellion in Thinis provoked a successful campaign against Asyut itself, and during the next eight years the powerful towns of Hermopolis and Herakleopolis also fell to Theban arms. With the loss of these centres it seems that the political and military authority of the 10th Dynasty was effectively eliminated, at least in the Nile valley, and troops loyal to the old regime were rounded up as fugitives. Although it is not known how Thebes came to dominate Lower Egypt, Montjuhotep II was subsequently able to perform a royal tour of the whole country. His achievement was announced in a new name—"Horus who unites the Twin Lands"—and immortalized in later tradition as the rebirth of a nation.

The entrance to the rock-cut tomb of Montjuhotep II and his queens at Thebes. The tomb was adorned with a mastaba raised upon terraces, and joined via a causeway to a splendid valley-temple. The whole complex evoked the magnificence of the Old Kingdom pyramids, whilst echoing the natural beauty of the Theban hills.

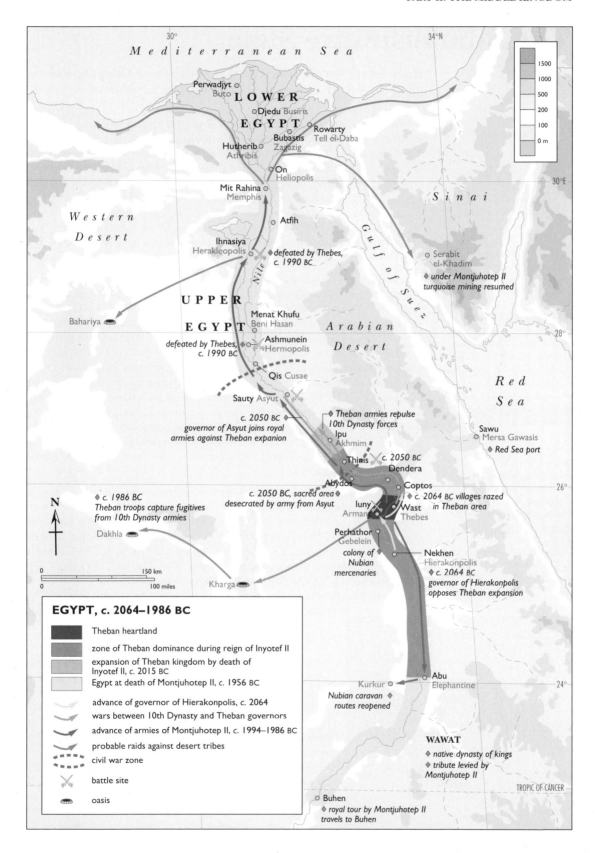

Mediterranean Sea

Perwadjyt
Buto
LOWER
Djedu Busiris
EGYPT
Rowarty
Bubastis Tell el-Daba
Hutherib Zagazig
Athribis
On
Heliopolis

Mit Rahina
Memphis

*Western
Desert*

Atfih

Ihnasiya
Herakleopolis ◆ defeated by Thebes,
c. 1990 BC

Sinai

○ Serabit
el-Khadim
◆ under Montjuhotep II
turquoise mining resumed

Gulf of Suez

**UPPER
EGYPT**

Menat Khufu
Beni Hasan

*Arabian
Desert*

Baharaya

defeated by Thebes,
c. 1990 BC
Ashmunein
Hermopolis

Qis Cusae

*Red
Sea*

Sauty Asyut

c. 2050 BC
governor of Asyut joins royal
armies against Theban expanion

◆ Theban armies repulse
10th Dynasty forces
Ipu
Akhmim

Sawu
○ Mersa Gawasis
◆ Red Sea port

◆ c. 1986 BC
Theban troops capture fugitives
from 10th Dynasty armies

Thinis ✗ c. 2050 BC
Dendera

c. 2050 BC, sacred area ◆
desecrated by army from Asyut

Abydos
Coptos
◆ c. 2064 BC villages razed
in Theban area

Iuny
Armant
Wast
Thebes

N

Dakhla

Perhathor
Gebelein
*colony of
Nubian
mercenaries*

Nekhen
Hierakonpolis
◆ c. 2064 BC
governor of Hierakonpolis
opposes Theban expansion

0 ———— 150 km
0 ———— 100 miles

Kharga

Abu
Kurkur ○ Elephantine
*Nubian caravan
routes reopened*

EGYPT, c. 2064–1986 BC

▮ Theban heartland

▮ zone of Theban dominance during reign of Inyotef II

▮ expansion of Theban kingdom by death of
Inyotef II, c. 2015 BC

▯ Egypt at death of Montjuhotep II, c. 1956 BC

╲ advance of governor of Hierakonpolis, c. 2064

╲ wars between 10th Dynasty and Theban governors

➤ advance of armies of Montjuhotep II, c. 1994–1986 BC

➤ probable raids against desert tribes

╌╌╌ civil war zone

✗ battle site

⬯ oasis

WAWAT
◆ native dynasty of kings
◆ tribute levied by
Montjuhotep II

TROPIC OF CANCER

○ Buhen
◆ royal tour by Montjuhotep II
travels to Buhen

The Administrative State

Amenemhat I was able to reinvent the kingship by combining the royal traditions of the Old Kingdom with reforms of the administration.

"The king has commanded you to travel south to Thinis and Abydos to perform a dedication for my father, Osiris Khenyimentu: to refurbish his secret cult-image with the electrum which he caused me to bring back from the far-end of Nubia in victory and justification."
Stela from Abydos of the courtier Iykhernofret

The tomb of Amenemhat III at Beni Hasan. The tombs of Middle Kingdom governors rank amonst the largest and most attractive of any period.

Following the success of Montjuhotep II in unifying the kingship, certain provincial governors were replaced by Theban loyalists, but most were assimilated into the new regime; at some centres, like Menat Khufu, a family ruling since the Old Kingdom remained in power. The king's power base, however, was Thebes, and the most influential positions at court were filled by his supporters. It fell to the vizîr's office to supervise the critical process of reunifying the administration, and every vizîr of the 11th Dynasty was a Theban. Two decades after the death of Montjuhotep II, an able and active vizîr named Amenemhat came to the throne, in a peaceful succession, as the first king of the 12th Dynasty.

Amenemhat I set about re-establishing the kingship as the central presence in the nation by combining the traditional royal authority of the Old Kingdom with various administrative reforms. The principal royal residence was moved to a new site at Itjtawy, south of Memphis on the northern edge of the Faiyum region. Nearby the king arranged for the construction of a funerary complex on a scale equal to that of the pyramids at Giza, so that the king and his pyramid were seen to be the living heart of Egypt once more. The structure of the unified government was based upon that of the later Old Kingdom: the king was the central source of authority, and his officials were empowered by attendance at the palace to act as his agents throughout the country; every official of the palace and the provinces was subject to the will of the king. Although many older offices were reformed or replaced, the key figures in central and local administration (the vizîrs and district governors) remained constant.

The potential of this centralized system to organize labour is manifest in records of expeditions sent to mine semi-precious stones in the harsh eastern desert and Sinai. In the first two centuries of the Middle Kingdom there were nearly 700 such expeditions; for example, an expedition to Sinai in Year 2 of Amenemhat III (*c.* 1816 BC) numbered 734 men. The turquoise and copper mines at Serabit el-Khadim and Wadi Maghara were exploited more extensively in the Middle Kingdom than in any other period of pharaonic history. The expeditions were organized by the highest-ranking palace officials: the earliest (and perhaps largest) may have been the expedition sent to quarry amethyst at Wadi el-Hudi, led by the future Amenemhat I whilst still a vizîr.

In the art and literature of the 12th Dynasty the humanity of the king, burdened by earthly responsibilities, was glimpsed, and there may have been terrible pressures to endure: according to one tradition—albeit a literary tradition—Amenemhat I was eventually assassinated by members of his own court, and the succession of his son, Senusret I was far from certain at that moment. Nevertheless, building on his legacy, the kings of the 12th Dynasty were able to forge a system of government in which the king was once more a unifying presence in Egypt, and the tendency to allow power to devolve to the provinces was subjugated to the king's personal charisma.

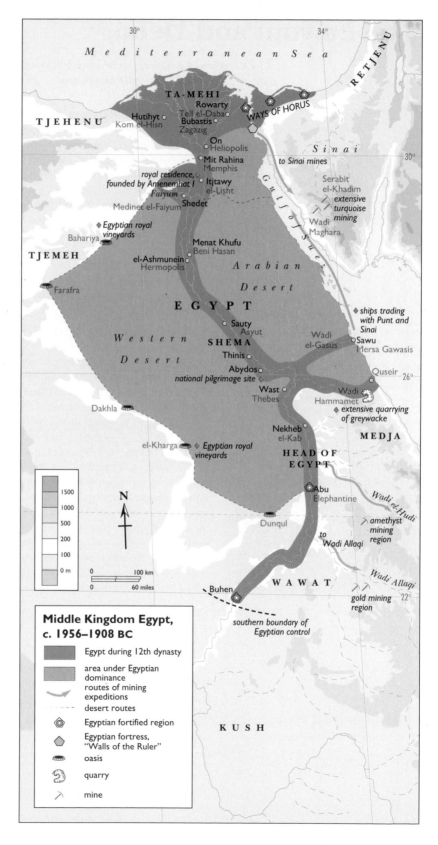

M e d i t e r r a n e a n   S e a

RETJENU

TA-MEHI

TJEHENU

Rowarty
Tell el-Daba
Hutihyt
Kom el-Hisn
Bubastis
Zagazig

WAYS OF HORUS

On
Heliopolis

S i n a i

to Sinai mines

Mit Rahina
Memphis

royal residence,
founded by Amenemhat I

Itjtawy
el-Lisht

Faiyum

Serabit
el-Khadim

extensive
turquoise
mining

Medinet el-Faiyum

Shedet

Wadi
Maghara

◆ *Egyptian royal
vineyards*

Bahariya

TJEMEH

Menat Khufu
Beni Hasan

el-Ashmunein
Hermopolis

A r a b i a n

D e s e r t

Farafra

EGYPT

Sauty
Asyut

W e s t e r n

D e s e r t

SHEMA

Thinis

◆ ships trading
with Punt and
Sinai

Wadi
el-Gasus

Sawu
Mersa Gawasis

Abydos

national pilgrimage site

Quseir

Wast
Thebes

Wadi
Hammamet

◆ extensive quarrying
of greywacke

Dakhla

el-Kharga

◆ *Egyptian royal
vineyards*

Nekheb
el-Kab

MEDJA

**HEAD OF
EGYPT**

Abu
Elephantine

Wadi el-Hudi

amethyst
mining
region

Dunqul

to
Wadi Allaqi

Wadi Allaqi

Buhen

WAWAT

gold mining
region

*southern boundary of
Egyptian control*

KUSH

1500
1000
500
200
100
0 m

N

0   100 km
0   60 miles

Middle Kingdom Egypt,
c. 1956–1908 BC

Egypt during 12th dynasty

area under Egyptian
dominance

routes of mining
expeditions

desert routes

Egyptian fortified region

Egyptian fortress,
"Walls of the Ruler"

oasis

quarry

mine

The Faiyum and Delta

The delta and the Faiyum were much wetter regions in ancient times, largely submerged by the Nile inundation.

"If the 11 enlistees are still waiting there for their reimbursement, all good and well— you are the one who can deal with matters within your own responsibility, if it pleases you."
Letter from Kahun

The pyramid of Senusret II at Illahun has a mud-brick core surrounded by the remains of a limestone casing.

Since the earliest settlement of Egypt, its outlying areas have tended to become drier, partly through the activities of farmers reclaiming arable land. In ancient times, settlements in the delta were sited only on the fringes or on sandy mounds known as turtle-backs; the area's ancient name was *Ta-mehi*, marsh land. Settlement in the Faiyum was similar in many ways: Lake Moeris was then much higher, and the area generally was so wet that settlement was limited to the fringes and a few specific areas. The ancient name of the region was the 'great lake' (*mer wer*, hence *Moeris* in Greek), or it was referred to simply as 'the water', *payom*, hence Faiyum. The arrival of the inundation wrought its most dramatic changes to the landscape in these regions: the low-lying delta marshes were flooded as far as the horizon, and water flowing into Lake Moeris could not disperse at all. At that moment the delta and Faiyum became, according to ancient texts, part of the 'Great Green'—the sea—and the turtle-backs were stranded like islands.

Administrative changes during the Middle Kingdom meant that the settlement of the delta and the Faiyum were given official priority. The government fortified its north-eastern border, and tightened its grip on outlying delta districts. The new royal residence at Itjtawy and the removal of the royal cemetery from Sakkara to the Faiyum increased the demands on settlement and agriculture in that region. Steps were taken to reduce the level of Lake Moeris and so increase the available land. A new town of the period was Hetepsenusret ("Senusret is at rest"), built beside the mortuary temple of Senusret II at Kahun to house the workmen of the royal pyramid and the priests who served his funerary cult. The town flourished for almost two centuries and contained about 250 regularly-arranged houses and was large enough to need its own mayor. An exceptional villa upon a rock outcrop (dubbed 'the acropolis') may hint at the occasional presence of the vizîr or even the king. A large number of papyri from two ancient archives discovered in Kahun are currently being studied, and should offer a unique insight into life in Middle Kingdom Egypt.

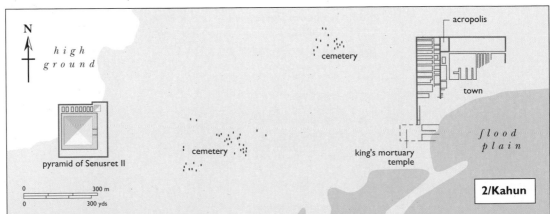

N

high ground

pyramid of Senusret II

0 300 m
0 300 yds

cemetery

cemetery

acropolis

town

king's mortuary temple

flood plain

2/Kahun

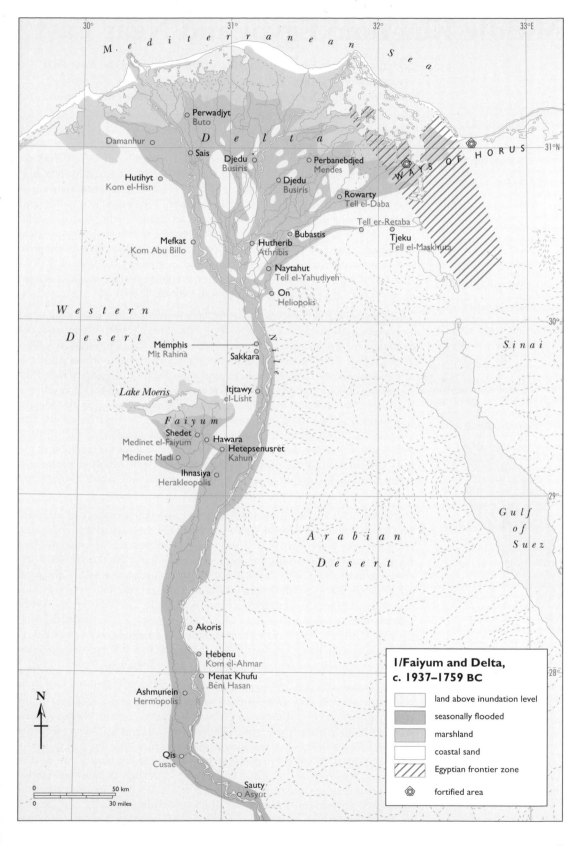

M e d i t e r r a n e a n S e a

Perwadjyt
Buto

Damanhur

D e l t a

Sais

Djedu
Busiris

Perbanebdjed
Mendes

WAYS OF HORUS

Hutihyt
Kom el-Hisn

Djedu
Busiris

Rowarty
Tell el-Daba

Tell er-Retaba

Mefkat
Kom Abu Billo

Hutherib
Athribis

Bubastis

Tjeku
Tell el-Maskhuta

Naytahut
Tell el-Yahudiyeh

On
Heliopolis

W e s t e r n

D e s e r t

Memphis
Mit Rahina

Sakkara

S i n a i

Lake Moeris

Itjtawy
el-Lisht

F a i y u m

Shedet
Medinet el-Faiyum

Hawara

Medinet Madi

Hetepsenusret
Kahun

Ihnasiya
Herakleopolis

G u l f
o f
S u e z

A r a b i a n

D e s e r t

Akoris

Hebenu
Kom el-Ahmar

Menat Khufu
Beni Hasan

Ashmunein
Hermopolis

N

Qis
Cusae

Sauty
Asyut

0   50 km
0   30 miles

**I/Faiyum and Delta,
c. 1937–1759 BC**

land above inundation level

seasonally flooded

marshland

coastal sand

Egyptian frontier zone

fortified area

47

Middle Kingdom Egypt and Near East

Middle Kingdom Egypt traded widely with the lands of the Near East, principally via the port of Byblos. Contacts with southern Palestine flourished, although royal policy avoided direct military intervention.

"This servant set out south. I paused at the Ways of Horus so that the commander who was in charge of the patrol there might send a message to the palace to let them know. The king arranged for a capable overseer of labourers on the royal estate to come, and with him ships loaded with gifts from the king for the natives who had accompanied me to lead me to the Ways of Horus."

The Story of Sinuhe

Scarabs—official seals and tokens—found throughout Palestine (Retjenu), Syria and Turkey, indicate extensive commercial links with Middle Kingdom Egypt. This network existed on two levels. Firstly, there were strong local links between peoples of the eastern delta and of southern Palestine, conducted informally on the basis of tradition, credit and perhaps kinship. Palestinian caravans regularly brought resins, spices and minerals such as malachite and galena; the largest caravans were received at the palace and the provincial capitals, but smaller groups frequently visited eastern delta towns such as Rowarty. Egypt also provided refuge for those fleeing political or climatic traumas in Palestine, like Jacob's family in the stories of Genesis. Palestinians and Syrians were also employed as servants and labourers or as slaves. During the 13th Dynasty the material culture of eastern delta villages developed a distinctive Egypto-Palestinian hybridization.

The other aspect of commerce was royal trade by which the palace obtained Lebanese timber and resin, as well as lapis lazuli, copper and ivory, in exchange for spices, gold and African trade goods. Contemporary Egyptian artefacts have been found throughout Retjenu, and royal monuments—statues and sphinxes—have been discovered from Beirut to Ugarit; finds within Egypt include objects from Minoan Crete. This trading network forged relationships with city-states in Syria and Babylonia, but there is no evidence of the formal royal bonding characteristic of trade in the New Kingdom. The crucial link in this network was Byblos, which had strong cultural affinities with Egypt, including the worship of Hathor, who was patron goddess of the port and mistress of the nearby cedar terraces. These affinities intensified during the Middle Kingdom, and the burials of the governors of Byblos eventually included Egyptian hieroglyphic texts.

During the 12th Dynasty it was royal policy to assert the existence of a distinct border separating Egypt from Palestine. In Nubia the southern border was a fixed line, but in the north-east it was a wide zone in which Egyptian military might was unchallenged. In the reign of Amenemhat I the border was made concrete in the form of "The Walls of the Ruler", a fortress which dominated all routes across northern Sinai. The most heavily used caravan routes—the "Ways of Horus"—were under Egyptian control, and so were policed by military patrols based in a series of fortified outposts. These roads and forts probably fell under the local administration of the 14th *nome* of Lower Egypt. "The Walls of the Ruler" also acted as a trading centre and a musterpoint for mining expeditions to Serabit el-Khadim and Wadi Maghara.

A provocative witness to this period is the group of objects called "execration texts": these pottery jars and figurines were inked over with the names of foreign regions and communities and then smashed as a curse. Names written on them include places throughout Retjenu, Shuwet and Api, even including Byblos, which ultimately was foreign and therefore "hostile". Despite the curses, Egypt rarely sought to promote her security or her trading interests in the north through the use of force. The only campaign certainly attested—although others are hinted at in various texts—was led by Senusret III as far as *Sekmem* (presumably Shechem), before turning back in the face of engagements with local troops.

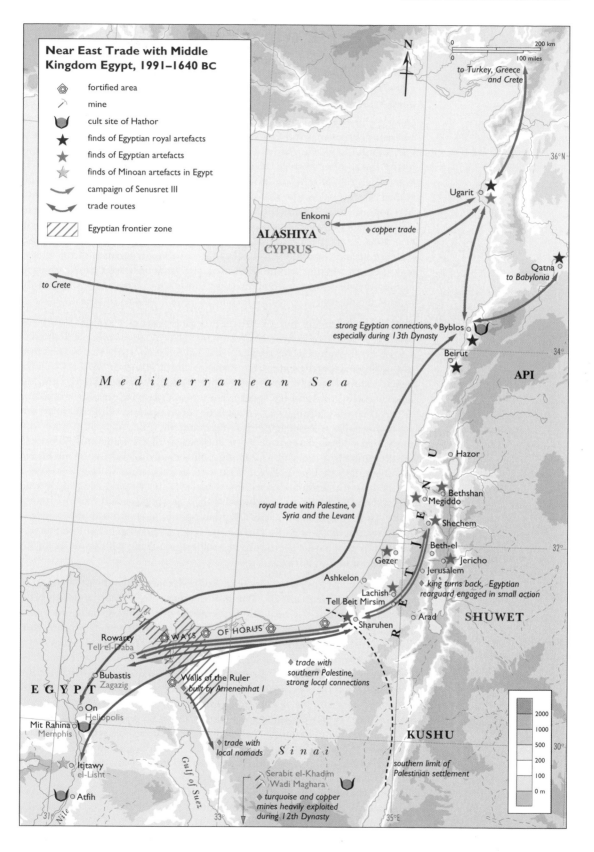

Near East Trade with Middle Kingdom Egypt, 1991–1640 BC

- ⊚ fortified area
- ⟋ mine
- ☻ cult site of Hathor
- ★ finds of Egyptian royal artefacts
- ★ finds of Egyptian artefacts
- ★ finds of Minoan artefacts in Egypt
- ⌣ campaign of Senusret III
- ⟶ trade routes
- ▨ Egyptian frontier zone

0 — 200 km
0 — 100 miles

N

to Turkey, Greece
and Crete

36°N

Ugarit ★

Enkomi ○   ◆ copper trade

Qatna
to Babylonia ★

ALASHIYA
CYPRUS

to Crete

strong Egyptian connections, ◆ Byblos
especially during 13th Dynasty

34°

Beirut ○ ★

API

M e d i t e r r a n e a n   S e a

Hazor ○

royal trade with Palestine, ◆
Syria and the Levant

U

Bethshan ○
★ Megiddo

Shechem ★

32°

Beth-el ○

Gezer ★

Jericho ★
Jerusalem ○

Ashkelon ○

◆ king turns back, Egyptian
rearguard engaged in small action

Lachish ○
Tell Beit Mirsim ★

Sharuhen ⊚

Arad ○

SHUWET

R E T J E N

Rowarty
Tell el-Daba   ⊚ WAYS ⊚ OF HORUS ⊚

◆ trade with
southern Palestine,
strong local connections

Bubastis ○
Zagazig

EGYPT   ⟋ Walls of the Ruler
built by Amenemhat I ⊚

On ○
Heliopolis

KUSHU

Mit Rahina ☻
Memphis

◆ trade with
local nomads   *S i n a i*

30°

southern limit of
Palestinian settlement

Itjtawy ★
el-Lisht

Gulf of Suez

Serabit el-Khadim ☻
⟋ Wadi Maghara

Atfih ☻

31°   33°   35°E

◆ turquoise and copper
mines heavily exploited
during 12th Dynasty

2000
1000
500
200
100
0 m

49

Middle Kingdom Egypt and Nubia

The Middle Kingdom army and administration systematically enriched Egypt's economy by dominating, and eventually annexing, Wawat and northern Kush.

"The southern boundary which is made in year 8 under Senusret III in order to prevent any Nubian passing it travelling north—overland or in a boat—or any Nubian cattle, except a Nubian coming to trade at Iken or upon business that one may properly do with them. Yet no boat of the Nubians shall be allowed to travel beyond Heh forever."

First Semna Boundary Stela of Senusret III

During the war against the 10th Dynasty, Montjuhotep II consolidated Theban control of southern Egypt by constructing a series of forts from Hierakonpolis to Elephantine, he then pressed into Wawat, in order to secure the southern border and safeguard the flow of Nubian goods. In his Year 15 (*c.* 1993 BC). Montjuhotep also strengthened his army by employing Nubian mercenaries, who distinguished themselves in combat with the loyalist troops of Asyut. Having successfully concluded the war, the new regime set about enhancing its trading position in Nubia; Kurkur was occupied as part of a wider strategy for controlling the southern caravan routes, and Wawat suffered at least one more military attack. Although Egypt did not seek to annex Wawat, regular tribute was levied, and Buhen was re-established as an Egyptian trade centre, at which the king himself stayed during his tour of the reunified country.

Subsequently, the policy of the 12th Dynasty kings towards Nubia was blunter. In the decade from his Year 5 (*c.* 1913 BC), the armies of Senusret I systematically reduced Wawat to formal Egyptian control. The cornerstone of this process was the extension of the southern group of forts as far as the second cataract; new forts were strategically placed to control both river and desert traffic, and served principally as secure stations for garrisons, although several were large enough to accommodate administrative and economic offices. Regular patrols operating via a network of military outposts made detailed records of the movement of caravans and potentially hostile nomads as part of a policing policy co-ordinated by the provincial administration of Upper Egypt. The forts at Ikkur and Kuban were also a secure base for mining expeditions, especially in the gold regions of Wadi Allaqi. New trade centres were established at Mirgissa and Sai in order to trade directly with Kush, and Egyptian agents were presumably active at Kerma in the heart of Kush. During the reign of Senusret II, a Red Sea port was founded at Sawu in order to re-establish sea trade with lands as far distant as Punt in East Africa.

The character of Egyptian control in Nubia was intensified by the expansionist ambitions of Senusret III. Troop movement into Nubia was made easier following the construction at the first cataract of a fortified road, and a canal allowing free passage on the Nile. Senusret's armies then drove into Kush itself on three campaigns during Years 8 to 19 (*c.* 1829–1818 BC). Mirgissa was fortified—thereby extending Egypt's border south of the second cataract for the first time in history—and a further series of forts was built from Askut to Semna. At Semna the desert invaded the river, and the military architects exploited the site to spectacular effect: the watercourse was partially dammed to restrict passage to the width of a single vessel isolated between forts at Semna and Kumma; approach to this channel was surveyed by a fort at Semna South, and passage beyond was dominated by a cluster of forts and a fortified road. A group of stelae was erected in the region to celebrate the Egyptian victory, along with a statue of the king which glowered over the border at the Kushites. In the king's own words, travel beyond Semna was now impossible without his consent, and future generations were challenged to maintain Egypt's grip on Nubia.

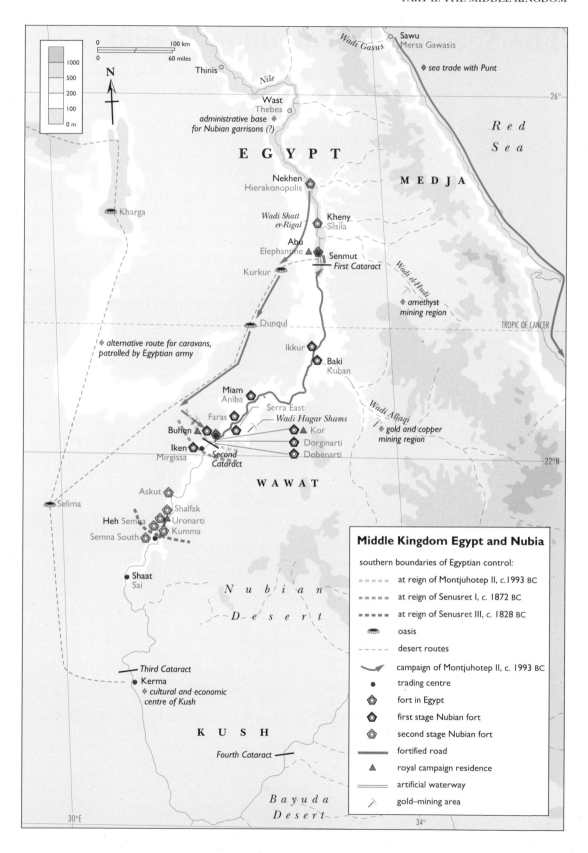

N

Wadi Gasus

Sawu
Mersa Gawasis

◆ sea trade with Punt

Thinis

Nile

Wast
Thebes

administrative base ◆
for Nubian garrisons (?)

EGYPT

MEDJA

Red
Sea

26°

Nekhen
Hierakonopolis

Kharga

Wadi Shatt
er-Rigal

Kheny
Silsila

Abu
Elephantine ▲

Senmut
First Cataract

Kurkur

Wadi el-Hudi

◆ amethyst
mining region

TROPIC OF CANCER

Dunqul

◆ alternative route for caravans,
patrolled by Egyptian army

Ikkur

Baki
Kuban

Miam
Aniba

Serra East
Wadi Hagar Shams

Wadi Allaqi

Faras

Buhen ▲

Kor ▲

◆ gold and copper
mining region

Iken
Mirgissa

Second
Cataract

Dorginarti

Dobenarti

22°N

WAWAT

Askut

Selima

Shalfak
Heh Semna ▲ Uronarti
Semna South Kumma

Shaat
Sai

N u b i a n

D e s e r t

Third Cataract
Kerma

◆ cultural and economic
centre of Kush

K U S H

Fourth Cataract

B a y u d a
D e s e r t

30°E

34°

Middle Kingdom Egypt and Nubia

southern boundaries of Egyptian control:

- - - - at reign of Montjuhotep II, c.1993 BC

– – – at reign of Senusret I, c. 1872 BC

▪▪▪▪ at reign of Senusret III, c. 1828 BC

⬭ oasis

- - - - desert routes

↘ campaign of Montjuhotep II, c. 1993 BC

● trading centre

⬡ fort in Egypt

⬡ first stage Nubian fort

⬡ second stage Nubian fort

━ fortified road

▲ royal campaign residence

═ artificial waterway

↗ gold–mining area

0 — 100 km
0 — 60 miles

1000
500
200
100
0 m

51

The Second Intermediate Period

The end of the Middle Kingdom saw Nubia lost from Egyptian control, the emergence of a Theban monarchy, and the division of the delta into several kingdoms.

"We are content with our Black Land: Abu is strong, and the heartland is with us as far as Cusae."
First Karnak Stela of Kamose.

No sharp division in administrative or political history marks the end of the Middle Kingdom: gradually the territorial authority of the 13th Dynasty diminished and the country was divided amongst several kings. Obscurity clouds most of these reigns and the political geography of the Second Intermediate Period is enormously problematic (although, ironically, important monuments and papyri have survived that offer a more detailed glimpse of the administration and demographics of society than in any preceding period). Royal burials at Memphis, Avaris and Thebes represent a tiny fraction of the number of kings known from texts: the Turin Royal Canon lists up to 175, few of whom reigned even five years. Evidence from monuments is far from harmonious, and so we rely on a conventional distillation of the data, according to which kings ruling from Itjtawy or Memphis are assigned to the 13th Dynasty, the kings of Avaris to the 15th Dynasty, and the kings of Thebes to the 17th Dynasty. The 14th and 16th dynasties thus became a

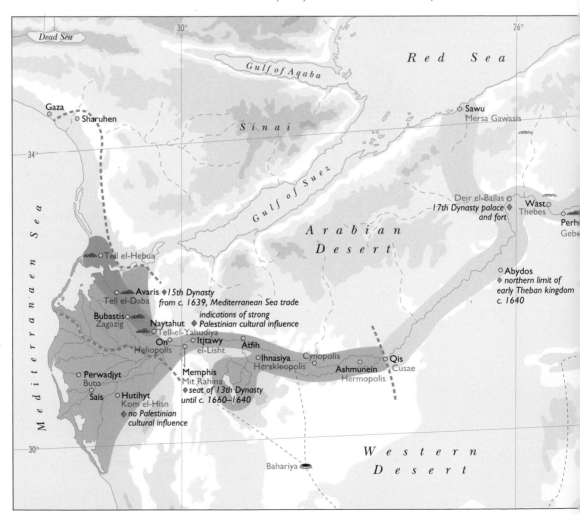

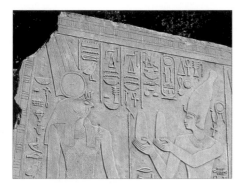

Relief from Karnak temple of Sobkemsaf, one of the few kings of Thebes in the Second Intermediate Period who left significant monuments. His exact position in history is unknown, although a document survives detailing robbery of his tomb more than 450 years after his death.

convenient repository for the remaining, intractably obscure kings.

The break-up of Middle Kingdom Egypt was determined by three processes: the loss of Nubia, the apparent division of the delta into several small kingdoms, and the rise to power of the Theban 17th Dynasty. In Nubia, the confederation of Nubian chiefs had rejected Egyptian rule during the 13th Dynasty, and recognized its own king, with Kerma in Kush as his power-centre. This kingdom consolidated its political and economic authority until it rivalled Egypt for pre-eminence on the Nile. Amongst its subjects were communities descended from the garrisons of Egyptian forts, and its armies recruited mercenaries from Egypt. Circumstances in the Nile delta are a matter of inference. Ay, one of the longest reigning kings of the 13th Dynasty, was buried near Avaris rather than Memphis, suggesting that the fragmentation of the north was already taking place. It seems likely that many kings were "small fry" subject to those wielding greater economic authority, and, in this sense, none held more power than the six kings of the 15th Dynasty who ruled Avaris, probably for 108 years, until the arrival of the Theban armies heralded the advent of the New Kingdom.

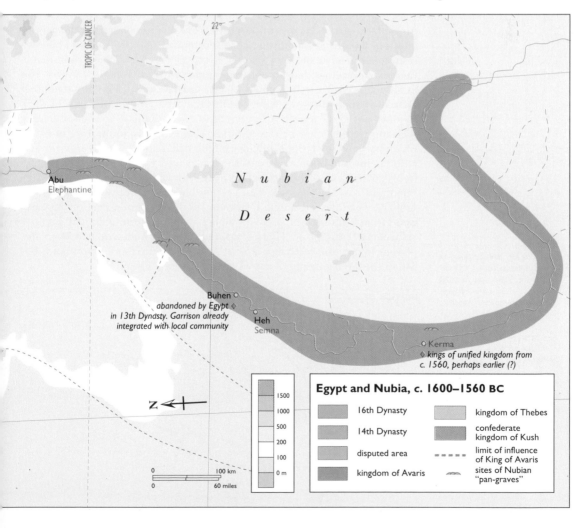

TROPIC OF CANCER

22°

Abu
Elephantine

N u b i a n

D e s e r t

Buhen
*abandoned by Egypt
in 13th Dynasty. Garrison already
integrated with local community*

Heh
Semna

Kerma
◇ *kings of unified kingdom from
c. 1560, perhaps earlier (?)*

Z

1500
1000
500
200
100
0 m

0   100 km
0   60 miles

Egypt and Nubia, c. 1600–1560 BC

16th Dynasty	kingdom of Thebes
14th Dynasty	confederate kingdom of Kush
disputed area	limit of influence of King of Avaris
kingdom of Avaris	sites of Nubian "pan-graves"

Thebes, Kush and the Hyksos Kings

The kings of Avaris and Kush were confronted by the aggression of Kamose and the armies of Thebes.

"You have been driven back with your army, and your speech is so miserable—in making me a chief whilst you are a ruler—as to demand for you the chopping-block to which you will fall! Watch your miserable back because my army is after you!" Kamose's speech to Apophis (Second Karnak Stela).

Out of the division of Egypt arose three kings, at Avaris, Thebes and Kush, who negotiated and traded as equals. On stelae erected by Kamose of Thebes in the Temple of Amun, his courtiers expressed their satisfaction at this situation in committed terms: "We are content with our Black Land ... the flattest of their lands are ploughed for us, cattle graze for us in the marshes, and emmer is sent for our swine ... Should someone come who would act against us, then we will act against him!" Nevertheless, the resolve to end partition came from the Theban king himself. Bemoaning the economic restraints imposed upon him by the king of Avaris, he complained: "Why do I bother to contemplate my victories when there is a chief in Avaris and another in Kush, and I am bound to an Asiatic and an Nubian, each man holding his own slice of this Black Land and dividing the country with me?" Kamose's motivation, therefore, was partly economic (he resented not having direct access to the trade routes of Palestine or to the mineral wealth of Nubia), and partly based on a profound belief in the integrity of the land along the Nile.

An initial attack on Kush is known only from oblique reference, but monuments of Kamose at Buhen survive as testimony to his success; the king also instituted the office of "King's Son of Kush" (Viceroy of Nubia), presumably thereby confirming that he had regained control of Wawat. However, the assault on Avaris is well detailed on the Karnak stelae. The population of Nefrusy were the first to pay for the insult to his dignity, with many of their number put to the sword. A force sent to cover the oasis roads at Bahariya then intercepted a letter from Apophis, king of Avaris, to the king of Kush, which betrayed the Hyksos' military impotence. Kamose's account is broken at this point, and resumes with Avaris already under attack—the king "flying" in his golden boat at the head of his fleet. This city, however, was heavily fortified and could not be razed as Nefrusy had been; instead its estates and orchards were ravaged, and its chariot-teams, bronze battle-axes, oil, incense, wood from Palestine, and precious metals and stone were all looted. Kamose returned in triumph to Thebes, satisfied that his authority had been displayed. In fact, the campaign against Avaris was little more than a raid, but with it the die was cast for a war which would unify Egypt.

The key to the attack on Avaris were marines, moving quickly by ship before landing to raid the estates and villages that surrounded Apophis' fortress. In the initial approach, the fleet was arrayed like a swooping falcon with the king at the head in his golden falcon-ship.

2/Kamose's raid of Avaris, c. 1540 BC

- marshland
- residential area
- movement of Egyptian fleet
- movement of marines through local estates

Egyptian fleet moored, Apophis' fleet plundered ◆

upstream ferry

The Asiatic Water

Kamose ◆ crosses river to taunt Apophis

Apophis' fortress

sacred precinct of Avaris

royal falcon ship

◆ briefly beseiged

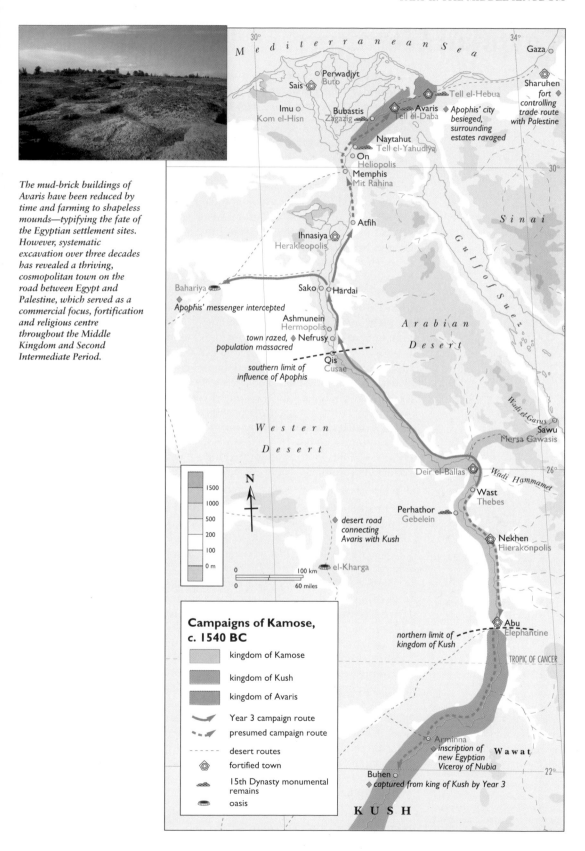

The mud-brick buildings of Avaris have been reduced by time and farming to shapeless mounds—typifying the fate of the Egyptian settlement sites. However, systematic excavation over three decades has revealed a thriving, cosmopolitan town on the road between Egypt and Palestine, which served as a commercial focus, fortification and religious centre throughout the Middle Kingdom and Second Intermediate Period.

Mediterranean Sea

Gaza

Sharuhen fort controlling trade route with Palestine

Perwadjyt
Buto

Sais

Tell el-Hebua

Imu
Kom el-Hisn

Bubastis
Zagazig

Avaris
Tell el-Daba

Apophis' city besieged, surrounding estates ravaged

Naytahut
Tell el-Yahudiya

On
Heliopolis

Memphis
Mit Rahina

S i n a i

Atfih

Ihnasiya
Herakleopolis

G u l f   o f   S u e z

Bahariya

Sako   Hardai

Apophis' messenger intercepted

Ashmunein
Hermopolis

town razed,   Nefrusy
population massacred

Qis
Cusae

A r a b i a n

D e s e r t

southern limit of influence of Apophis

W e s t e r n

D e s e r t

Wadi el-Gasus

Sawu
Mersa Gawasis

Deir el-Ballas

Wadi Hammamet

Wast
Thebes

Perhathor
Gebelein

desert road connecting Avaris with Kush

Nekhen
Hierakonpolis

el-Kharga

TROPIC OF CANCER

Abu
Elephantine

northern limit of kingdom of Kush

N

1500
1000
500
200
100
0 m

0   100 km
0   60 miles

Arminna
inscription of new Egyptian Viceroy of Nubia

W a w a t

Buhen
captured from king of Kush by Year 3

Campaigns of Kamose, c. 1540 BC

kingdom of Kamose

kingdom of Kush

kingdom of Avaris

Year 3 campaign route

presumed campaign route

desert routes

fortified town

15th Dynasty monumental remains

oasis

K U S H

Egyptian Literature

Egyptian literature as composed in the Middle Kingdom, proved hugely influential for later generations; a central theme is understanding how to live a decent life in harmony with the greater scheme of the created world.

"Listen to me, my captain, I do not speak out of turn. Cleanse yourself, and pour water on your fingers. Then speak up when you are addressed, speak to the king with your wits about you, and speak without stammering. A man's speech can save him. His words can earn him indulgence. Still, you do what you like—talking to you is tiresome!"

The Story of the Shipwrecked Sailor

In the late-12th and 15th Dynasties, the earliest Egyptian literature was written for consumption in life, but it was inspired by the funerary texts of officials; these quasi-biographies used typical phrases to define a life lived properly, as befitted a responsible member of society, and to claim the resultant rewards—royal favour, a good reputation and a place in the after-life. A central ideal in tomb biography, and hence in literature, was *maat*, the proper order of creation; to understand *maat* was to understand what is ethical and just, and also to understand the intentions of the creator god. In texts such as *The Laments of Khakheperrasonb*, the chaos is imagined of a world in which *maat* was neglected, although the possibility that this could ever happen is denied. Other texts, known as "Instructions", simply try to define a good life lived ethically; they recommend adherence to tradition, and claim to be based on the teachings of wise officials, especially Old Kingdom courtiers such as the legendary Imhotep, or on the sayings of kings. The most famous collection was attributed to Ptahhotep, said to be vizîr of King Izezi of the 5th Dynasty, although he may be an entirely fictional character; his sayings espouse virtues of moderation, generosity, and truth—tempered by discretion. Ptahhotep fosters the ideal of a man who accepts his lot in life; a compelling variation on the same theme is *A Man's Dispute with his Own Soul*, preserved in a single 12th Dynasty copy. For the man, the human condition is an intolerable burden, but death offers a longed-for release; the soul responds that death is a melancholy business and it is not for us to rid ourselves of life as if it were something we control. Eventually, the two are reconciled to the inevitability of death, and anticipate the new awareness it may bring.

Old Kingdom funerary texts also inspired accounts of fictional lives, which draw upon the oral story-telling traditions of Ancient Egypt. *The Story of the Shipwrecked Sailor* is the earliest example of a genre in which a perilous journey becomes a voyage of understanding, like the stories of Odysseus and Aeneas, or Conrad's *Heart of Darkness*. It is also a picturesque drama, and—as we might expect of a story which treats religious themes in a folktale—has an underlying moral: a wise, mystical serpent exhorts the stranded sailor to learn self-control and accept what has befallen him (including the deaths of his companions), to be content with an eventual return to his family and to look forward to a dignified burial. However, the text most popular amongst Egyptians themselves was *The Story of Sinuhe*, several copies of which survive, including two major Middle Kingdom papyri and an *ostracon* with an updated New Kingdom text. Sinuhe is a courtier who flees to Palestine, filled with fear and guilt, following the murder of his king, Amenemhat I. In exile he becomes a wealthy and celebrated warrior, but this cannot calm his anxieties, and ultimately he is forced to forsake even his family in order to gain the one thing which can offer peace of mind: reconciliation with the new king of Egypt and his own people. Sinuhe's story is a profound account of human hopes and fears, and a moving insight into what it once meant to be Egyptian.

Middle Kingdom literature was so influential that the "classics" were still read centuries later, and new compositions generally conformed to established

Detail on this page. Part of the passage from The Story of the Shipwrecked Sailor *translated above; the single surviving copy of the tale is a 12th Dynasty papyrus, probably originally prepared for use in a scribal school.*

Painting from the tomb of Sennefer at Thebes (18th Dynasty). There were strong links between the themes of Egyptian art and literature. For example, the journeys of self-discovery made by Sinuhe and the shipwrecked sailor are the subjects of two of the most engaging ancient stories; in this painting, the same theme is translated into a funerary context, depicting the journey of the dead man's soul to Abydos, to leave behind the anxieties of life and dwell in the blessed kingdom of Osiris.

genres. The wisdom of Ptahhotep was echoed in the New Kingdom by *The Instructions of Amenemope*, and later by *The Instructions of Ankhsheshonky*. The fairytale quality of *The Story of the Shipwrecked Sailor* is also apparent in *The Doomed Prince* or *The Tale of Two Brothers*, both of which involve adventures abroad in strange lands; in the Late Period, cycles of mythical adventures became popular, involving quasi-historical figures such as Setne-Khaemwast (a son of Ramesses II) and the rebel Inaros. A taste for satire, apparent in scurrilous Middle Kingdom stories about the courts of Snofru and Khufu, resurfaced in humorous tales about kings such as Apophis and Amasis, and even about the gods themselves. Dozens of copies of Middle Kingdom writings were held by the sophisticated villagers at Deir el-Medina, including *Ptahhotep* and *Sinuhe*; some were placed in tombs as treasured wisdom, whilst others were used to educate children. One scribe, Keniherkhopeshef, collected a library of over forty papyri, on one of which was asked the question: "Is there anyone now like Hardjedef? Is there another like Imhotep?... Is there another like Ptahhotep or Kaires?". A New Kingdom lyric, known as *The Song of the Harper*, has an unexpected but pointed rejoinder: "I have heard the words of Amenhotep and Hardjedef, whose sayings are recited faithfully, although their tombs have crumbled as if they have never been. No-one comes back from beyond to say what it is like, to speak their needs or soothe our hearts until we must go where they have gone!

III: The New Kingdom

The New Kingdom was a time of unity, during which the policy of annexing Nubian gold-mines made Egypt the major commercial power in the ancient world. Extensive trading networks with other great kings were built upon ties of mutual respect.

"If (the king) were to spend a moment enjoying himself hunting on any desert, the number of what he brought himself would be more than the spoils of the entire expedition. He slew seven lions by archery in the space of a moment, after he had brought the hides of twelve bulls in a single hour: the period for breakfast came and their tails were at his backside. He toppled 120 tuskers on the desert of Nii, returning from Naharin after he had crossed the Euphrates, and crushed the villages on both its sides, which are reduced to ashes for eternity."

Stela of
Thutmose III
from the temple
of Armant

The renaissance during the 18th Dynasty began with the reunification of Egypt in the reign of Ahmose, son and heir of the 17th Dynasty, but founding father of the New Kingdom. He inherited the belief that the kings of Thebes in the Second Intermediate Period were the legitimate successors to the Middle Kingdom, upon whom fell the obligation to reunite the Black Land, the Nilotic kingdom of Egypt and Nubia together. The sequence of events by which this came about in Ahmose's reign is unclear: the final war against Avaris was launched late in the new king's reign (perhaps as late as Year 20), but it seems that Memphis—crucially outside Kamose's control—had fallen into Theban hands already, and so the intervening years may have witnessed ongoing Theban aggression. Apophis and Khemudy, the last kings of Avaris, saw their town assaulted by Theban marines on as many as five separate campaigns, each characterized by savage fighting between fellow-Egyptians in the surrounding canals and estates. After the great fortress itself fell, an army crossed Sinai to besiege Sharuhen, a Palestinian fort and trade centre within Hyksos dominion which had helped to maintain the commercial authority of Avaris. The siege was ended after three years *c.* 1518 BC, and the victorious Egyptians were ruthless in slaughtering the population, thereby asserting that the route across Sinai—and hence the passage of trade between Egypt and Palestine—was in Theban control. Even if Khemudy had survived the downfall of Avaris, he would have found his economic power base shattered.

There is no evidence to suggest that Theban armies pursued their success by advancing into Palestine during the reign of Ahmose; in fact, there is no evidence of any Egyptian campaigns in Palestine at all until the 22nd Year of Thutmose III, some 61 years later. Archaeological evidence indicating that several sites such as Jericho were burned or abandoned at about this time, has been mooted as evidence of Egyptian aggression, but these destructions took place over a long period and are better explained as the result of protracted, localized fighting between Palestinian and Canaanite city-states. An inscription of the female king Hatshepsut—in a temple built shortly after this period near Beni Hasan—suggests that Avaris under the 15th Dynasty kings had been a haven for Palestinian refugees, who were perhaps displaced from their homeland during this difficult period. In fact, the destruction of strategic towns in Syria or Palestine would have been self-defeating for Egypt, since these were the very places which organized the movement of trade. Later New Kingdom records indicate that pharaoh preferred to leave these towns in the hands of their own rulers, once he had extracted an oath of loyalty; more troublesome chiefs were sometimes deposed in favour of a more amenable character, but atrocities such as that at Sharuhen were repeated only rarely, and there is no compelling evidence of the deliberate, wholesale destruction of the fabric of large towns.

Ahmose's victory in the north of Egypt was apparently complete by the end of his reign, but the army was required to suppress two uprisings in defiance of the new order. A rebellion in Nubia was perhaps not unexpected, and could even be interpreted as a war provoked by continued Egyptian expansion. Monuments of this period have been discovered as far south as the island of Shaat, 120 kilometres beyond the Middle Kingdom border at

Semna; although Shaat had, in earlier times, been populated by Egyptian merchants, the presence of royal monuments probably indicates more direct intervention; certainly the town had been turned into an Egyptian fort by the reign of Thutmose I (*c.* 1493–1481 BC). The second incident was probably a genuine rebellion within Egypt itself, led by a shadowy figure called Tetian, and indicated that the process of reunification was still not without its enemies. Ultimately, however, the Theban vision of a reunified Black Land was fulfilled, and Amenhotep I succeeded his father *c.* 1514 BC as the king of all Egypt. Even though Amenhotep died 21 years later without a surviving son as heir, the succession passed without incident to a Theban courtier, Thutmose—possibly related to the dead king by marriage—who fathered a line of kings that retained the throne until the death of Tutankhamun 175 years later. The royal family of the 18th Dynasty is probably the best documented in pharaonic history, and certainly the most written about in modern times. Royal texts from this period normally refer only to religious performances by the king and little else, but a wealth of art has survived, several palaces have been excavated, and the tombs of courtiers throughout the country have been surveyed; even the corpses of many New Kingdom pharaohs, and several of their queens, are miraculously still preserved. Such evidence offers the tantalizing impression that we can get to know these ancient rulers; surely if we can gaze upon their mortal faces, then we can understand what motivated them? Of course, this is foolish; nevertheless kings like Thutmose III, Akhenaten and Tutankhamun have long established roles in a modern mythology (or soap opera) of Ancient Egypt, which is far more potent than any diligent academic analysis of the evidence.

The two defining characteristics of royal art in the 18th Dynasty were the identification of the king as an incarnation of the sun god, and the prominence given to queens as his female counterparts. The first of these was a belief dating back to the Old Kingdom, and the 18th Dynasty pharaohs were fascinated by the ancient pyramids at Giza, near which they built a palace and several temples. The prominence of the queens was apparent in monumental art from the beginning of the dynasty; wives, mothers and daughters were frequently shown accompanying the king, whereas royal men were generally unseen. Beginning with Ahhotep and Ahmose-Nefertiti the mother and wife respectively of Ahmose, a series of queens assumed exceptional religious and

Detail from reliefs in the temple at Deir el-Bahri depicting the expedition to Punt during the reign of Hatshepsut. This scene shows Parehu, ruler of Punt, and his wife Ati, followed by a retinue bringing local goods to Egyptian ships on the Red Sea shore. Like many other African nations, Punt was a valued trading partner of Egypt, and never a military opponent, although the artist has characteristically implied that the bearded Puntites brought their produce as a tribute to pharaoh. The depiction of the queen's obesity was unusual in Egyptian art, which usually portrayed idealized bodies, especially for women.

Detail of the 19th Dynasty Hypostyle Hall in the temple of Amun-Ra at Karnak. Many of Egypt's greatest temples originally date from the New Kingdom, although many, like Karnak, were built on the sites of earlier shrines. In the New Kingdom, the size of temples—in terms of buildings, staff and, importance to the administration— was generally very much greater than before.

economic authority. The most significant was Hatshepsut: as the daughter of Thutmose I, and the half-sister and wife of Thutmose II, her authority was barely distinguishable from that of the kings, and eventually she became king herself in the reign of her step-son, Thutmose III. She then ruled as his co-regent until her death *c.* 1458 BC. Hatshepsut was not succeeded as king by her own daughter as she had planned, and her reputation suffered at the hands of later generations who felt that the distinction between king and queen could not be so completely disregarded. Nevertheless, the prominence of the queens was maintained into the reign of Ramesses II (*c.* 1279–1213 BC), whose principal wife, Nefertari, was worshipped as an incarnation of the goddess Hathor in her own temple at Nubia.

Both aspects of 18th Dynasty kingship reached their most pronounced form during the reigns of Amenhotep III and of his son Amenhotep IV, when conscious reflection on the nature of kingship led to the development of a startling new art style with which to express new ideas. After the death of Amenhotep III, the ancient iconography of the sun-god Ra-Horakhty was changed from a disc with a falcon's wings to a disc with human arms in order to represent the sun as the spirit of the dead king nurturing his living son. In the same period, the principal queens—Tiy and Nefertiti respectively—were shown slaughtering the enemies of Egypt as if they were kings; eventually, under the name Nefernefruaten, Nefertiti became titular king alongside her husband. Both Amenhotep III and his son built temples expressing their new ideas at ancient religious centres such as Thebes and Hermopolis; but eventually Amenhotep IV ordered the building of a city on a virgin site called Akhetaten ("horizon of the sun-disc") in which religious practices could be developed which were pure and free from any unwanted associations with the past. The king also changed his personal name to Akhenaten ("the spirit of the sun-disc"), although the rest of his titulary was unaltered. The Amarna period (so-called after the site of Akhetaten) was reviled by later kings for having distorted fundamental beliefs about the kingship, but it can be seen as the final step, albeit a step too far, along a path which guided the whole of the 18th Dynasty.

Kush and the Nubian Gold Mines

Following the annexation of Wawat in the 17th Dynasty, large tracts of Nubia were assimilated into Egypt for almost 500 years, as a result of which the economic wealth of the vast southern land played a formative role in the historical development of the New Kingdom. The occupied territories were so important that their administration was fully integrated into the central administration of Egypt; the office of "King's Son of Kush" (which, despite appearances, was never occupied by the natural son of any king) held the same responsibilities within Nubia that the vizîrs held within Egypt, and the incumbent had available to him a comparable staff of agents. An administrative infrastructure modelled directly on the Egyptian government—including privileged trading centres, military forts and temple-towns—was set in place swiftly, principally during the reigns of Thutmose I and Thutmose II; significant differences in the administration of Nubia were those dictated by security issues in the border areas and deserts. The indigenous chiefs of Wawat—and eventually also the chiefs of many

Head of a colossal statue of Hatshepsut with the beard and crown of king. The role of principal queen became increasingly close to that of king during the early 18th Dynasty, and eventually c. 1473 BC Hatshepsut—who was the daughter of Thutmose I, and queen of Thutmose II—ascended the throne as king in her own right alongside her stepson, Thutmose III.

parts of Kush—were accorded the same status in government as high-ranking courtiers, and encouraged to participate actively in the subjugation of their own homeland; indeed, many native rulers sent their children to the Egyptian palace to be raised in the presence of the king and his future successor.

New Kingdom policy with regard to Wawat and Kush was essentially determined by two considerations. On the one hand, as Nilotic lands they were an integral part of the Black Land; this belief intensified the potential threat—both political and economic—from the kingdom of Kush, which was thereby seen as a pretender to rightful Egyptian hegemony. On the other hand, the enormous mineral resources of Nubia, especially in gold, were the foundation on which the 18th Dynasty built a formidable commercial economy. These two aspects of policy had different geographical implications—the determination to extend Egyptian control of the Black Land involved expansion along the river, whereas the search for gold required mining expeditions to trek ever deeper into the eastern desert—but they were, of course, inextricably linked, since any enlargement of territory or wealth on Egypt's part was made directly at the expense of Kush.

The annexation of Wawat had predictably plunged Egypt and Kush into direct conflict at the very beginning of the New Kingdom. Wawat was the principal gold-producing region of Nubia, and could act as a strategic buffer zone in front of Kush. However, during the reign of Amenhotep I (if not before), it became Egyptian policy to extend the southern boundary further than it had existed during the Middle Kingdom. Thutmose I subsequently brought the third cataract region under his control, and established a fortress on the river at Tombos, barely thirty kilometres north of the cultural heartland of Kush at Kerma. He also arranged for Wawat to be carved into five new administrative districts, presumably in order to ensure that rebellion could not crystallize within the traditional tribal structure of the region. Around *c.* 1481 BC a rebellion sponsored by Kush was suppressed with greater ferocity by the armies of Thutmose II, and thereafter any aspirations towards independence in the population of Wawat were effectively eliminated. The co-regency between Thutmose III and Hatshepsut seems to have been the key period in which attempts to resist Egyptian domination of Kush itself were effectively overcome; after Hatshepsut's demise, the sole reign of Thutmose III was for a long time dominated by political and military manoeuvring in Syria and Palestine, suggesting that Egypt's strategic interest in the south was secure. Following a campaign beyond Kerma deep into Kush in Year 47 of Thutmose III (*c.* 1433 BC), a granite stela of the king was erected at Gebel Barkal near the fourth cataract in connection with the building of a

The "colossi of Memnon", over 60 feet high, now stand in splendid isolation at Western Thebes, but originally they flanked a gateway within the mortuary complex of Amenhotep III. The seated king is flanked at his feet by the principal queens. His mortuary complex was the most massive in the New Kingdom, and included an artificial harbour which allowed sea-going vessels to bring tribute directly from the Near East to his funerary temple.

fort; an Egyptian town was founded nearby at Napata in the reign of his son, Amenhotep II (*c.* 1427–1392 BC). This site probably represented the southernmost limit of Egyptian control along the Nile during the New Kingdom, beyond which the arid region of Karoy formed a natural frontier.

The foundation of Napata indicated a turning point in relations between Egypt and Kush, since the town was probably isolated in an area of the Nile still largely controlled by independent Kushites; however, the unified kingdom of Kush had obviously by that time fragmented under economic and military pressure from Egypt, and the indigenous chiefs were in no position to resist the presence of agents from a nation now significantly more powerful than their own. Periodic uprisings against Egyptian domination as late as the reign of Amenhotep III (*c.* 1382–1344 BC) became increasingly routine incidents with which to deal. Napata itself was principally a trading centre, in which dealings between Egypt and Kush were now conducted purely on a commercial basis, and the local chiefs flourished by co-operating with Egypt in conveying trade to and from lands to the south and east. However, Egyptian officials were not content always to deal with middle-men, and constantly promoted direct contact with the suppliers of necessary goods. It is likely that all traffic through Nubia as far south as Tombos was entirely controlled by Egypt after the reign of Thutmose I. During the Hatshepsut co-regency, commercial links were established with countries south of Kush, such as Irem and Nmayu, and members of the ruling families of these lands were welcomed at pharaoh's palace. The most fabulous of the African trading partners was the chiefdom of Punt on the Red Sea coast: it was the land from which came the highly-desirable incense known as *antyu*, and other goods handled there included ivory, ebony, gold and exotic animal skins. Egypt had been in indirect contact with Punt since the Old Kingdom, and occasional expeditions had braved the sea in order to reach it, but direct contact had been lost during the Second Intermediate Period. A celebrated expedition, therefore, was despatched by Hatshepsut *c.* 1460 BC to "open the way" to Punt, and other expeditions followed occasionally throughout the New Kingdom. Nevertheless, the majority of Puntite goods still reached Egypt by land on the caravans of merchants from Kush.

Gold-mining in Nubia was not straightforward: the majority of the mines were in the eastern desert and so presented enormous logistical difficulties, not least with regard to safety in an area that was hostile to Egyptians in terms of both its geography and its semi-nomadic populations; the muster points for expeditions were typically military forts. Nevertheless, the 18th Dynasty kings exploited the mines on a previously unimagined scale, and one which increased cumulatively as Egypt's commercial authority in Africa and the Near East increased. The exploitation began no later than the reign of Thutmose I: an inscription in his name at Kurgus—midway between the fourth and fifth cataracts on the Nile—is best understood as marking the spot at which a mining expedition travelling from Wawat via the valleys of the eastern desert emerged beside the river several hundred kilometres further south. The aggressive intent of this broken inscription, hammered into an isolated rock, is a vehement echo of the 12th Dynasty boundary stelae of Senusret III:

"If any Nubian oversteps the decree which my father Amun has given to me, (his head?) shall be chopped off ... for me ... and he shall have no heirs."

Alongside, an exact copy of the inscription was carved by an expedition during the reign of Thutmose III. As the threat from Kush receded, so greater manpower and resources could be devoted to mining: expeditions sent by Amenhotep III (*c.* 1382–1344 BC) systematically opened up whole new areas of the desert, and penetrated so far east that they could be supported by moving troops and provisions in ships along the Red Sea coast. However, the dangers were not inconsiderable, and, for example, a hostile uprising in the region of Ikuyta *c.* 1334 BC in the reign of Akhenaten required the intervention of troops under the command of the King's Son of Kush, Thutmose. Nevertheless, the same region was still being exploited by Egyptians during the reign of Ramesses III, over 150 years later.

Egypt and the Near East

New Kingdom Egypt had no ideological purpose to serve by conquering lands beyond the Nile comparable to the belief in the integrity of the Black Land which motivated her expansion into Nubia. Therefore, her long and far-reaching involvement with Syria and Palestine was essentially shaped by political and commercial considerations. Our knowledge of the subject during the 18th Dynasty is largely based on evidence from two periods: the campaigns of Thutmose III and Amenhotep II (*c.* 1458–1418 BC), and finally the period covering the transition between the reigns of Amenhotep III and Amenhotep IV (*c.* 1345–1330 BC). On the basis of this evidence, it is possible to determine a consistent policy of defending commercial interests assertively but with the minimum of direct military intervention. Egypt was most interested in the ports of the Levantine coast from Tyre to Sumur—through which passed the commercial traffic of the Near East and the Eastern Mediterranean—and in the Syrian towns which dominated the caravan routes running to the other great kingdoms of the era. The thorny and intractable politics of Palestine and Canaan, characterized by ruthless brinkmanship and sporadic in-fighting in often treacherous terrain, were best avoided, although the king of Egypt was well able to use the threat of his armies and his considerable presence in Syria to impose a stranglehold on any enemies who sought to jeopardize the unrestricted passage of his caravans.

Between the siege of Sharuhen and the campaigns of Thutmose III, the only records of Egyptian intervention in Syria or Palestine concern a campaign of Thutmose I which reached Byblos, presumably by ship, before marching north to cross the Orontes river, and then pressing ahead to the Euphrates river in the lands of the king of Mittani. The purpose of the campaign is entirely unknown, although contact with Byblos had been integral to Egyptian trade during the Middle Kingdom, and the intention was perhaps to re-establish a dominant presence in the port itself and at the same time confirm Egypt's intention to police the surrounding region. However, the seventeen campaigns of Thutmose III were undoubtedly a systematic attempt to affirm Egypt's pre-eminence in the commercial life of Syria and Palestine; the campaigns were a potent mixture of grandiose pharaonic display and decisive military action, although most of the crucial military incidents occurred on the first campaign *c.* 1458 BC, when the king's armies took control of Gaza and Joppa, before defeating the armies of a coalition of city-states in battle at the city of Megiddo, which controlled the major trade routes through the north of Palestine. Thereafter, the campaigns of Thutmose III were typically concentrated north of Megiddo, especially in the area of Byblos. The same campaigning pattern re-emerged in the reign of Amenhotep II, and throughout this whole period the consistent feature of Egypt's involvement was an interest in the Levantine ports and the cities which bordered the inland trade-routes from Megiddo to the lands of the king of Mitanni.

One of the greatest difficulties in interpreting the history of pharaonic Egypt is the nature of royal monumental inscriptions like temple reliefs and stelae, which often are the only real source of information about political events—the campaigns of Thutmose III and Amenhotep II being conspicuous examples. Such monuments were never erected to commemorate history but in order to act as a witness to the authority and divine nature of the king of Egypt, and as such were mostly concerned with traditional rhetoric about the king and with records of temple building. Events like alliances and battles were usually mentioned only in passing or ignored altogether; for example, the wars of Ahmose are not mentioned on any surviving royal monuments. Therefore, the Battle of Megiddo is so prominent on monuments of Thutmose III—it is mentioned on stelae from Thebes, Armant and Nubia, as well as a long annalistic inscription in the temple of Karnak—because it was an unequivocal demonstration of certain truths about the king: firstly, his success was sponsored by the gods; secondly his authority over every land was exemplified by the defeat of a coalition of forces from dozens of states; finally, his success was seen to be compromised only by the stupidity of the ordinary mortals around him—the enemy which opposed his interests, and his own army which looted the camp of the routed defenders instead of pressing ahead to capture Megiddo on the day of the battle itself. While there is no reason to doubt the significant political and economic advantage gained by Egypt in the Battle of Megiddo, it seems likely that other campaigns directed at key commercial targets, such as the port of Sumur or "the fortress of" Kadesh in the Orontes valley, were equally significant in political terms, although they are barely visible in the royal record.

With regard to the last quarter of the dynasty, however, the so-called Amarna letters—an archive of international correspondence from the royal palace at Akhetaten—provide a distinctly different kind of information about the politics of the Near East. Many of the letters were sent to or from the major kings of the Levant and the Near East who styled themselves "brothers" of pharaoh; the principal subject of correspondence was the exchange of gifts and daughters which created communal ties of credit and kinship. Since the movement of goods in and out of Egypt was only possible by the will of the king, these ties were the basic channels through which international commerce was conducted; Egypt exported gold, ivory and African trade goods—as well as craftsmen and physicians—in return for silver, copper, timber and various oils. Although the major kings were obviously those with the greatest commercial muscle, not all of them—especially the kings of Alashiya and Arzawa—were necessarily the rulers of great empires.

The remaining letters in the archive were sent by the rulers of various city-states in Syria and Palestine, who self-consciously presented themselves as the inferiors of pharaoh. Their letters have a typical structure in which the ruler prostrated himself before pharaoh and then typically demanded gold and troops in extravagant quantities. The demands are essentially stereotyped and calculated to display how dependent the local rulers were on their royal patron; usually their requests went unheeded. On the other hand, the loyalist addresses of rival chiefs reflect a culture of constant brinkmanship which was not entirely to the benefit of the king of Egypt, since it also entailed

View of the columns originally supporting the roof of a chapel of the goddess Hathor in the temple at Deir el-Bahri; each capital has been carved in the form of Hathor— human-headed with a large wig and the ears of a cow. Hathor represented sexuality and motherhood, and was incarnate in the women of the royal household; elsewhere in the same temple, reliefs depict the king's mother conceiving her royal child (in this case Hatshepsut) with the god Amun. The prominence of Hathor in this important temple must relate to beliefs which led to Queen Hatshepsut's assumption of the kingship, and most representations of her in the Hathor chapel were obliterated at a later date.

commercial and territorial disputes which had the potential to destabilize areas through which regular Egyptian caravans required safe passage; some of the rulers were even prepared to trade their loyalties elsewhere, such as Aziru of Amurru, who defied Akhenaten by pledging his allegiance to Hatti. However, another defiant chief, Labayu from the hill-country of Canaan, threatened the security of the crucial area around Megiddo, and so was defeated and killed by a coalition of Palestinian city-states acting on the orders of the king of Egypt.

The archive from Amarna is unique—no other extant source is so rich in detail about Egyptian politics at any time until the Late Period—and the formulaic addresses of the correspondents present a bizarre mixture of regal indifference on the part of the major kings and frenzied impotence on the part of the local rulers, most of which is to do with conforming to the hierarchy of power in the Near East and cannot be taken at face value as a record of the contemporary political scene. It is not surprising, therefore, that the picture of Syria and Palestine painted in the letters sometimes seems more chaotic than the picture derived earlier in the dynasty entirely from Egyptian monumental sources. It has been suggested that the letters detail a period of decline in which internal difficulties obliged the king of Egypt to neglect his foreign responsibilities, but other sources tend to dispute this conclusion, including the evidence of contemporary campaigns in Nubia. The king of Egypt in the late 18th Dynasty was willing to allow the local rulers of Syria and Palestine to conduct their interminable disputes, but the circumstances surrounding the death of Labayu alone are sufficient to show that he was not prepared to let those troubles destabilize the region in any way that adversely affected his commercial interests. New Kingdom Egypt was no imperial war machine: she was a self-confident, cultural and commercial giant, linking the highways of Africa to Europe and the Near East.

The Wars of Ahmose

Ahmose defeated the kings of Avaris and so created a realm as extensive as that of the Middle Kingdom.

> *"Then came that enemy, Tetian by name, who had collected all the disaffected to himself, but the king slew him, and his force was obliterated. Thereafter, three heads and six aurorae of land in my home town were given to me."*
> Tomb inscription of Ahmose-Saibana

The temple at Deir el-Bahri is the greatest monument of the early 18th Dynasty. Its terraced architecture elaborates the design used for the adjacent tomb of Montjuhotep II.

The political map of Egypt at the death of Kamose is conjectural, but we can be sure that the ideological and commercial imperative for reunifying the Nile lands had been demonstrated, and that Theban authority had been extended into Nubia as far as Buhen. Kamose's probable son and successor, Ahmose, was still a child at his accession, but was eventually to conclude that process of reunification, and so attain a stature in later tradition equal to that of the other celebrated architects of a united Egypt, Menes and Montjuhotep II.

The campaigns of the new king against his northern enemy Apophis, and subsequently Khemudy, probably began late in his second decade as king; they are well documented in the tomb inscriptions at el-Kab of Ahmose-Saibana and Ahmose-Pennekhbet, who began long military careers at this time and were keen to record the decorations, slaves, and grants of land which they earned as a result. Apparently the Theban regime had gained control of Memphis before war was launched against Avaris, and certainly Ahmose-Saibana began his career as a marine in the "Northern Fleet" of Thebes. As many as five separate campaigns against Avaris entailed protracted fighting on land and in the extensive waterways surrounding the great fortified city, but eventually, the marine relates: "Avaris was plundered, and I took plunder away from it—one man, three women, i.e. four heads—and the king gave them to me for slaves." The king immediately prosecuted the Hyksos' Palestinian associates by beseiging Sharuhen, eventually plundering its wealth and massacring its population. In doing so Ahmose brought under his unquestioned control the roads across Sinai, and also reasserted the sort of boundary between Egypt and Palestine that had existed during the Middle Kingdom, before its erosion by the independent knigdom of Avaris.

Victorious in the north, Ahmose subsequently led an army through Nubia in order to confirm his authority at the southern border of his dominion. Nevertheless, the difficulties still facing the new regime were realized when he was obliged to put down two rebellions. The first was led by Aata, perhaps a Nubian chieftain, "whose fate hastened his doom" Ahmose-Saibana grimly warned. The second was led by Tetian, who was probably Egyptian and perhaps from the newly-conquered north country. With Tetian perished the last opposition to the new era from within Egypt itself; in time the succession would pass smoothly via Ahmose's own son Amenhotep I to Thutmose I, who, if related at all, was so only by marriage.

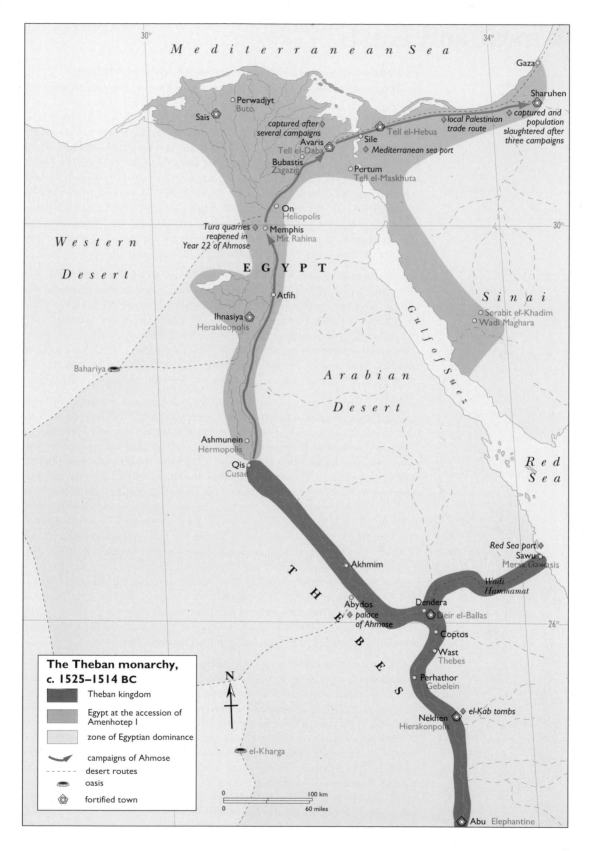

Mediterranean Sea

Gaza

Sharuhen

○ Perwadjyt
Buto

Sais ◎

captured after
several campaigns

◇ local Palestinian
trade route

◇ captured and
population
slaughtered after
three campaigns

Avaris
Tell el-Daba

Sile

◇ Mediterranean sea port

Tell el-Hebua

Bubastis
Zagazig

Pertum
Tell el-Maskhuta

W e s t e r n

On
Heliopolis

Tura quarries
reopened in
Year 22 of Ahmose

Memphis
Mit Rahina

E G Y P T

D e s e r t

○ Atfih

S i n a i

○ Serabit el-Khadim
○ Wadi Maghara

Ihnasiya
Herakleopolis

A r a b i a n

Baharia

Ashmunein
Hermopolis

D e s e r t

Qis
Cusae

Gulf of Suez

*R e d
S e a*

Red Sea port
Sawu
Mersa Gawasis

○ Akhmim

T

*Wadi
Hammamat*

H

Abydos
palace
of Ahmose

Dendera

Deir el-Ballas

E

B

Coptos

Wast
Thebes

E

Perhathor
Gebelein

S

el-Kab tombs

Nekhen
Hierakonpolis

el-Kharga

Abu Elephantine

**The Theban monarchy,
c. 1525–1514 BC**

Theban kingdom

Egypt at the accession of
Amenhotep I

zone of Egyptian dominance

campaigns of Ahmose

desert routes

oasis

fortified town

N

0   100 km
0   60 miles

Wawat and Kush

The Theban annexation of Wawat was consolidated by extending Egyptian control into Kush itself: the prize was the Nubian gold supply.

"Now, there was a chieftain in the north of impotent Kush, who had drifted into a time of conspiracy with a pair of Nubians in the southern plain ... The king raged about this like a panther after he heard, and said: 'As I live! As Ra loves me! As I praise my father, the lord of the gods, Amun! ... I will not let a single man amongst them live! I will set death amongst them! Then the king sent a great army to Nubia, on his first occasion of victory, to overthrow all those who had plotted against the king and rebelled against the Lord of the Twin Lands."
Stela of Thutmose II near Aswan

Immediately south of Egypt, Wawat was a populous land which gave access to deserts exceptionally rich in gold. During the Second Intermediate Period it had been transformed into a border separating the kingdoms of Thebes and Kush, which held until Kamose calculated that his defences would be better served by bringing the region directly under his control. In so doing he was resurrecting the occupationist policy of his Middle Kingdom predecessors, and inevitably his aggression plunged Egypt and Kush once more into conflict. But for Egypt there was more than security at stake: the Theban authorities recognised that the Nubian gold mines were the foundations on which Egypt could be reconstructed as a formidable commercial power.

A policy of conquest directed towards the kingdom of Kush itself emerged when Amenhotep I founded a fortified Egyptian town at Shaat, beyond the Middle Kingdom border in Nubia; the king was determined "to extend the boundaries of the Black Land", according to Ahmose-Saibana. His successor, Thutmose I, subsequently extended his authority along the river to Tombos, at the third cataract on the Nile, barely thirty kilometres north of the Kushite capital at Kerma, and also sent a small force along the gold-mining routes of the desert wadis to lay claim to the richest sources of the commercial prize.

At the death of Thutmose I, half a century after Kamose's accession, the borders of the Black Land—Egypt and Nubia as a unified Nilotic kingdom—had been recast into what would be their essential form for the next 450 years; in Nubia, an area of rich grassland beyond the third cataract eventually gave way to the less hospitable region of Karoy, and this would henceforth be the southern boundary. Egyptians later established a fortified town at Napata, deep within Kush, during the reign of Thutmose III, and a major cult site for the god Amun at nearby Gebel Barkal. The new regime would quickly resort to force to quell any disturbance which they considered to be treasonous rebellion in the Nubian domains, or to repel attacks sponsored by the chiefs of Kush. With time, this became an increasingly routine exercise. The Egyptian government quickly installed its own administration, the old forts were rebuilt, and new forts and temple-towns were sited throughout Wawat and Kush as instruments of economic integration. In the chiefdoms of Wawat, native rulers now served as Egyptian officials and were typically buried in Egyptian-style tombs, whilst the material culture of the indigenous population assumed pronounced Egyptian characteristics.

Egypt's success in Nubia was confirmed in the latter half of the reign of Thutmose III, when even unconquered territories of Kush accepted the reality of Egyptian domination, and consented to act as trading partners. Thereafter, children of Kushite chiefs were sent to the Egyptian court to be educated in the new order, and Egyptian activity in the region assumed an air of confidence: new temples were occasionally built outside the protected fortress-compounds. This situation allowed the Egyptian army to concentrate on the expansion of Egyptian gold-mining activity, and, during the reins of Thutmose IV and Amenhotep III, it pushed systematically eastwards to the distant mines of Ikuyta and Ibhet. To the south, Egypt was apparently able to impose herself on the rulers of Irem in such a way as to forestall any interference from there.

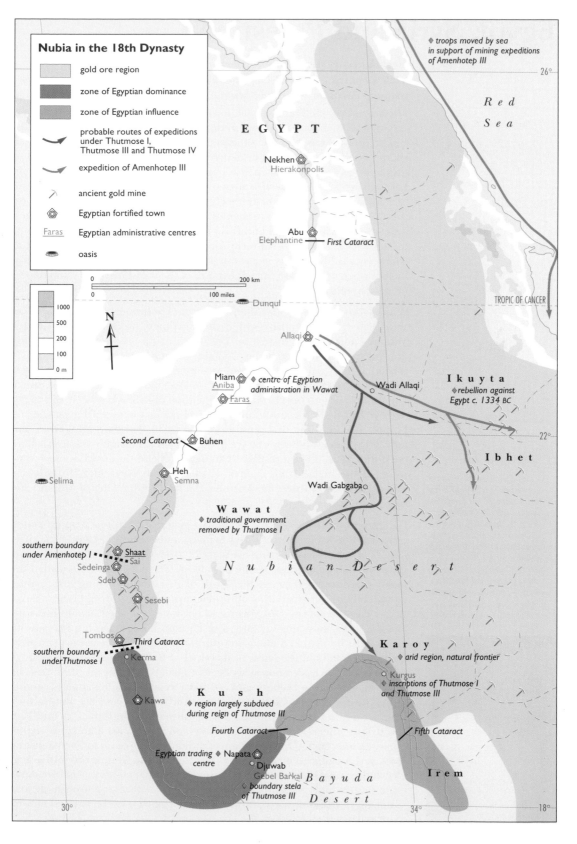

Nubia in the 18th Dynasty

- gold ore region
- zone of Egyptian dominance
- zone of Egyptian influence
- probable routes of expeditions under Thutmose I, Thutmose III and Thutmose IV
- expedition of Amenhotep III
- ancient gold mine
- Egyptian fortified town
- *Faras* Egyptian administrative centres
- oasis

0 ——— 200 km
0 ——— 100 miles

1000
500
200
100
0 m

N

EGYPT

Nekhen
Hierakonpolis

Abu — First Cataract
Elephantine

◆ troops moved by sea in support of mining expeditions of Amenhotep III

26°

Red Sea

TROPIC OF CANCER

Dunqul

Allaqi

Wadi Allaqi

Ikuyta
◆ rebellion against Egypt c. 1334 BC

22°

Ibhet

Miam
Aniba ◆ centre of Egyptian administration in Wawat
Faras

Second Cataract — Buhen

Selima
Heh
Semna

Wadi Gabgaba

Wawat
◆ traditional government removed by Thutmose I

Nubian Desert

southern boundary under Amenhotep I Shaat
Sedeinga Sai
Sdeb
Sesebi

Tombos — Third Cataract
southern boundary under Thutmose I Kerma

Karoy
◆ arid region, natural frontier

Kurgus
◆ inscriptions of Thutmose I and Thutmose III

Kush
◆ region largely subdued during reign of Thutmose III

Kawa

Fourth Cataract —

Fifth Cataract

Egyptian trading ◆ Napata
centre ◇ Djuwab
Gebel Barkal
◆ boundary stela
of Thutmose III

Bayuda Desert

Irem

30° 34° 18°

Egypt, Syria and Palestine I

Egypt's armies secured her commercial interests by re-establishing her traditional influence at Byblos, and by gaining control of the inland trade routes to Palestine, Syria and Mittani.

"I will perform a miracle for you: I grant you valour and victory over all the hills, I place your power and your fearfulness in all the plains, and the dread of you up to the very pillars of the sky."
The Poetical Stela of Thutmose III

There is no compelling evidence to suggest that Ahmose exploited his success at Sharuhen by continuing his campaigns further into Palestine; his son and successor, Amenhotep I, appears not to have campaigned in Palestine at all. Although archaeological evidence for the burning and abandonment of sites such as Jericho has, in the past, been ascribed to the activities of Egyptian armies, these destructions were in all probability the result of protracted, localized troubles between Canaanite chiefs. Written records suggest that New Kingdom Egyptian armies rarely destroyed lands or fortresses; instead success is recorded in terms of the quantity of plunder captured for the temples as tribute or in terms of the number of prisoners awarded to courageous soldiers. This behaviour seems consistent with that of an urban society which understood the importance of the Palestinian city-states for the movement of trade.

Within thirty years of Sharuhen, however, Thutmose I had led Egyptian armies as far as Naharin (which the Egyptians used as a synonym for Mittani), and erected a stela on the banks of the Euphrates proclaiming the northern boundary of his domain. A list of place names apparently related to this campaign, inscribed on a monumental gate at Karnak, covers the area from Byblos along the coast toward Sumur, and across the mountains of Lebanon to the Orontes. The mention of Byblos is crucial: this major seaport had been the traditional point of contact between Egypt and the Levant. It is possible that Thutmose I avoided Palestine altogether and moved his armies to Byblos by sea, focussing his campaign (which may have been little more than a display of strength) inland on a region crossed by some of the major trade routes of the ancient Near East, linking the Levantine ports to Palestine, Anatolia, the lands of the king of Mittani, and beyond to Assyria.

An aerial view of the modern tell at Megiddo looking towards the Egyptian advance. The direct approach from the southwest, via the Aruna Pass, was so narrow and difficult that it was left undefended by the coalition facing Thutmose III, but the king himself led his forces, including chariots and horses, in single file and pounced on the enemy camp unawares.

His grandson, Thutmose III, adopted a systematic approach to affirming Egypt's influence in Palestine and Syria by undertaking 17 campaigns virtually on an annual basis during his Years 22 to 42. On the first he marched via Gaza and a siege of Joppa to the key city of Megiddo, which controlled the major trade routes through the north of Palestine. Catching his enemies completely by surprise after an audacious advance through the narrow Aruna Pass, he defeated an alliance of city-states and their armies in battle, and eventually took the city after a seven month siege. On his 5th and 6th campaigns, he marched along the northern part of the coastal plain near Byblos and attacked the lands of the chief of Kadesh (another city strategically located on trade routes) as far as Galilee. Then, in his 33rd Year, he made his own way to Naharin and erected a stela alongside that of his grandfather (unfortunately these stelae have not survived and are known only from ancient references). Subsequently, during his 9th, 10th, 13th and 17th campaigns, there was further military activity against Canaanite cities. However, only during his first campaign did the king claim to have captured cities and humiliated or replaced their leaders, and in only one other Year (39) did he campaign in southern Palestine, on that occasion with the deliberate intention of punishing a major local disturbance. On at least four "campaigns" the king apparently avoided any fighting and restricted himself to formal displays of authority.

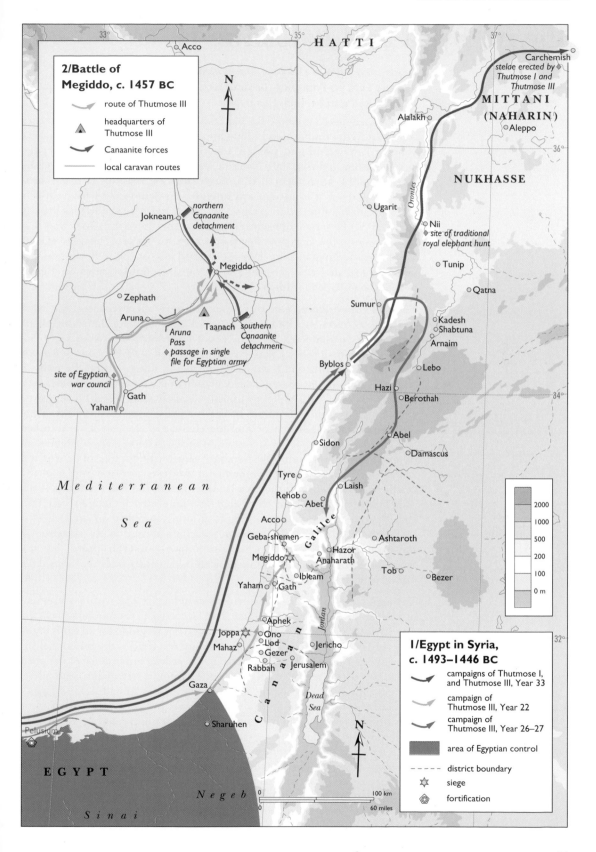

2/Battle of Megiddo, c. 1457 BC

→ route of Thutmose III

▲ headquarters of Thutmose III

➤ Canaanite forces

— local caravan routes

HATTI

Acco

Carchemish
stelae erected by Thutmose I and Thutmose III

MITTANI (NAHARIN)

Alalakh

Aleppo

NUKHASSE

Ugarit

Nii
site of traditional royal elephant hunt

Tunip

Qatna

Sumur

Kadesh
Shabtuna

Arnaim

Byblos

Lebo

Hazi

Berothah

Abel

Damascus

Sidon

Tyre

Laish

Rehob

Abet

Acco

Ashtaroth

Geba-shemen

Megiddo
Anaharath
Hazor

Ibleam

Tob

Bezer

Yaham
Gath

Aphek

Joppa
Ono
Lod
Jericho
Mahaz
Gezer
Rabbah
Jerusalem

Gaza

Dead Sea

Sharuhen

Pelusium

EGYPT

Mediterranean Sea

Galilee

Canaan

Jordan

Negeb

Sinai

Inset — Battle of Megiddo:

Jokneam
northern Canaanite detachment

Megiddo

Zephath

Aruna

Taanach
southern Canaanite detachment

Aruna Pass
passage in single file for Egyptian army

site of Egyptian war council

Gath

Yaham

1/Egypt in Syria, c. 1493–1446 BC

➤ campaigns of Thutmose I, and Thutmose III, Year 33

➤ campaign of Thutmose III, Year 22

➤ campaign of Thutmose III, Year 26–27

■ area of Egyptian control

--- district boundary

✡ siege

⬡ fortification

0   100 km

0   60 miles

2000
1000
500
200
100
0 m

Egypt, Syria and Palestine II

In his campaigns in Palestine Amenhotep II displayed a continuity of purpose with his immediate predecessors. His primary goal was regional stability and uninterrupted commerce.

"At daybreak, the king approached at the reins, equipped with a sceptre and the regalia of Montju ... Anukharta was plundered ... The king reached the area of Megiddo. The chief of Qebaasumin, whose name was Qaqa, was caught—his wife, his children and his household likewise—and another chief was put in his place. The king reached Memphis with his will satisfied in all the hills, and all the plains beneath his sandals."

Stela of Amenhotep II from the temple of Ptah at Memphis

The campaigns of Thutmose III, like that of his grandfather, had been concentrated in the coastal area of Retjenu and lands north of the hill-country (Canaan), Megiddo and Galilee, the coast around Byblos (Djahy), the Orontes valley, and eventually Naharin. Only on his first campaign can we be certain that his armies marched through Palestine in order to reach these areas; perhaps that campaign was intended to demonstrate his authority throughout Palestine once and for all, allied perhaps to the fact that he could not yet be certain of his reception in the northern sea-ports. After that time, however, the king probably transported the bulk of his army and its supplies from Egypt by ship; when he crossed into Naharin, Byblos was certainly his logistical base according to his own account inscribed on a great stela at Gebel Barkal in Nubia.

The same campaigning pattern re-emerged in the first decade of the reign of Thutmose's son, Amenhotep II. In Year 3, the king campaigned in Takhsy, from where he abducted seven dissident chiefs who were later sacrificed in Egypt (the bodies of six were publicly displayed at Thebes, whilst the seventh was paraded through Nubia before being hung outside the walls of Napata). In Year 7, he marched an army across the Orontes and then south through Takhsy and Galilee to punish towns that opposed his authority (including Nii, where Thutmose III had once displayed his authority in traditional pharaonic manner by hunting elephants). In Year 9, he travelled from Perunefer, the port of Memphis, in order to depose Qaqa, chief of an otherwise unknown town (Qebaasumin) near Megiddo: this, of course, was crucial territory for Egypt's commercial interests, and the gravity of the threat posed by rebels in the area is evident from the fact that Qaqa is the only Palestinian or Syrian chief actually mentioned by name in an 18th Dynasty royal inscription. According to accounts inscribed on royal stelae at Memphis and Karnak, this campaign was characterized by the slaughter of the population of Iturin (location unknown)—notable proof that the Egyptians were not afraid openly to acknowledge atrocities that they committed against foreign cities.

Throughout this whole period, the consistent feature of Egypt's involvement in Canaan and the Levant was her interest in the Levantine ports and the cities that bordered the inland trade-routes from Megiddo to the lands of the kings of Hatti, Mittani and Babylon. This interest reflects the traditional significance of Byblos and, more especially, the crucial importance of the ports and roads which moved trade between Egypt and her major commercial partners, the great kings of the Near East. Thutmose III had secured Egypt's influence in the region, and thereafter direct military intervention arose only from the need to punish rebellion (as Egypt interpreted any opposition to her interest) and restore the status quo. In general, the cities of Palestine were far from being enslaved or conquered, but they found themselves squeezed between Egypt to the south and her dependencies and trading partners to the north, and so it fell to the local rulers to play their part as loyal servants of a king whose long shadow fell across their land, and whose caravans and armies demanded the freedom to move in whatever direction they pleased.

Egypt in Syria, c. 1425–1418

Amenhotep II in Year 7

Amenhotep II in Year 9

zone of Egyptian influence

zone of Egyptian dominance

Punt and God's Land

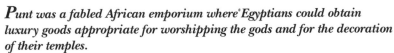

Punt was a fabled African emporium where Egyptians could obtain luxury goods appropriate for worshipping the gods and for the decoration of their temples.

"It is the sacred region of God's Land; it is my place of distraction; I have made it for myself in order to cleanse my spirit, along with my mother, Hathor…the lady of Punt."
Speech of Amun in the Punt Reliefs at Deir el-Bahri

For many centuries, the African chiefdom of Punt, characterized by beehive-shaped houses raised above water on stilts, seemed to the Egyptians to be the most exotic of lands to visit, and in return Puntites regularly paid their respects at the court of pharaoh. Punt's importance was as an emporium with a unique richness of available goods, of which the most typical was the incense known as *antyu*, produced in vast resinous lumps in the nearby region of *Utjenet* (God's Land). Punt was also a commercial centre for goods from elsewhere in Africa, such as ivory, ebony, gold and animal skins. Egypt grew rich by re-exporting these goods to Europe and the Near East, and as a result we still use the words "ebony" (*hebny*) and "gum" (*kemy*) employed by the ancients themselves (possibly originally as words from the languages of Punt or Nubia).

Punt was reached from Egypt by sailing on the Red Sea: in the Old Kingdom this meant crossing the desert east of Memphis to the Gulf of Suez, or setting sail out of Sinai, from where Pepynakht had recovered the bodies of the ill-fated expedition massacred whilst building boats for the Punt trade in the 6th Dynasty. From the Middle Kingdom onwards, Red Sea journeys usually began from Coptos via the port at Sawu, or via Wadi Hammamat and Quseir; possibly in the New Kingdom there was an even more southerly port at Head of Nekheb. Because of its exotic, "overseas" character, it has often been suggested that Punt was located as far away as the coast of modern Eritrea, Somalia or Yemen. However, it is nowadays accepted that goods from Punt also reached New Kingdom Egypt on land via Nmay and Irem, and that the children of the chiefs of Punt were raised at the Egyptian court alongside children from Kush and Irem, and therefore that Punt was not so far distant from Egyptian lands in Nubia as used to be supposed. Nevertheless, there is no evidence to suggest that there was ever any military conflict between the two nations.

The importance of the expedition sent to Punt by Hatshepsut, the stepmother and co-regent of Thutmose III, is apparent from the extensive record of it in her mortuary temple at Deir el-Bahri. This detail shows members of the expedition carrying aromatic herbs to their ships.

Punt was not simply exotic, it was also a mystical place from which came many extraordinary goods for the adornment of the homes of the gods, such as incense for purification, and the skins of giraffes, panthers and cheetahs worn by the priests. Another mystical region was the Lebanese mountains (*Lemnon*), which sustained the tall, straight timber used for the flagstaffs adorning the temple facades, and the bark-shrines in which the gods were paraded in festivals. Punt and Lebanon were therefore both identified as regions of God's Land. The most famous expedition to Punt was actually proposed by an oracle of a god, Amun, which instructed Hatshepsut to organize the first large-scale expedition of the New Kingdom after contact between the two lands had been suspended during the Second Intermediate Period. Hatshepsut's mortuary temple in Western Thebes includes detailed depictions of the expedition, the journey by sea, and the reception offered by the chief of Punt. The visitors left behind a shrine dedicated to Amun in a land which, they supposed, he had made as his personal pleasure garden.

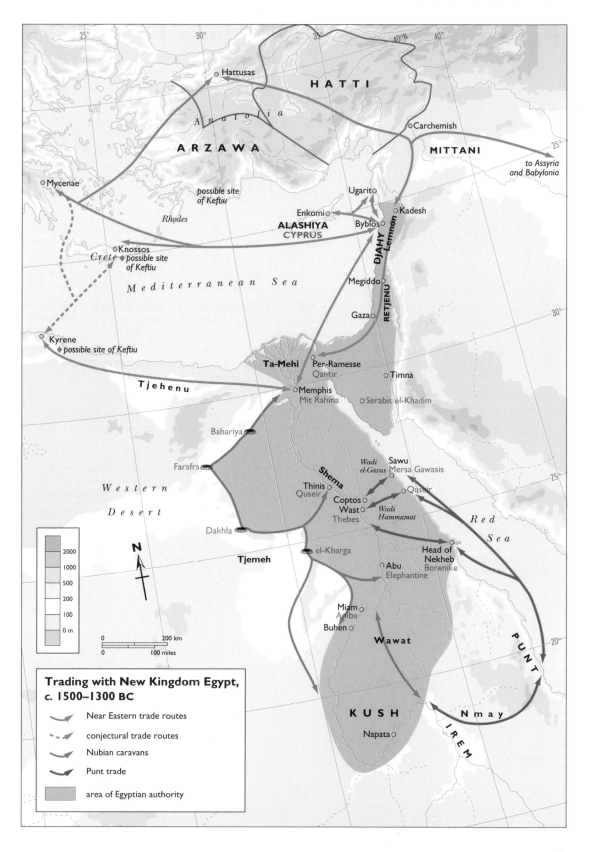

Power and the Royal Palace I

The New Kingdom court was an itinerant institution gathered around the king, and comprising officials, priests and family, together with many hundreds of retainers and servants.

"On this day, the king was in Akhetaten ... and appeared at the reins of his great electrum chariot like the sun when it rises in the sky, so that he filled the Twin Lands with love for him."
The Boundary Stelae of Akhetaten

The spiritual heart of the New Kingdom Egypt was the court, traditionally known simply as "the interior". It embodied two separate domains: the "harîm", devoted to the care of the royal family, and the central administration. Each had its own officials and quarters; the link between them was the throne-room, in which the king received regular reports from his administrators. A third group of officials and palace buildings represented the prosaically-named "stores".

In order to display the king's authority and allow him to perform rituals in every major temple, it seems that the court was generally itinerant, spending only a few weeks at a time in any one of a number of palaces, and often travelling abroad into subject territories. As the court travelled, its provisions were supplied by local officials and major temples, and probably also by the king's own estates. Palace architecture was typically a variation upon that of the temple, except that the throne-room took the place of the god's sanctuary. There are also obvious differences in the size and function of palaces: some could accommodate only brief stays, whilst the enormous palace complex of Amenhotep III at Western Thebes was created as the location for the celebration of ancient kingship festivals.

King and court were so intimately connected that the definitive word for the court as a royal institution—"the great estate", *p^erro*—eventually became a synonym for "king", and has since passed into the modern world, via the Bible, as *pharaoh*.

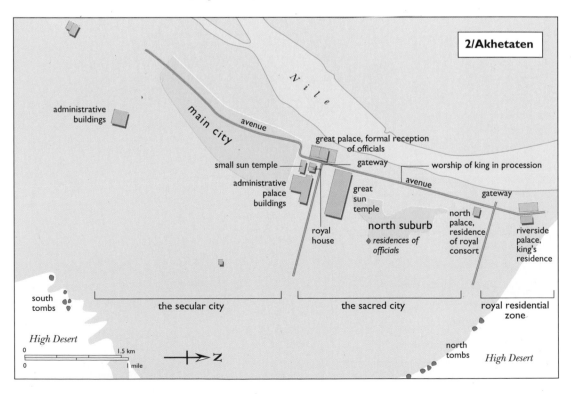

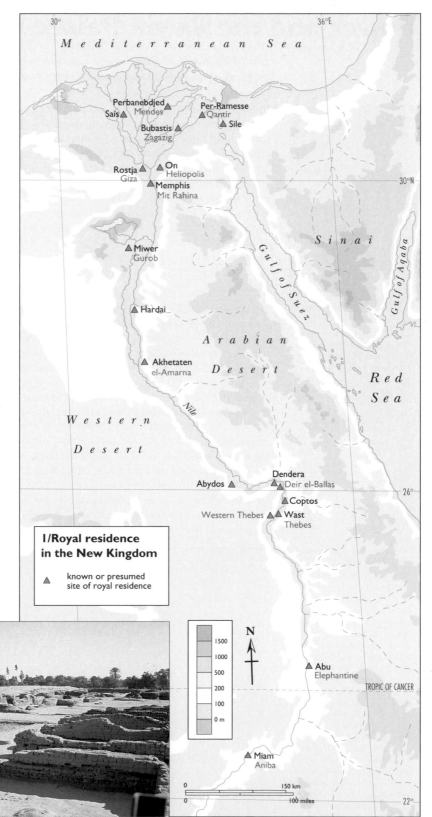

Akhetaten was built c. 1341 BC by Amenhotep IV as a royal residence and cult site for the sun-god, Ra Horakhty. Its main feature is an avenue running from the northern palaces to the central temple and palace area, along which the king would process each morning he was resident. As he passed, officials in the north suburb would line the route to worship and be near him. The king then conducted the worship of the sun in the temples, before appearing with his family at a window overlooking the avenue to distribute gifts to loyal officials.

1/**Royal residence in the New Kingdom**

▲ known or presumed site of royal residence

Power and the Royal Palace II

Distribution of authority through association with the king empowered the court officials and temples as the central administrative agencies of the country.

Above: The mortuary complex, or Ramesseum, of Ramesses II. Although the temple's orthogonal plan is unusual, its ornate interior remains fairly orthodox.

In New Kingdom Egypt, power still depended upon proximity to the king, at least in the sense of having privileged access to him. Therefore, each department of the administration was headed by a single man who swore an oath of office to the king, and would then regularly represent his department in the king's presence. Likewise, the children of foreign rulers favourable to Egypt were often brought to the palace harîm in order to be introduced to the culture of pharaonic authority. However, the officials who accompanied the king at court, and so generally had his ear, were potentially the most divisive influences in the country. If there was civil strife during this era, the activities of high officials were often an integral part of the problem: for example, an astonishing group of legal documents from the 20th Dynasty indicate that key figures in the harîm were directly involved in a plot to assassinate Ramesses III.

Notionally, all of Egypt was in the care of the king; in practice, responsibility for much of the land and its people was turned over to the temples in order to furnish the vast quantities of produce needed for religious offerings and the maintenance of large staffs of priests, officials, workmen, and soforth, together with their families. The sheer scale of temple rituals ensured that they now became the basic agency by which to organize available land and labour. According to the Great Harris Papyrus, Ramesses III alone endowed the services of over 86,000 people to the cult of Amun-Ra, and of thousands more to the cults of other gods. Some of these would have been slaves or prisoners, but most would have been tied by contract and tradition to their own farm land, and their produce made available to the temple in the form of taxes. In return their status and security would have been guaranteed by the royal court, although temporary conscription was still a common way of mobilizing labour for great state projects. For most communities, therefore, the temples became the guarantors of material well-being, even more perhaps than of their spiritual well-being.

Far right: The mortuary complex of Ramesses III at Medinet Habu illustrates the association of the king and court with the civil administration and priesthood. The temple of the king's mortuary cult, built of stone, is surrounded by royal palaces and a mud-brick town housing the priests and other temple staff. This town includes the storage magazines and administrative offices for the west bank community at Thebes in general: it has been estimated that Medinet Habu was directly responsible for the lives of over 62,000 Egyptians living here and at nearby communities. In this capacity, it replaced an earlier royal complex, the Ramesseum.

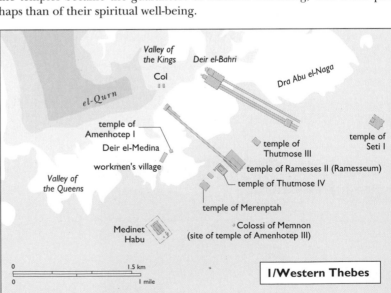

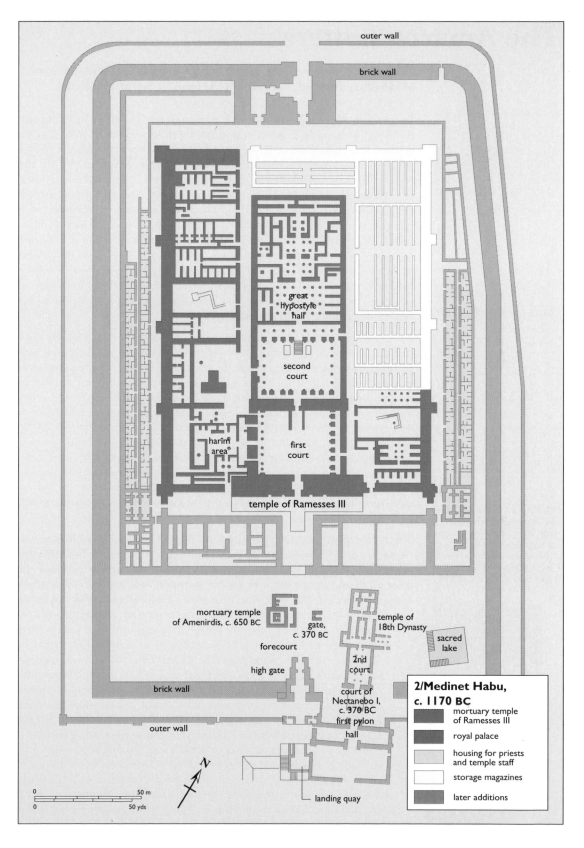

outer wall

brick wall

great
hypostyle
hall

second
court

harîm
area

first
court

temple of Ramesses III

mortuary temple
of Amenirdis, c. 650 BC

gate,
c. 370 BC

temple of
18th Dynasty

sacred
lake

forecourt

high gate

2nd
court

brick wall

court of
Nectanebo I,
c. 370 BC

first pylon

hall

outer wall

**2/Medinet Habu,
c. 1170 BC**

mortuary temple
of Ramesses III

royal palace

housing for priests
and temple staff

storage magazines

later additions

N

0   50 m
0   50 yds

landing quay

The Amarna Letters

An archive of international correspondence with the 18th-Dynasty court has illustrated the politics of the ancient world in exceptional detail.

"Let the king heed the words of his servant ... Rebels killed Aduna, the chief of Irqata, but nobody said anything to Abdiashirta and so they have gone on taking territory for themselves ... I am afraid ... Send archers."

Letter from Ribhadda, chief of Byblos, to the Egyptian court

A letter from Tusratta, King of Mitanni, to Amenhotep IV. In this letter Tusratta complains of the detention in Egypt of his envoys who should have returned with messages and gifts from the Egyptian king.

The chance discovery in 1887 of an archive in a royal palace at Akhetaten furnished a uniquely detailed source for the study of ancient Near Eastern politics. It included over 350 letters circulated between the King of Egypt and his ruling contemporaries during the last years of Amenhotep III, the reign of his son Amenhotep IV, and the early years of Tutankhamun—perhaps 25 years in total. The letters can be divided into two groups: those from kings whose status was equal to that of pharaoh, and those from rulers who subordinated themselves to him. The other major players were in Babylonia, Assyria, Mittani, Hatti, Arzawa and Alashiya. Letters between these kings are composed of stereotyped salutations and rhetorical effusions on the subject of their relationship as brothers. There is little talk of politics; brotherhood is exhibited through extravagant gift-giving (i.e. trade) and the exchange of daughters as brides, thus creating the communal ties of credit typical of the non-monetary societies of the ancient Near East.

Other correspondents were city-state rulers whose own authority was measured in strictly local terms. Their letters to Egypt are, in their own way, equally stereotypical—kings prostrate themselves before a more prestigious king to express their servility. These "servants" tried to outdo one another in exaggerated claims of loyalty and in demands for gold, troops and other indulgences that only a great king could supply, and they were ever ready to denigrate their peers with reports of disloyal conduct (hence the political situation in Syria and Palestine is recounted in absurdly anarchic terms). Frequently, however, their faithful addresses are followed by calculated reports of their own deeds, which betray the fact that they were prepared to risk their master's wrath in order to gain local political and economic advantage. Seemingly, the shadow cast by Egypt was not sufficient to dominate day-to-day political realities.

Nearly one-quarter of the letters are from Ribhadda, the chief of Byblos, and his successor: Ribhadda was the only subordinate whose tone is sufficiently familiar to have inquired after pharaoh's health, and he was certainly the most frank and demanding, so we can presume that the "special relationship" continued. The politics of Ribhadda's Byblos were dominated by the emergence of a major power in Amurru and the aggression of Suppiluliuma I, King of Hatti. With Sumur captured and Byblos virtually besieged, Amenhotep IV was obliged to summon the ruler of Amurru, Aziru, to court, where he was detained for several months. Subsequently, however, Aziru stepped up the pressure on Byblos and switched his allegiance to the King of Hatti. The politics of Palestine, on the other hand, were dominated by local power-games in which Egypt intervened as little as possible. However, the raiding of Labayu and his sons near Megiddo was one local irritation which grew into a threat to trade. Avoiding direct intervention, Amenhotep IV demanded that a group of Palestinian city-states put aside their own differences and co-operate in order to eliminate Labayu. Probably we should see in the strategy of protecting the trade routes with the minimum of direct intervention, the blueprint for New Kingdom policy generally towards the thorny politics of Bronze-Age Palestine.

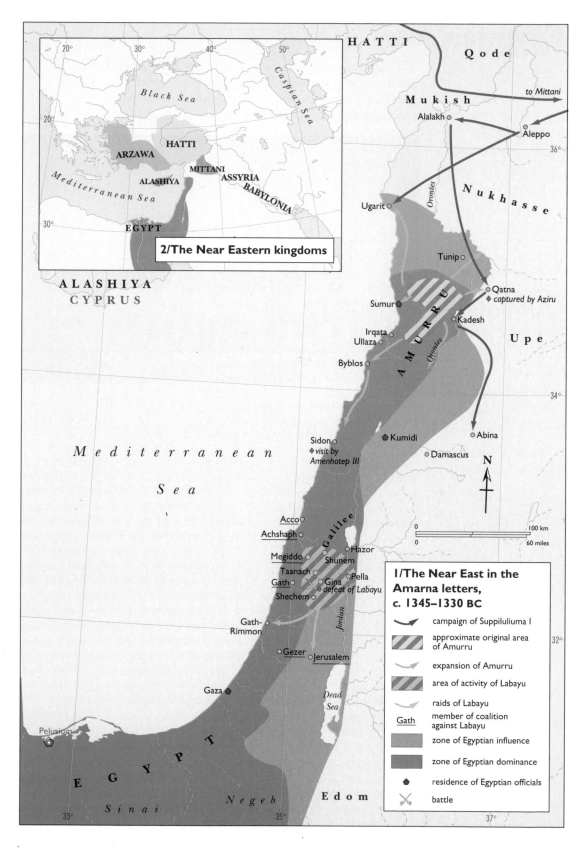

2/The Near Eastern kingdoms

1/The Near East in the Amarna letters, c. 1345–1330 BC

- campaign of Suppiluliuma I
- approximate original area of Amurru
- expansion of Amurru
- area of activity of Labayu
- raids of Labayu
- <u>Gath</u> member of coalition against Labayu
- zone of Egyptian influence
- zone of Egyptian dominance
- residence of Egyptian officials
- battle

Egyptian Art

The distinctive religious and funerary art of Ancient Egypt was characterized by the formality of the canon of proportion; a style was developed and maintained which expressed dignity, authority and spirituality in a clear and elegant manner.

"Greetings, perfect of face, possessor of radiance, whom Ptah-Sokar has completed, whom Anubis has exalted, to whom Thoth has given the beautiful visage of the gods. Your right eye is the evening sun, and your left eye is the morning sun. Your eyebrows are the Nine Gods, and your forehead is Anubis. The back of your head is Horus, and your braided hair is Ptah-Sokar."
Golden Funerary Mask of Tutankhamun

Above right: *Painting from the tomb of the vizîr Ramose at Thebes, showing funeral furniture being brought to the tomb. Egyptian artists were skilled at exploiting the possibilities of art: here the grief of women—reflected in their extravagant gestures and twisted bodies—seems dramatic in comparison with the rigid formality which predominates in funerary art.*

The early development of Egyptian kingship was mirrored in the formulation of the principles which characterized religious and funerary art throughout the whole dynastic period. At the heart of the distinctive pharaonic style was a structured formality already apparent in monuments of the 1st Dynasty—such as the Narmer palette—which was achieved by locating figures on a perfectly flat baseline: the absence of this organizing feature in prehistoric scenes makes them seem random and "un-Egyptian". All other lines used for drafting scenes, in two or three-dimensions, were drawn parallel to this baseline, or at right-angles to it. In the Middle Kingdom, the procedure was developed into a proportional canon or grid-of-squares, laid upon the stone surface in ink. The canon most commonly used divided the human figure into simple proportions: one-third of the height from the soles of the feet to the knee, halfway to the buttocks, two-thirds of the height to the elbow, etc. In this way figures were sketched typically, and portraiture was generally reserved only for the face. A particular version of the canon would predominate at a given time, and so determine the perceived "flavour" of the art of that period; for example, 19th Dynasty figures have longer legs and shorter, more slender torsos than those of the earlier periods because the line of the buttocks was located one square higher on the grid. The art of the Amarna period is immediately distinctive, partly because it was based upon an entirely new canon of proportion. A grid was rarely used to draft every figure in a scene, but lines in the grid of a major figure could be extended across the whole composition in order to co-ordinate the positions of other figures.

Human bodies were sketched as composites built up from individual parts: the resultant figures are unnatural, but nonetheless elegant and intriguing. For example, shoulders are shown from the front, beside which the torso seems extremely slender because it is presented in profile and only one breast is observed. The eye—seen in full—seems unusually large and attrac-

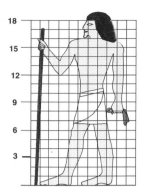

Above: *The typical canon of proportion used by an Egyptian artist divided the human figure into 18 squares from the baseline to the hairline; the parts of the body were then plotted at regular intervals. In this way, the artist created "typical" figures, exhibiting the characteristic formality of pharaonic art.*

tive since it is set in a face shown in profile. Such "typical" bodies are often idealized, especially for women: the figures of a man's wife and mother would both be shown in young womanhood, apparently indistinguishable in age. Colours were expressive rather than natural: red skin implied vigorous, tanned youth, whereas yellow skin indicated women or middle-aged men who worked indoors; blue or gold indicated divinity because of their unnatural character and association with precious materials; the occasional use of black for royal figures expressed the fertility of the Nile soil out of which Egypt was born. Stereotypes were frequently employed, especially to indicate the geographical origins of foreigners.

The formality of religious and funerary art upheld established principles. Firstly, art was required to be truthful; like Plato, Egyptian artists considered observations such as perspective or emotion to be momentary distortions, and as such peripheral to their work (although they could be indicated if appropriate). Canonical scenes were intended to convey more permanent ideas such as social status, authority or spirituality. It was equally important that these abstract ideas should be shown as obviously as possible, and so symbolism is everywhere apparent. Important figures were given noble features and powerful bodies adorned with symbols of high office—like Holbein's potent images of the Tudor court in 16th century England. A woman was normally seen in sheer fabric or sheathed in an impossibly tight dress; alongside, her husband—wearing only a kilt for modesty—would typically be shown directing workers in his estate, hunting water fowl or spearing fish. In this way, the sexuality of their relationship was made conspicuous, but so too was the relative passivity of the woman. A successful composition became part of every artist's repertoire, to be repeated for centuries, and, at its worst, the art of the temples and tombs of Ancient Egypt can be stereotyped and mechanical. However, in talented hands, Egyptian formal art was an attractive and inspiring style which could evoke a variety of feelings and express difficult and profound ideas clearly and concisely.

Left: *The most distinctive art of Ancient Egypt was the delicate, melodramatic—but occasionally aggressive—style of the Amarna period. In this scene the life-bearing hands of the sun-god Ra are seen to stream down and caress the worshipping figures of the king and queen, Akhenaten and Nefertiti. A characteristic feature of this art—the distorted bodies of the royal family, with exaggerated hips and breasts even on men— was based on the iconography of hermaphrodite fertility gods, and indicated a conscious use of symbolism.*

IV: The Late New Kingdom

Egypt in the Late New Kingdom enjoyed prosperity and international influence. However, the loss of Nubian gold and the division of the kingship ushered in a difficult era of civil disturbance, exacerbated by the royal family itself.

"You are like the Sun in all that you have done; what your heart desires comes to pass. If you wish a plan by night, at dawn it comes instantly to pass. We are used to seeing your many miracles since you ascended as king of the twin lands, but even if we had not heard, if our eyes had not seen, still they would all have come to be... What land do you not know? Who has embraced it like you? Have you not seen the unformed land even as it takes shape? Is there any foreign land which you have not trodden?"

Speech of the court to Ramesses II from a stela at Quban

The history of Egypt from *c.* 1295 BC to the traumatic invasion by Assyria in 664 BC can be divided into two periods: the 19th and 20th Dynasties represent a period of political unity and international supremacy, in which the policies of the 18th Dynasty were extended, and their achievements built upon; subsequently, the Third Intermediate Period was an era of division, in which native armies once more clashed on Egyptian soil, and when, for the first time, a lack of political purpose threatened to leave the land of the pharaohs at the mercy of foreign kings. Nevertheless, there are strong currents of continuity running throughout the centuries, especially in foreign policy, by which the Third Intermediate Period can be seen to develop straightforwardly out of the New Kingdom. Collectively, the 19th and 20th Dynasties are the Ramesside period, dominated by the royal name Ramesses, which was adopted by no less than nine kings of the 20th Dynasty in honour of their most magnificent predecessor Ramesses II. In addition to their family names, the kings of Egypt had several throne-names; those adopted by the Ramessides were echoed in the throne-names of the kings of the Third Intermediate Period, who were obliged to walk in the sunshine of reflected glory.

A new era of kingship began *c.* 1315 BC with the accession of Horemheb, although he is conventionally listed by scholars as the last king of the 18th Dynasty; it seems that later Egyptian tradition credited Horemheb with sweeping away a period of bogus rule by the pharaohs of the so-called Amarna period—Akhenaten, Nefernefruaten, Tutankhamun and Ay. There is some doubtful evidence to suggest that Horemheb's move from vizîr to king provoked conflict within the palace community, but any such difficulties were swiftly overcome; his own successor was in turn another vizîr, Ramesses I, who fathered the 19th Dynasty line. The new dynasty was originally from the delta although this had no significant impact on the administration of the country: the major palace officials were retained in office, including several appointed before the reign of Horemheb, and the great southern city of Thebes—ancestral home of the 18th Dynasty—retained its traditional prominence as the cultic home of Amun-Ra and the cemetery of the kings.

From a foreign policy perspective, the decades after the events chronicled in the Amarna letters are poorly documented, but crucial developments can be recognized.; the most significant was certainly the demise of the kingdom of Mittani, squeezed by the expansionist ambitions of Hatti to its north west and Assyria to its south east. The implications of this event were twofold for the Egyptians: firstly, the long-standing division of authority in Syria, from which Egypt gained the commercial advantage, was overturned; secondly, areas dominated by Egypt—though largely only on the basis of guarantees of loyalty made by local chiefs—were threatened by the machinations of two regimes disturbingly more aggressive than Mittani had ever seemed to be. The most immediate issues were the loyalty of Canaan—a traditionally troublesome region bound to Egypt only loosely—and the security of the Orontes valley, an area vital to the movement of trade northwards and eastwards from Egypt's Syrian ports such as Byblos and Sumur. Ramesses' son, Seti I, undertook a series of campaigns in which potentially disloyal elements

The temple of Ramesses II at Abu Simbel in ancient Wawat. The temple was dedicated to the cults of the greatest gods of New Kingdom Egypt: Ptah, Amun-Ra, Ra-Horakhty and the king himself. Egypt's earlier temples in Nubia were usually built inside forts, but this majestic facade trumpets the confidence with which Wawat was ruled after three centuries of continuous occupation.

were forced once more to acknowledge Egyptian hegemony, notably Canaan itself, and the kingdom of Amurru, which stood on the boundary with Hittite territory and had continued to defy Egypt since the reign of Aziru of the Amarna letters. Seti's success in Palestine was considerable, but in Syria served only to set the stage for a seemingly inevitable head-on conflict with Hatti.

In the 13th century BC, the city of Kadesh controlled the movement of trade in the Orontes valley, and had been within Egyptian hegemony for nearly 200 years since the reign of Thutmose III. During the period of the Amarna letters, the Hittite king Suppiluliuma I had led his army onto Mittanian lands, and subsequently manoeuvred them along the boundary of Egyptian territory towards Kadesh in a clearly provocative and threatening gesture. In the following years, the Hittites probably took control of the city and Seti himself was obliged to engage an army in battle nearby. The issue was unresolved at his death and became part of the legacy to his son, Ramesses II, who began systematically to whittle away territories gained by Hatti at Egyptian expense: *c.* 1276 BC, the new king led his armies along the Palestinian coastal plain to Byblos, and then advanced into Amurru; the next year he attacked Kadesh itself, although the battle was fought to a stand-off costly to both sides, in which the king himself was nearly killed after his vanguard was ambushed and surrounded. Subsequently, Hittite armies briefly regained control of Amurru, but Ramesses returned three years later to reverse his losses and make his own territorial gains in the Orontes valley. Thus nothing was achieved.

A modern audience tends to be astonished by the sheer audacity with which Ramesses II paraded the events of the battle of Kadesh on the walls of his five greatest temples, and even commissioned a poem to be written in celebration. His behaviour could be interpreted as bombastic arrogance in which his considerable achievement in fighting to save the day was allowed to obscure the naive recklessness with which he had led his men into a blatant ambush. Alternatively, it could be seen as revisionist history of the crudest kind, in which the king trumpeted his "victory" so loudly and so often that the real story would hopefully be forgotten. In fact, a more charitable interpretation would recognize that the records of the battle constitute a pious hymn of thanksgiving for the king's deliverance to the god Amun, who was seen to fight alongside the king that day. It has also been suggested that the records were intended to undermine the influence of the army officers—whose actions nearly precipitated total disaster—in a post-war environment which recognized that a diplomatic solution to the Hittite problem was the only feasible option. This last suggestion is perhaps speculating further than the evidence would allow; moreover, in the end the role of the military had been decisive since it had forced Hatti to recognize that the military conquest of Egyptian Syria was impossible. Therefore, *c.* 1259 BC, representatives of Ramesses II and Hattusili III of Hatti agreed to a formal division of control over the Syrian trade routes, which held throughout the rest of the New Kingdom. Thereafter, the attention of the Hittite king was generally turned elsewhere in his lands, and the few Egyptian "campaigns" in Syria or Palestine undertaken as late as the reign of Ramesses VII (*c.* 1136–1129 BC) were rather more displays of royal authority intended to impress than military manoeuvres designed to subdue.

The Village at Deir el-Medina

Ironically, although the Ramesside period is overshadowed by one king and the monumental accounts of his wars, the Late New Kingdom is a period exceptionally well documented from a more humdrum and informal perspective, the workmen's village at Deir el-Medina. The village is sited in the desert on the west bank at Thebes and was abandoned by its inhabitants in favour of the fortified temple of Medinet Habu at the end of the 20th Dynasty, when civil disturbances threatened their security. Thereafter, the site was largely forgotten until it attracted the interest of 19th century antiquarians, and its exceptional location away from the flood-plain allowed the village to survive in a far better condition than would be expected of such an ancient settlement. Ongoing and systematic study of the masses of documentation and items of everyday life from Deir el-Medina has revealed a community that was as exceptional in its life as it was in its death: "the servants in the place of harmony", as the villagers were known, have since turned out to be scribes, craftsmen, and masons (along with their families and servants) whose only official employment was to build the royal tombs in the Valley of the Kings.

The village is arranged around a central street, so narrow that it is possible to touch both sides at once, and is surrounded by a 20-foot high wall with just one door opening to the north. At its zenith about 70 houses were arrayed along the street and adjoining alleys, each quite regular and perhaps more compact than was usual in a typical ancient village. Because of the solemn nature of the villagers' work, they were accorded a very high social status, and everything necessary for their working and domestic lives was supplied, in Egypt's non-monetary economy, in kind from the magazines of the royal mortuary temples. A scribe or foreman expected to receive sufficient quantities of emmer and barley to support a household with up to a dozen members, and there were other regular rations such as vegetables, fish, salt, chickpeas, fats and oils, as well as juniper berries and cumin for spicing the cooking. Effectively, the welfare of the workmen and their dependents was the direct responsibility of the office of the vizîr of Upper Egypt, and the maintenance of the village generated an enormous quantity of documentation; in addition, the villagers themselves were an exceptionally literate group who composed their own letters and work-records, copied out literature, poetry and hymns, and left personal graffiti in the surrounding hills. Most of this documentation was abandoned with the village and as a result such a wealth of detail has been preserved, that Deir el-Medina as it existed during the last two centuries of the New Kingdom is easily the best documented community in the whole ancient world. It is possible today to identify the homes of named individuals, and to recount some of the gossip about what once took place behind closed doors!

The Egyptian version of the treaty agreed c. 1259 BC between Ramesses II and the Hittite king, Hattusili III, in which control over Syrian towns and trade routes was formally divided between the two kingdoms after 50 years of conflict. This text covers a 13 feet-high wall in the temple of Karnak; by contrast, a version discovered in the archives of Hattusas, the capital of Hatti, was written on a clay tablet just a few inches high.

The End of the New Kingdom

The transition from the 19th to the 20th Dynasty was not without difficulties, all of which seem to have stemmed from within the royal family. The succession of Seti II as heir of Merenptah (*c.* 1213–1203 BC) was usurped, at least in the south of the country, by Merenptah's half-brother Amenmesse. The resultant dynastic confusion was ended only by a new royal family headed by Sethnakht (*c.* 1186–1184 BC). However, Sethnakht's own son, Ramesses III (*c.* 1184–1153 BC), was subject to an

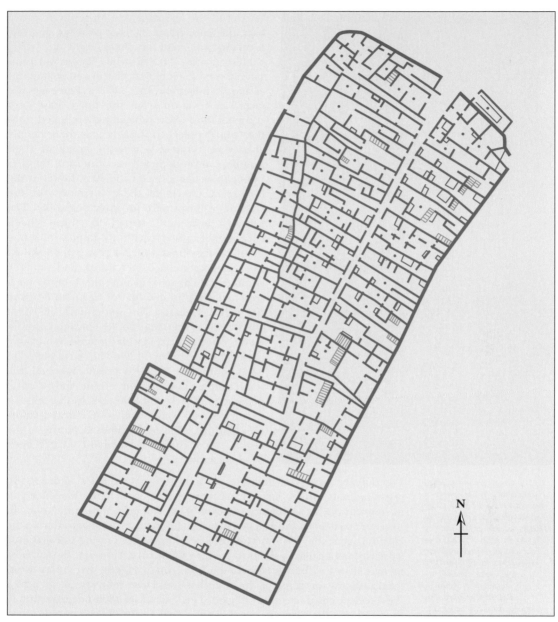

Plan of the workmen's village at Deir el-Medina. The village was purpose-built during the reign of Thutmose I, and has a designed plan based around a central street. In the reign of Horemheb, the village was extended northwards beyond the original wall, and southwards through an area that had previously been stables. At the height of its occupation in the 19th Dynasty, the village housed nearly 70 families resident in nine distinct districts.

assassination plot hatched by officials and queens of the harîm; apparently the plot failed, although the formal wording of the subsequent legal proceedings leaves some doubt. Evidence from Deir el-Medina suggests that these dynastic crises adversely affected society in general, at least by creating a climate of doubt, but that, in the long run, the country was largely unaffected.

During this period Egypt was faced with a disturbing series of invasions from Libya: based on the sketchy details available, a straightforward explanation would be that famine forced refugees to flee in their tens of thousands towards the north west of Egypt, where smaller numbers of their kinfolk had peacefully been working, trading and settling for nearly a century; a more sinister explanation is that Libyan settlement threatened to overwhelm the Nile delta, and so undermine the Egyptian administration in that region.

Detail from a relief of Shoshenk I in the temple of Amun-Ra at Karnak, in which a personification of the city of Thebes delivers captive enemy cities to the king. The name of each city is written within a ring representing a fortified wall, surmounted by a stereotyped Syrian or Palestinian head; this information can be used to reconstruct the details of the campaign c. 925 BC.

Whatever the explanation, Merenptah drove back the immigrants by force of arms, and any problem was held in check until the years *c.* 1180 BC and *c.* 1174 BC, when Ramesses III was again forced to employ armies to defeat attempts at mass immigration. In *c.* 1177 BC Ramesses also faced an invasion from the north east by a confederation often misleadingly referred to as the "Sea Peoples". It is likely that these people also were refugees—certainly many of their number were depicted as itinerant families rather than marauders. Ultimately, however, the long-term effects of these invasions on the stability of Egypt were probably negligible. The Libyan invasions seem to have been exceptional episodes within a long-term settlement process from which Egypt gained skilled workers, experienced merchants, and valuable commercial contacts; in time the Libyan rulers spawned a traditional line of Egyptian kings in the 22nd Dynasty. No settlement of Egypt resulted from the "Sea Peoples" invasion; however, it is often associated with the sudden break-up of the Hittite empire *c.* 1200–1175 BC in the reign of Suppiluliuma II, which presumably had dramatic implications for the ethnic and political geography of Syria and Palestine. In this sense, it may have been symptomatic of political developments which affected Egyptian authority in the region, although whether for good or bad is open to speculation.

The military success of Ramesses III indicates that he led a vigorous and organized state, which pursued its commercial interests in the Near East and maintained the infrastructure of government and gold-mining in Nubia. In these circumstances, the absence of any major military campaigns during the later reigns of the 20th Dynasty reflected Egypt's continuing international authority, rather than a creeping military impotence. However, two developments during the final decades of the 20th Dynasty suggest that the nature of royal authority was changing in a way that would have major implications for the future political make-up of Egypt. The first was an apparent reduction in the touring of the king, who increasingly relied on the presence of his representatives to control the provincial administration rather than expecting provincial officials to attend him at court on a regular basis. The second development was the emergence of a divine state-within-a-state at Thebes: here oracles of the gods Amun-Ra, Mut and Khonsu increasingly assumed the king's role to appoint officials, and the distinction between the high priest of Amun and the king as a living representative of the gods became increasingly unclear. In the reign of Ramesses IX (*c.* 1126–1108 BC), the high priest Amenhotep had been depicted at Karnak with a stature virtually equal to that of the king, indicating equality of status in iconographic terms; during the reign of Ramesses XI (*c.* 1099–1069 BC), the vizir and general of the king's armies, Herihor, actually adopted the titles of a king whilst serving as high priest within the sacred city.

Nevertheless, indications of a reduction in the authority of pharaoh at the

A view of the interior of the mortuary temple of Ramesses III at Medinet Habu. The royal tomb and temple took the place of the pyramid as the country's major building project during the New Kingdom, even though the temples of other gods were generally built on a much larger scale than previously. Medinet Habu continued as a town and place of worship beyond the reigns of the last pharaohs.

end of the 20th Dynasty may be more apparent than real. Developments at Thebes were confined to the temple estate at Karnak—off-limits to the masses—and were essentially a cultic phenomenon which affected the iconography, but not the importance, of the institution of kingship. Other indications are circumstantial but inconclusive. The story of *The Voyage of Wenamun* is often mooted: Wenamun was an official from Karnak sent to Byblos in the reign of Ramesses XI in order to obtain wood for the sacred boat of Amun-Ra, but he was robbed *en route* and subjected to a series of humiliations in various Palestinian ports, including Byblos itself. Wenamun had such a distressing time because he had arrived in Byblos without gifts or documentation, and was on the run for robbery; the response of the local rulers to such a bedraggled and unlikely ambassador was understandable, and his treatment, in what may be a fictional tale, was not necessarily symptomatic of a decline in Egypt's regional authority. Another source, damning on the face of it, is a conspiratorial letter to a scribe at Deir el-Medina written by the general of pharaoh's armies, Piankh, regarding the interrogation and possible murder of two security guards, which included the words:"Another point: As for pharaoh, how will he reach this land? As for pharaoh, whose superior is he?"Probably, however, these seemingly treacherous remarks should be paraphrased: "Who is pharaoh's representative—I am! Therefore, who is answerable to him and will have to do any talking—me!" In this sense it is presumably meant to reassure the nervous recipient about the safety of becoming involved in such a clandestine affair.

The Third Intermediate Period

The beginning of a new era was was brought about by a political event, a civil war which raged in Upper Egypt and resulted in the loss of the occupied Nubian territories after nearly 500 years of Egyptian rule. The war began *c.* 1087 BC in the reign of Ramesses XI, when the armies of Panehsy, viceroy of Nubia, occupied Thebes, possibly at the invitation of the king; seven years later, the "treacherous" general Piankh pursued these troops back south, and Panehsy wrested Nubia from Egyptian control once and for all. As a result, there was a sudden and dramatic reduction in the supply of Nubian gold and trade goods, which must have seriously reduced Egypt's commercial authority within the international community. In the aftermath, Ramesses passed away without an heir, and a new line of kings, the 21st Dynasty, came to power, headed by Smendes (*c.* 1069–1043 BC). The centre of authority of the new dynasty was the delta city of Tanis, although strong links with the priest-kings of Thebes were formalized by dynastic marriages, and the civil disturbances in Upper Egypt caused by the war of Panehsy, because of which Deir el-Medina was finally abandoned, seem to have been checked.

The throne apparently passed without incident from the last king of the 21st Dynasty to his adopted heir, Shoshenk I (*c.* 945–924 BC), a man of Libyan descent. Shoshenk I reasserted Egypt's historic dominance in Palestine with a campaign *c.* 925 BC against the kingdom of Israel, and key commercial towns such as Megiddo and the port of Gaza. Despite this vigorous beginning, the effectiveness of the new dynasty was restricted by the diminished wealth of the nation and by the increasing power of the regional administrations. Successive kings sought to hold emerging divisions in check by retaining major offices within a small circle of royal family members, or by awarding concessions to office holders as royal favours, thereby fostering a culture of obligation amongst the ruling class. Ultimately, however, these policies only succeeded in weakening the structural unity of the country, whilst simultaneously generating tensions within the royal family itself, which became a much more political instrument than it had ever previously been.

By the mid-9th century BC, bitter disputes over the boundaries of authority had begun to break out between the regions and within the dynasty—often as two sides of the same coin, since dynastic princes increasingly established *de facto* kingdoms in provincial power centres. Such bitterness inevitably led to warfare, and once again Egyptian armies took to the field against fellow-Egyptians, although civil war was far from typical of the period. By the time of Shoshenk III (*c.* 825–773 BC), it had become apparent that the ruling dynasty was on the verge of fragmenting, so the king himself took the initiative in establishing princes from his own family as titular kings in key provincial cities; presumably he hoped to control a process that was inevitable in any case, and so ensure that the country ultimately remained within the control of his own dynasty. Again, however, the policy was far from successful, and led to a much greater multiplication of autonomous regimes than Shoshenk had intended. Ironically, some of the most assertive rulers were the chiefs of Libyan descent, amongst whose number the 22nd Dynasty had originally been counted. Another assertive, if not aggressive, regime was that of prince Tefnakht of Sais during the late 8th century BC, who had sufficient influence to support Hosea, king of Samaria, in opposition to Assyria. Tefnakht also fostered in the city of Sais a sense of independence which would have a profound influence on the history of Egypt after her involvement with Assyria degenerated into war.

Post-Imperial Nubia

The history of Nubia after the regime of Panehsy renounced Egyptian control is a notorious dark age in our knowledge, but one which ended in a manner as abrupt as it was unforeseen, when the armies of a Kushite pharaoh brought Egypt temporarily under his sway. For three centuries, the evidence falls silent: the handful of texts securely dated to this period seem to indicate that a small number of quasi-royal families challenged one another for power in the vacuum created by the withdrawal of the Egyptian administration; with the summit of the administration effectively eliminated for at least a century, the structures of centralized power unravelled, and the tangible remains of a settled, bureaucratic state disappeared. In Wawat especially, the population seems to have melted away: perhaps less certain patterns of agriculture outside the Egyptian system obliged people to resort to a semi-nomadic lifestyle on the desert fringes, or perhaps there was an exodus to more fertile and stable areas in Kush, precipitated initially by the invasion of general Piankh and thereafter by political uncertainty. It is unfortunate, however, that the building of the el-Sadd el-Ali High Dam in the 1960s has drowned most of ancient Wawat under the waters of Lake Nasser, and so no answer to the depopulation conundrum is likely to emerge on the basis of systematic archaeological excavation in the foreseeable future.

No tangible details can be discerned until the middle of the 8th century BC, when the ruling family of Napata emerged as overlords of a united Kushite kingdom, although the process by which this came about is entirely unknown. The royal culture of this family, as expressed in their art and funerary customs, was essentially that of the New Kingdom administration in Nubia, and from the reign of Kashta (c. 760–747 BC) onwards the Napatan rulers styled themselves as traditional pharaohs identified in Manetho's List as the 25th Dynasty. Their beliefs also recognized pharaonic obligations towards the Nilotic kingdom as a whole, and especially towards the cults of the Egyptian gods; kingship at Napata was dominated by the oracle of Amun at Gebel Barkal, where the new kings built on an enormous scale in the sacred area founded by Egyptians almost 700 years earlier. The Napatan kings knew, however, that the ancient cult centre of Amun—and hence the source of their own authority—was Thebes, and so Kashta's son and successor, Piy, resolved to celebrate the ancient festival of Opet in the city. Initially, he promoted his presence politically by arranging for his sister, Amenirdis, to be adopted as the eventual successor to the incumbent God's Wife of Amun—the most influential office in the sacred city at that time—but by c. 728 BC an army was sent to force acceptance of Piy's authority on the population of Upper Egypt. In Egypt of the late 8th century BC, his troops could not hope to control large areas of the Nile valley without arousing the hostility of the powerful Tefnakht of Sais; Tefnakht, indeed, organized a coalition of delta rulers—kings, princes, and Libyan chiefs—to oppose growing Napatan influence. However, the swiftness with which the Kushite armies had arrived allowed them the initiative, and Tefnakht was attacked and then besieged at Hermopolis for several weeks, until Piy himself arrived to end the siege. He then travelled to Memphis and Heliopolis in order to worship the ancient gods, whilst also receiving the homage of other Egyptian rulers in formal recognition of his dominion throughout the lands of the Nile. Piy could claim to hold what he believed was his rightful pharaonic inheritance, and but now that a Nubian pharaoh dominated a fragmented kingdom of limited international influence, the long-standing order of the New Kingdom had finally been turned on its head.

The 19th Dynasty Osireion at Abydos is an astonishing subterranean temple built to celebrate the ancient cult of Osiris, the resurrected king. The temple's plan is not unconventional, but it was otherwise unique; the main building was originally covered with a mastaba-like mound of soil, planted with trees—representing the primaeval mound of creation—and could only be approached via a descending ramp over 100 metres long.

The Road to Kadesh

The impact of the Hittite Empire on the trade routes of the Orontes Valley forced a climactic battle with Egypt, and the creation of a new political order in Syria.

"I found that Amun came when I called him, and gave me his hand, and I rejoiced; he called from behind, as if next to me: 'Forward, I am with you!'"
Poem of the Battle of Kadesh

In the years following the Amarna period, the expansionist policies of Hatti and Assyria had led to the virtual eclipse of Mittanian independence. Of greater concern to Egypt, however, was the situation of Kadesh, the great trading centre of the Orontes Valley, whose chiefs felt increasing pressure to ally with Hatti. In spite of peace treaties between the two nations, Hittite and Egyptian armies had clashed near Kadesh at some point during or after the reign of Tutankhamun, (*c.* 1327–1318 BC). A new dynasty, the 19th, had a military background, and felt it was time to reassert the role of the king as war-leader. Initially Seti I (*c.* 1294–1279 BC) took the field against the Shasu (a troublesome group of stateless people in southern Palestine), briefly returned Amurru to Egyptian control, and then engaged a Hittite army near Kadesh. However, Seti's successes were only preliminary skirmishes in which the two armies appraised the gathering storm: it was his son, Ramesses II, who was destined to meet the armies of Muwatalli of Hatti in the climactic battle for control of the Orontes.

In his 4th Year, Ramesses led his armies through the subject ports of the Palestinian coast to Byblos, and then advanced into Amurru once more. The following year he was in position to pounce on Kadesh itself. In the event, the Egyptian army was tricked and outmanoeuvred by a Hittite-sponsored coalition: its four brigades were strung out approaching the city and the king, with the vanguard, was ambushed. The disaster for Egypt was nearly total, but Ramesses' own leadership, and the timely arrival of reinforcements, allowed him to fight his way out of a stalemate in which the enemy lost several key leaders. Ramesses would later present a monumental account of this battle on the walls of his five greatest temples, and a poem was created in celebration. Modern commentators have seen this as lying, boasting or revisionist history: in fact, the king's valour and leadership were the stuff of legend, and there is sincere humility in his thanksgiving to the god Amun for his deliverance.

The immediate aftermath of this inconclusive battle was to upset the *status quo* in Syria and Palestine, and the armies of Mutwatalli were quick to seize the initiative by regaining control of Amurru and then invading Upe. Ramesses, however, was far from subdued, and led two more campaigns in the next five years to reassert his authority in Canaan, the coastal ports and Amurru—indeed he was able to wreste several towns in the Orontes valley from Hittite control. However, neither country could fail to recognize that the stand-off established at Kadesh was ultimately immovable, and that dissent in their subject territories was being stirred up by local chiefs skilled at exploiting political confusion. In addition, the aggressive regime of Shalmaneser I in Assyria posed a mutual threat. Therefore, in his 21st Year, Ramesses II agreed with the new Hittite emperor, Hattusili II, to a division of control over Syrian territories and the caravan routes crossing them, formally recognized by a treaty of which copies have survived from Egypt and Hatti. The Hittite version was scratched on a clay tablet filed away in a palace archive, whereas the Egyptian hieroglyphic version was inscribed, more than twice human-size, on a wall in the temple of Karnak to celebrate the beneficent intervention of the gods in the affairs of men. Such divinely-inscribed peace was destined to hold throughout the next century.

Kadesh was the first battle in history of which a detailed account survived. Hittite spies convinced the Egyptian officers that their enemy, hidden on the blindside of Kadesh, had actually withdrawn. Ramesses and his forward brigade (Amun) therefore pressed ahead and camped near the city. When the suprise attack came, the Brigade of Ra was routed and fled towards the vanguard.

The king rallied his two forward brigades, and the timely appearance of élite Ne'arim reinforcements allowed the Egyptians to survive until the arrival of the Brigades of Seth and Ptah forced the stalemate.

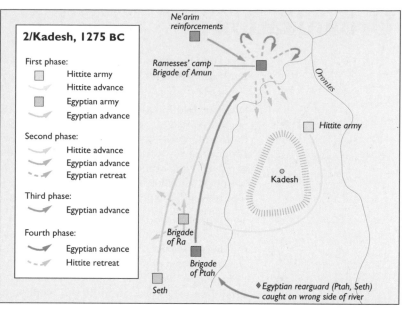

2/Kadesh, 1275 BC

First phase:
- ☐ Hittite army
- Hittite advance
- ☐ Egyptian army
- Egyptian advance

Second phase:
- Hittite advance
- Egyptian advance
- Egyptian retreat

Third phase:
- Egyptian advance

Fourth phase:
- Egyptian advance
- Hittite retreat

Ne'arim reinforcements

Ramesses' camp Brigade of Amun

Orontes

Hittite army

Kadesh

Brigade of Ra

Brigade of Ptah

Seth

◆ Egyptian rearguard (Ptah, Seth) caught on wrong side of river

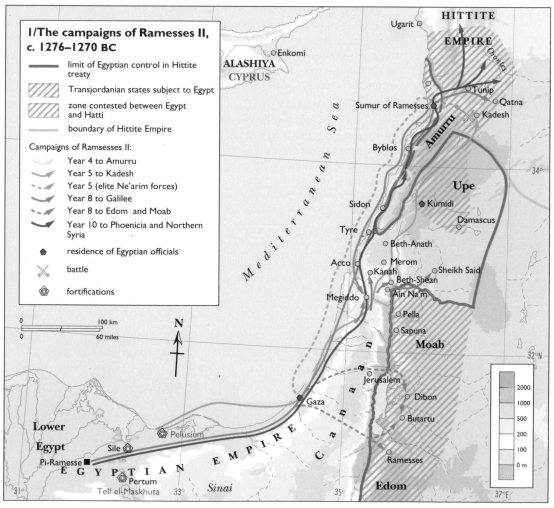

1/The campaigns of Ramesses II, c. 1276–1270 BC

- ▬▬ limit of Egyptian control in Hittite treaty
- ▨ Transjordanian states subject to Egypt
- ▨ zone contested between Egypt and Hatti
- ▬▬ boundary of Hittite Empire

Campaigns of Ramesses II:
- Year 4 to Amurru
- Year 5 to Kadesh
- Year 5 (elite Ne'arim forces)
- Year 8 to Galilee
- Year 8 to Edom and Moab
- Year 10 to Phoenicia and Northern Syria
- ⬠ residence of Egyptian officials
- ⚔ battle
- ◎ fortifications

0 ____ 100 km
0 ____ 60 miles

N

HITTITE EMPIRE

Ugarit

ALASHIYA CYPRUS

Enkomi

Orontes

Tunip

Qatna

Sumur of Ramesses

Amurru

Kadesh

Byblos

Mediterranean Sea

Upe

Sidon

Kumidi

Damascus

Tyre

Beth-Anath

Acco

Merom

Sheikh Said

Kanah

Beth-Shean

Megiddo

Ain Na'm

Pella

Sapuna

Moab

Canaan

Jerusalem

Dibon

Gaza

Butartu

Lower Egypt

Pelusium

Sile

EGYPTIAN EMPIRE

Ramesses

Pi-Ramesse

Pertum

Edom

Tell el-Maskhuta

Sinai

31° 33° 35° 37°E

34°

32°N

2000
1000
500
200
100
0 m

Urbanization

The New Kingdom saw dramatic changes in the urban development of Egypt as the largest settlements grew into huge, cosmopolitan cities.

"This flight your servant made was not premeditated; it was not my wish, I did not invent it. I do not know what took me from my home. It was like sleepwalking; like when a marsh-man finds himself in Elephantine—a man of the delta in the far south."
The Story of Sinuhe

Since the Old Kingdom, the Egyptians had distinguished three types of communities: villages, communities with a harbour—which became centres of trade and travel—and larger towns. The largest towns were the capitals of the administrative districts (*nomes*), which by the time of New Kingdom numbered 42. Each capital was densely populated and surrounded by other communities; sometimes there was another populous centre. Between these centres, however, the population could dwindle to almost nothing.

The population of Egypt as a whole increased dramatically during the New Kingdom: exact figures are hard to establish, but some estimates suggest that numbers increased from 1½ million to 2½–5 million during the 18th–19th Dynasties. Most of this increase occurred at Memphis and Heliopolis, where up to half of the entire population may have resided: Memphis may have been the world's first city with over 1 million people. Larger provincial centres such as Sais, Per-Ramesse, Herakleopolis and Thebes also expanded, swelled partly by large numbers of immigrants attracted by the wealth and stability of the country. These immigrants and their descendants formed tight-knit but generally well-respected communities which offered Egypt workers with crucial skills, such as seamen, merchants, mercenaries, translators and glassworkers. Texts from the New Kingdom manifest names from as far afield as Libya, Greece, Babylon and Kush.

These communities formed a cohesive society, its character dictated by local issues and the needs of the farmers who formed Egypt's economic base, but with a government which was still characteristically centralized. Social hierarchies ensured that the distribution of wealth was élitist, and the king made an elaborate show out of rewarding loyal officials at home and abroad. There was a permanent military administration but the army was never employed as a coercive arm of government; there were few garrisons in Egypt itself, and their role was to train and to register those liable for military service.

The Northern Palace of Akhetaten was part of a new city built for Amenhotep IV; possibly it housed his principal queen when the court was in residence. Even a great palace such as this was typically built with hard, but ultimately friable mud-brick, emphasizing the fleeting character of a living settlement in comparison with the permanence of stone-built tombs and temples, which tend to dominate the archaeological record of pharaonic Egypt.

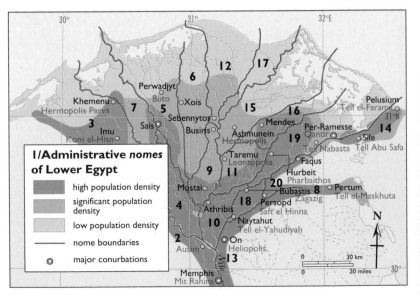

1/Administrative nomes of Lower Egypt

- high population density
- significant population density
- low population density
- nome boundaries
- major conurbations

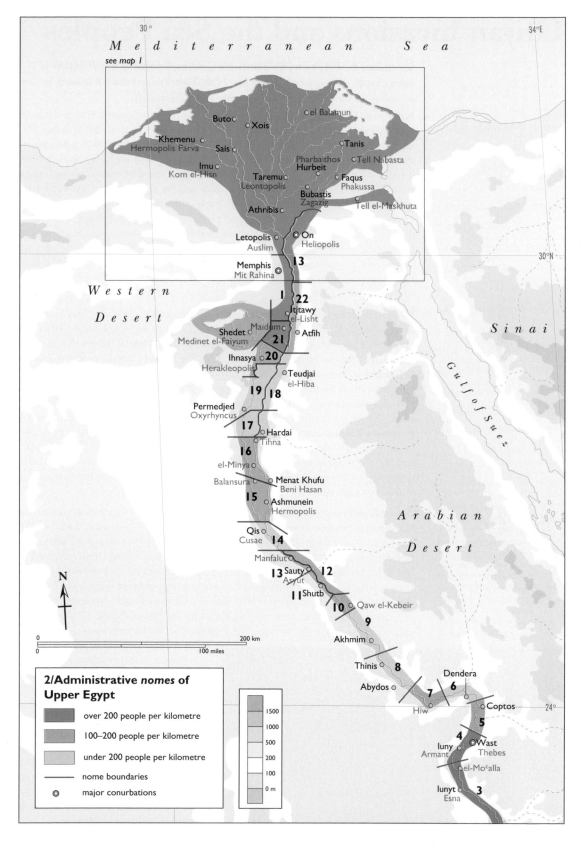

M e d i t e r r a n e a n   S e a

see map I

Buto
Xois
el Balamun
Khemenu
Hermopolis Parva
Sais
Tanis
Imu
Kom el-Hisn
Pharbaithos
Tell Nabasta
Hurbeit
Taremu
Leontopolis
Faqus
Phakussa
Bubastis
Zagazig
Tell el-Maskhuta
Athribis

Letopolis
Auslim
On
Heliopolis

Memphis
Mit Rahina
13

W e s t e r n

D e s e r t

1
22
Itjtawy
el-Lisht
Maidum
Atfih
Shedet
Medinet el-Faiyum
21
Ihnasya
Herakleopolis
20
Teudjai
el-Hiba
19 **18**
Permedjed
Oxyrhyncus
17
Hardai
Tihna
16
el-Minya
Menat Khufu
Beni Hasan
Balansura
15
Ashmunein
Hermopolis
Qis
Cusae
14
Manfalut
13
Sauty
Asyut
12
11
Shutb
10
Qaw el-Kebeir
9
Akhmim

S i n a i

G u l f   o f   S u e z

A r a b i a n

D e s e r t

N

0 _____ 200 km
0 _____ 100 miles

Thinis
8
Dendera
Abydos
7
6
Hiw
Coptos
5
4
Iuny
Armant
Wast
Thebes
el-Mocalla
Iunyt
Esna
3

30°N

24°

2/Administrative *nomes* of Upper Egypt

■ over 200 people per kilometre
■ 100–200 people per kilometre
□ under 200 people per kilometre
— nome boundaries
◎ major conurbations

1500
1000
500
200
100
0 m

Libyan Invasions and the Sea Peoples

Incursions by Libyan tribes across the western fringes of Egypt assumed a more threatening aspect during the 19th Dynasty, and were followed by the invasion of "Sea Peoples" in the reign of Ramesses III.

"The land of Tjehenu came all together, as the Libu, the Seped, and the Mashwash ... their intentions were 'Action!', and their wishes were filled with wrongdoing and perversion; but their plans were crushed and overturned by the wish of the god."
Inscription of Ramesses III, at Medinet Habu

A frieze carved at Abydos during the reign of Ramesses II portrays the Libyan invaders of Egypt, and the Sea Peoples as fierce warriors clad in battle helmets. Nevertheless, they brought their homes and families with them in carts, and are likely to have been desperate, displaced peoples rather than savage marauders.

Seti I and Ramesses II both conducted campaigns against the people of Tjehenu in the Western Desert. However, by the end of the 19th Dynasty, the settlement in Egypt of members of new tribes, the Mashwash and Libu, probably indicates the arrival of people from Kyrene and its hinterland, which stood further west than any Egyptian army had campaigned. Although they were mainly pastoral peoples, they had strong armies, were governed by established dynasties of kings, and their potential threat was recognized when Ramesses II constructed a series of forts along the coastal route into the western fringes of the delta to match the forts on the Sinai roads. Nevertheless, these people normally arrived peacefully to form a significant immigrant population, and many, especially amongst the Mashwash, had extensive trading interests which would certainly have been of benefit to the commerce of Egypt.

The *status quo* was upset when Merenptah resorted to military force in order to repulse a mass incursion from Libya, slaying nearly 10,000. His own account of the war, inscribed on the famous "Israel Stela", hints that famine may have displaced the refugees. On the other hand, many invaders belonged to non-Libyan tribes—Sherdan, Sheklesh, Turesh, Lukki—who may have been mercenaries or trading partners, in which case the very political and commercial future of the western-central delta may have been at stake. Such a disquieting movement was repelled again in Year Five of Ramesses III, and once more in Year Eleven; women and children, in depictions of the invaders at Ramesses' mortuary temple at Medinet Habu, imply further attempts at mass immigration. Apparently, the kings of Egypt trod a tightrope balancing the benefits of Libyan settlement against her security in an increasingly volatile region.

If, at this difficult time, Ramesses III depended on the established security of his eastern border, then another invasion in Year Eight must have galled him: a confederation of tribes (often referred to as "Sea Peoples", although Egyptian accounts identify only a minority as being "of the sea") arrived at the delta via Hatti and Syria, and the ensuing upheaval and unrest has been woven into a tale of marauders overthrowing mighty empires. In fact, amongst them were women and children, and they should probably be seen at least partly as refugees, perhaps victims of the collapse of the Hittite empire rather than its nemesis. In comparison with the threat from Libya, this displacement of people made no lasting impression on Egypt itself. However, it may have had dramatic implications for the ethnic and political geography of Syria and Palestine, fomenting raids against the Levantine ports and other important towns, and, in this sense, could have had major implications for Egypt's authority. At present, however, the evidence bearing directly on this matter is both limited and equivocal.

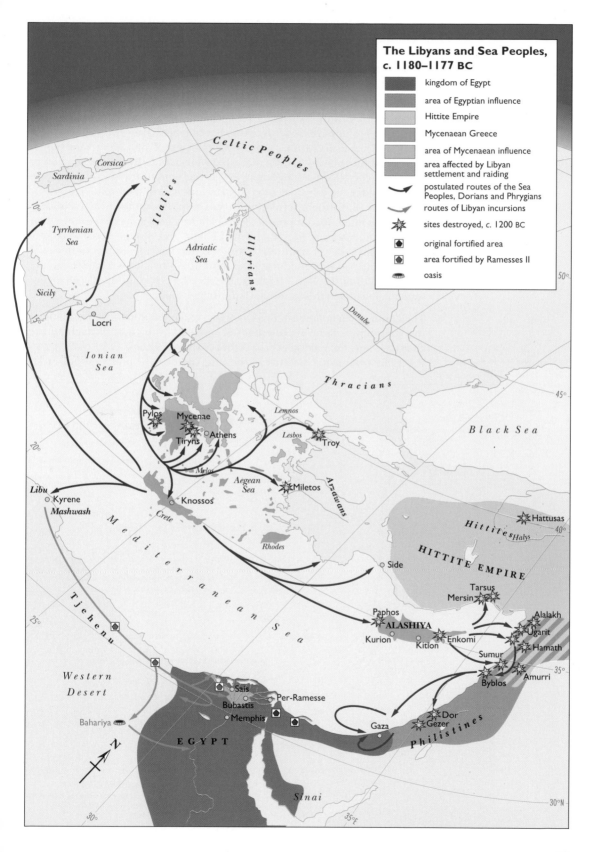

**The Libyans and Sea Peoples,
c. 1180–1177 BC**

kingdom of Egypt

area of Egyptian influence

Hittite Empire

Mycenaean Greece

area of Mycenaean influence

area affected by Libyan
settlement and raiding

postulated routes of the Sea
Peoples, Dorians and Phrygians

routes of Libyan incursions

sites destroyed, c. 1200 BC

original fortified area

area fortified by Ramesses II

oasis

Celtic Peoples

Sardinia

Corsica

Tyrrhenian
Sea

Italics

Adriatic
Sea

Illyrians

Danube

Sicily

Locri

Ionian
Sea

Thracians

Black Sea

Lemnos

Pylos

Mycenae

Lesbos

Troy

Athens

Tiryns

Melos

Aegean
Sea

Arzawans

Miletos

Libu

Kyrene

Mashwash

Knossos

Crete

Rhodes

Mediterranean

Hittites

Hattusas

Halys

HITTITE EMPIRE

Side

Tarsus

Mersin

Alalakh

Paphos

ALASHIYA

Ugarit

Kurion

Kition

Enkomi

Hamath

Sumur

Tjehenu

Sea

Byblos

Amurri

Western
Desert

Sais

Bubastis

Per-Ramesse

Memphis

Dor

Gezer

Bahariya

Gaza

Philistines

EGYPT

Sinai

N

97

The Decline of Royal Authority

A radical reconsideration of the personal authority of the last Ramesside pharaohs resulted in the division of the kingship of Egypt.

"Since there is no boat on the river that does not belong to Amun, and the sea belongs to him, therefore the Lebanon, which you say is yours, that also belongs to him."

The Voyage of Wenamun

In comparison with the earlier New Kingdom, monuments of the 20th Dynasty seem unimpressive, but this is not necessarily symptomatic of a decline in royal wealth or authority: Ramesses III had been vigorous in defence of his country, and there is no evidence of a dramatic reduction in trade with the Near East. In Nubia a vigorous administration retained control, and since the infrastructure of government and gold mining was now centuries old, further development was perhaps unnecessary. Periodic restrictions in the food supply at Deir el-Medina may indicate no more than the normal pattern of life in ancient Thebes, and though there were robberies in the Valley of the Kings, there was no challenge to the authority of the royal officials who conducted the ensuing prosecutions. However, in the final decades of the New Kingdom, the ideology of kingship was changing fundamentally, and this would have profound implications.

The defining phenomena in this change were a reduction in the travelling of the king (although his representatives were still prominent throughout the country), and the emergence of a theocracy in Thebes. The result was to lessen the charismatic presence of the king, increase the power of the oracles

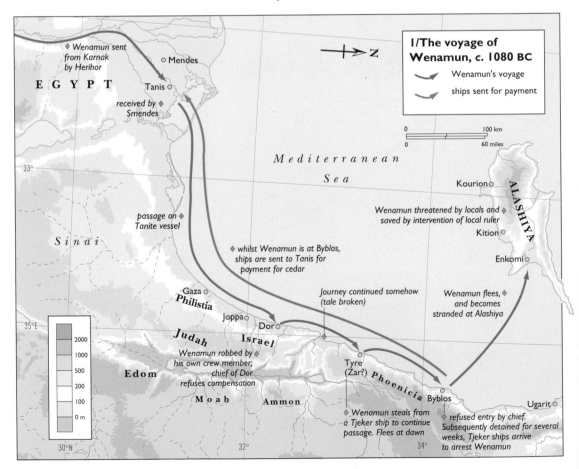

I/The voyage of Wenamun, c. 1080 BC

Wenamun's voyage

ships sent for payment

Wenamun sent from Karnak by Herihor

EGYPT

Mendes

Tanis

received by Smendes

Mediterranean Sea

Kourion

passage on Tanite vessel

Sinai

Wenamun threatened by locals and saved by intervention of local ruler

Kition

ALASHIYA

Enkomi

whilst Wenamun is at Byblos, ships are sent to Tanis for payment for cedar

Gaza

Philistia

Joppa

Dor

Journey continued somehow (tale broken)

Wenamun flees, and becomes stranded at Alashiya

Judah

Israel

Wenamun robbed by his own crew member; chief of Dor refuses compensation

Edom

Tyre (Zar?)

Phoenicia

Byblos

Ugarit

Moab

Ammon

Wenamun steals from a Tjeker ship to continue passage. Flees at dawn

refused entry by chief. Subsequently detained for several weeks, Tjeker ships arrive to arrest Wenamun

of the Theban gods, and blur the distinction between the authority of the high priest of Amun and that of the king himself. Around Year 12 of Ramesses XI, the armies of Panehsy, viceroy of Nubia, occupied Thebes, and confiscated temple lands on which to settle veterans; the high priest of Amun, Amenhotep, was deposed and chased to Hardai. The viceroy assumed control of the area but was an unpopular governor: seven years later, the commander of all Egypt's armies, Herihor (who may have been a son of Amenhotep by marriage) was recognized as the new high priest. His son, Piankh, pursued Panehsy's armies back to Nubia. Herihor then assumed the titles of vizîr, viceroy of Nubia, and, most significantly, a royal titulary, in which his fitness to rule was ascribed to his priestly authority. Although the rule of Ramesses XI remained unquestioned outside Thebes, a new era was generally acknowledged by dating legal documents to the time of the "Repeating (or Multiplying) of Births"; the significance of the phrase is unknown, but it may refer to the duplication of the earthly king, or indicate a period of renaissance. In this era also appear the earliest references to the shadowy figure of Smendes, *de facto* king at Tanis.

Dating to the seven years of the "Repeating of Births" is a remarkable text known as "The Voyage of Wenamun". There is disagreement amongst scholars about whether the story is an account of a real or fictional journey since it is so rich in characterization, has a vividness unexpected in a dry-as-dust document, and continues a theme—an Egyptian stranded abroad by circumstances beyond his control—familiar from literature. Nevertheless, the story has coloured most accounts of Egypt's declining authority in the Near East.

Wenamun is sent by Herihor to Byblos, on a ship sailing out of Tanis, in order to bring cedar for the sacred boat of Amun. *En route* he endures a series of humiliations. At Dor, he is robbed and left stranded, with only a portable statue of Amun for support. Having himself resorted to robbery in order to reach Byblos, once there Wenamun discovers that an Egyptian without documents or gifts cannot demand cedar, and is detained until payment is arranged and transported from Tanis. The governor's court takes advantage of this unexpected opportunity to humiliate the forlorn-looking official—having been dictated to by such people for centuries! Eventually, the wood is supplied, but Tjeker sailors, from whom Wenamun had stolen, demand his arrest. He flees and is stranded at Alashiya, where the locals threaten his life; at this point the story is abruptly broken off. Throughout, Wenamun demonstrates the determination and ingenuity which his countrymen would have admired.

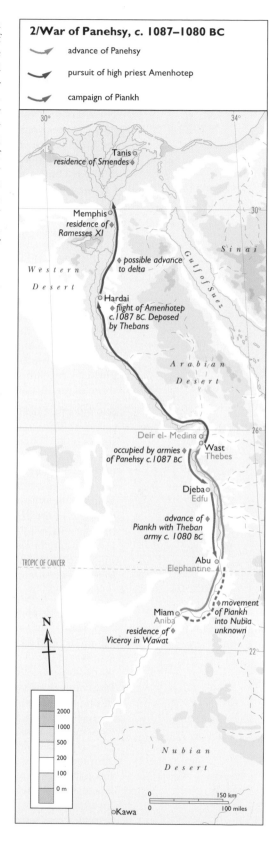

2/War of Panehsy, c. 1087–1080 BC

advance of Panehsy

pursuit of high priest Amenhotep

campaign of Piankh

Tanis
residence of Smendes

Memphis
residence of
Ramesses XI

possible advance
to delta

*Western
Desert*

Sinai

Gulf of Suez

Hardai
flight of Amenhotep
c. 1087 BC. Deposed
by Thebans

*Arabian
Desert*

Deir el- Medina
occupied by armies
of Panehsy c. 1087 BC

Wast
Thebes

Djeba
Edfu

advance of
Piankh with Theban
army c. 1080 BC

TROPIC OF CANCER

Abu
Elephantine

N

Miam
Aniba
residence of
Viceroy in Wawat

movement
of Piankh
into Nubia
unknown

2000
1000
500
200
100
0 m

*Nubian
Desert*

0   150 km
0   100 miles

Kawa

Tanis, Thebes and Libya

The death of Ramesses XI marks the beginning of the Third Intermediate Period, in which Egyptian dominance of Nubia and Palestine was ended.

"I ask Horus of Kuban, Horus of Aniba, and Atum, lord of this land ... to allow my sacred lord, Amun of Karnak, to bring me back alive from the hellhole in which I am stranded in this far-away land, so that I can hold you close ... Now my lord trusts me and does not neglect me: he has set aside for me a jug of wine every five days, five loaves per day, and a large container of beer - which has cured my sickness!"

Letter to Deir el–Medina from Thutmose, an official in Piankh's expedition to Nubia

The era of the "Repeating of Births" and subsequently the death of Ramesses XI are conventionally understood to mark a new phase of Egyptian history – the Third Intermediate Period. Although there was still a single line of kings for 250 years (not counting the priest-kings of Thebes), Panehsy effectively now ruled Nubia as an independent state that would never again fall under Egyptian control during the dynastic period. The result was a dramatic reduction in the supply of the gold and African goods on which the powerful New Kingdom economy had been founded: Egypt's commercial status in the ancient world suffered the inevitable adverse consequences.

Herihor had predeceased Ramesses XI and was succeeded by his son, Piankh, in all his offices except viceroy of Nubia and king. Piankh and his successors retained power for over a century, but ultimate authority at Thebes lay with the oracles of the gods Amun, Mut and Khons, which appointed temple officials and dictated the daily routine in the life of the high priest. Occasionally—as Pinudjem I and Menkheperra—the high priests again assumed royal titles, and a fortified residence was built at Teudjai, the northern limit of their effective authority. However, the kings normally recognized throughout the country, even in the sacred city, were those of the 21st Dynasty—successors to Smendes.

Smendes had become *de facto* king at Ramesses' death, with his centre of power at Tanis, a city built at the end of the New Kingdom from the very stones of Per-Ramesse. Little is known about his career, although as king he was active as far south as Gebelein; possibly he also came to power as a result of the increasingly regal authority of Amun, since Tanis was the major cult-site of the god in the north, and Smendes' royal descendants occasionally assumed the title of high priest of Amun. Links with Thebes were strong, and the kings of the 21st Dynasty often sent royal women as wives for the Theban high priests, who were therefore descended from the royal lines of both Herihor and Smendes (indeed, it had been suggested that Smendes himself was a son of Herihor); the logical conclusion came about when the Theban high priest Psusennes became king at Tanis as Har-Psusennes II.

The wars of Ramesses II had not stemmed the peaceful settlement of the Libyans in Egypt, who regularly appeared as far south as Thebes; the most important areas of settlement were the delta and the region between Memphis and Herakleopolis, where immigrants formed large communities, assimilated to the culture of the Nile valley but still respecting the hereditary authority of the Great Chiefs of the Libu and the Ma (i.e. Mashwash). Har-Psusennes II attended a formal dedication ceremony at Karnak conducted by one such chief, Shoshenk, son of Nimlot; although his relationship to the king is unknown, it may be assumed that he was the man who succeeded Psusennes as Shoshenk I, first king of the 22nd Dynasty. Shoshenk, though Libyan by name and descent, was traditionally Egyptian in his customs. He adopted Tanis as his own centre of authority, and was typically active throughout the country. The role of Teudjai was turned on its head, since it became the crucial centre for 22nd Dynasty government of the south, including Thebes. Despite political tensions, the Theban high priests were relegated to a supporting role.

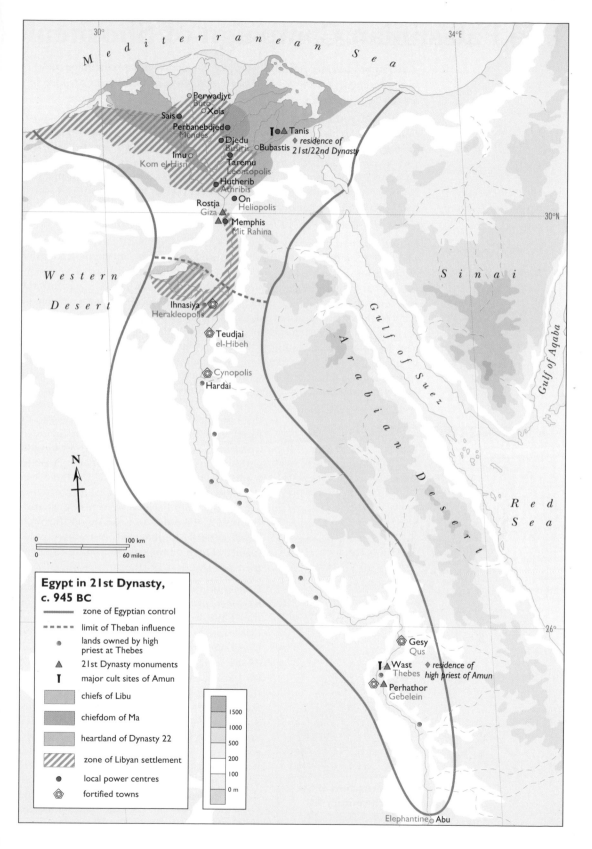

M e d i t e r r a n e a n S e a

30°

34°E

○ Perwadjyt
Buto
○ Xois
Sais ○
Perbanebdjed ●
Mendes
● Djedu
Busiris ○ Bubastis
Imu ○
Kom el-Hisn
Taremu
Leontopolis
● Hutherib
Athribis
Rostja ● ● On
Giza ▲ Heliopolis
▲ ● Memphis
Mit Rahina

Ι ● ▲ Tanis
◆ residence of
21st/22nd Dynasty

S i n a i

W e s t e r n

D e s e r t

◎ Ihnasiya
Herakleopolis

◎ Teudjai
el-Hibeh

◎ Cynopolis
● Hardai

Gulf of Suez

A r a b i a n D e s e r t

Gulf of Aqaba

30°N

N

↑

R e d

S e a

26°N

| 0 | | 100 km |
| 0 | | 60 miles |

◎ Gesy
Qus

Ι ▲ Wast
Thebes
◆ residence of
high priest of Amun

◎ ▲ Perhathor
Gebelein

Egypt in 21st Dynasty,
c. 945 BC

——— zone of Egyptian control

– – – limit of Theban influence

• lands owned by high
  priest at Thebes

▲ 21st Dynasty monuments

Ι major cult sites of Amun

▨ chiefs of Libu

▨ chiefdom of Ma

▨ heartland of Dynasty 22

▨ zone of Libyan settlement

● local power centres

◎ fortified towns

	1500
	1000
	500
	200
	100
	0 m

Elephantine ○ Abu

The Palestinian Campaign of Shoshenk I

The Palestinian campaign of Shoshenk I is widely considered to be the historical model for the Biblical story of the looting of Solomon's temple in the city of Jerusalem.

"In the fifth year of Rehoboam, Shishak the King of Egypt marched on Jerusalem. He took all the treasures from the Temple of Yahweh and from the royal palace. He took everything..."
I Kings, 14:25

Although Egypt's influence in the Levant seems to have dwindled significantly in the final decades of the New Kingdom, there is an apparent thread of continuity linking the military and commercial activities of the 18th and 19th dynasties with those of kings such as Siamun (21st Dynasty) and Osorkon I (22nd Dynasty). Presumably the kings of the Third Intermediate Period recognised that trading links with the kings of the Near East which had been fundamental to the stability of New Kingdom society could prove crucial in a potentially divisive era of competing dynasties.

During this period the one incursion into Palestine by an Egyptian army for which we have detailed testimony was presided over by Shoshenk I, founder of the 22nd Dynasty, who orchestrated a militaristic display of authority through key areas of Palestine in his 20th year as king. His own account was subsequently inscribed upon the south wall of the majestic new entrance to the Temple of Amun at Karnak which he initiated but never completed. In part, the list of towns and cities given there is strikingly reminiscent of the Year 22 campaign of Thutmose III and the Year 9 campaign of Amenhotep II in particular, and it has been suggested that it merely plagiarized earlier records; in fact, Shoshenk's inscription contains many place names not listed in any comparable New Kingdom monuments. The campaign, launched from Gaza, consisted of a strike into the Negeb, and a separate series of raids through the hill-country into the kingdom of Israel. The full list of "subject" towns (many of which may have formally recognized Egypt's authority without necessarily being cowed in battle) has not survived, but the total was considerably in excess of fifty. One place name which stands out because of its historical associations is Megiddo, and the march through Israel is easily understood as an attempt to reassert Egypt's long-standing authority over the trade routes of northern Palestine.

Conventionally, the campaign of Shoshenk I has been identified as the historical basis for the Biblical story of Rehoboam of Judah, in whose reign Shishak, king of Egypt, captured fifteen Judaean fortresses, and plundered all of the gold of Solomon's temple as his price for sparing the city of Jerusalem from destruction (I Kings, 14 and II Chronicles, 12). In fact, there is no compelling evidence to support this identification: Shoshenk's army attacked Israel, not Judah (of the fortified towns only Aijalon is definitely mentioned, whilst Jerusalem certainly does not appear) and ultimately there is no stronger correspondence between the two narratives than the coincidence between the name Shoshenk and the Biblical Shishak.

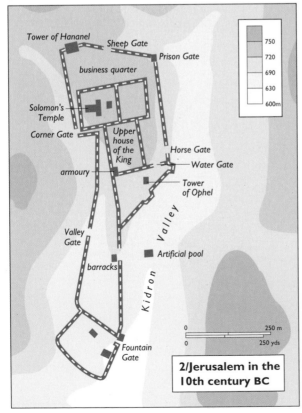

Tower of Hananel
Sheep Gate
Prison Gate
business quarter
Solomon's Temple
Corner Gate
Upper house of the King
Horse Gate
Water Gate
armoury
Tower of Ophel
Valley Gate
Kidron Valley
Artificial pool
barracks
Fountain Gate

750
720
690
630
600m

0   250 m
0   250 yds

2/Jerusalem in the 10th century BC

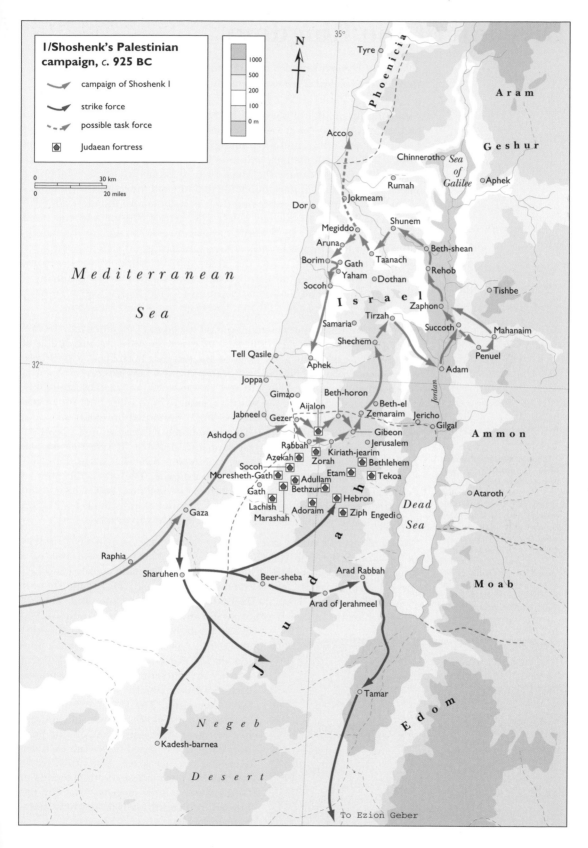

I/Shoshenk's Palestinian campaign, c. 925 BC

campaign of Shoshenk I
strike force
possible task force
Judaean fortress

30 km
20 miles

N

Tyre
Phoenicia
Aram
Geshur
Acco
Chinneroth
Sea of Galilee
Aphek
Rumah
Dor
Jokmeam
Megiddo
Shunem
Beth-shean
Aruna
Taanach
Borim
Gath
Yaham
Rehob
Socoh
Dothan
Tishbe
Israel
Zaphon
Samaria
Tirzah
Succoth
Mahanaim
Shechem
Penuel
Tell Qasile
Aphek
Adam
Joppa
Gimzo
Beth-horon
Jabneel
Aijalon
Beth-el
Gezer
Zemaraim
Jericho
Gilgal
Ammon
Ashdod
Gibeon
Rabbah
Jerusalem
Azekah
Kiriath-jearim
Socoh
Zorah
Bethlehem
Moresheth-Gath
Adullam
Etam
Tekoa
Gath
Bethzur
Lachish
Hebron
Ataroth
Marashah
Adoraim
Ziph
Engedi
Gaza
Dead Sea
Judah
Raphia
Moab
Sharuhen
Beer-sheba
Arad Rabbah
Arad of Jerahmeel
Negeb
Tamar
Edom
Kadesh-barnea
Desert
To Ezion Geber

Mediterranean Sea

1000
500
200
100
0 m

35°
32°

Jordan

Division of the Kingdom

The 22nd Dynasty presided over the division of Egypt amongst powerful local rulers, several of whom eventually assumed the status of king.

"Enemies were suppressed who were from within this land, which had sunk into confusion at this time."

The Chronicle of Prince Osorkon

Although the transfer of power to the 22nd Dynasty was apparently straightforward, processes were at work that would eventually result in the division of Egypt. For example, continued immigration into the delta had created a western chiefdom of the Libu only loosely bound to traditional Egyptian patterns of authority. Initially the kings held divisions in check by assigning major offices in the administration, the military and the temples to members of their own family, or by marrying their daughters into the most powerful provincial families. In this way power was restricted to people who owed their authority directly to pharaoh. Other concessions, such as the hereditary right to hold important offices, were granted to officials as rewards for loyalty. On the other hand, the geographical scope of most offices, including the vizîrate, was greatly restricted, so that the kingship stood alone as a powerful national institution. The result was a country structurally much less united than it had been in the New Kingdom.

Although the 22nd Dynasty sought to bind the country together with the fabric of the royal family, the result was the exact opposite. An inscription of Osorkon II (*c.* 874–850 BC) bemoaned the fact that even his own sons were now competitors: the Nile valley became divided between two competing centres of power, at Herakleopolis and Thebes, each governed by a royal son. The king sought to impose one prince as ruler of both cities, but without lasting effect; when Takeloth II (*c.* 850–825 BC) promoted his eldest son—also called Osorkon—as high priest at Thebes, family rivalries ignited a protracted dispute which periodically erupted into violence. The sacred city witnessed the undignified spectacle of priests and officials driving their own high priest—appointed by their king—into exile. The official account of events inscribed at Karnak temple, *The Chronicle of Prince Osorkon*, talks about the resultant "confusion" in terms of elemental disorder—a situation opposed to everything which Egypt valued as right and proper.

Shoshenk III eventually tried to reinvigorate the provincial authority of his family by dignifying his brother Pedubast with the status of a king at Leontopolis *c.* 818 BC (23rd Dynasty), but this merely provoked the claims of rival family member dynasties; the 22nd Dynasty eventually spawned kings at Herakleopolis, Hermopolis and Thebes. However, in the mid 8th century, the divisive Theban priesthood was finally neutralized by transferring supreme authority amongst the earthly population of the city to the God's Wife of Amun, an ancient office which henceforth would always be held by a king's daughter. The God's Wife held no hereditary right to office, but could appoint her successor. At that moment, Piy, the head of a royal house based at Napata in Kush, arranged for his sister, Amenirdis, to be accepted as the successor to the incumbent God's Wife. It now emerged that Piy saw himself as pharaoh, with far-reaching ambitions in Egypt.

A view of the sacred area of Tanis. The authority of Tanis stemmed from the presence of the temple of Amun-Ra, originally built with stone brought from the abandoned city of Per-Ramesse. The remnants of the blocks and obelisks of the temple itself lie scattered in the distance, beyond the rectangular tombs of the kings of the 21st-22nd Dynasties, in which the intact burials of several kings were discovered in 1939.

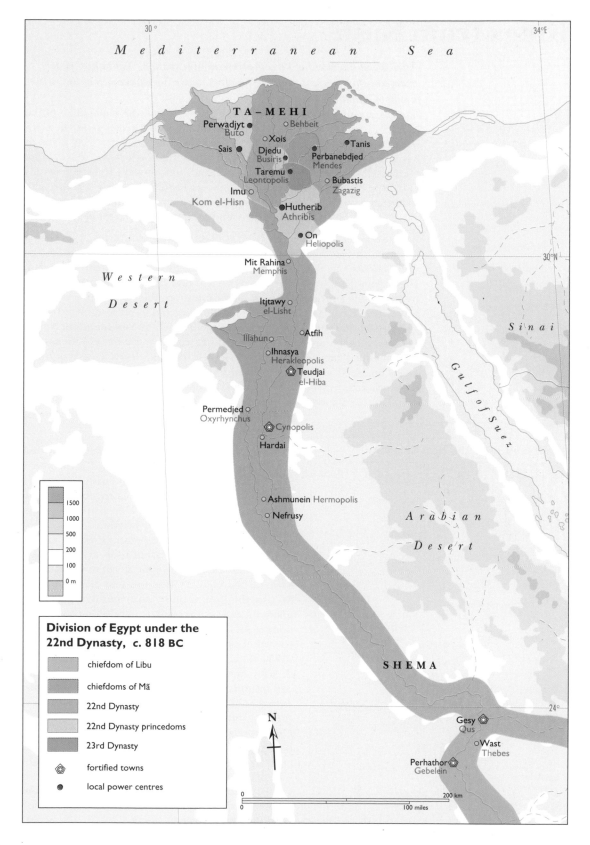

Mediterranean Sea

TA-MEHI

Perwadjyt ●
Buto
○ Behbeit

● Xois
Sais ●
Djedu ● ● Tanis
Busiris Perbanebdjed
● Mendes
Taremu ●
Leontopolis ○ Bubastis
Imu ○ Zagazig
Kom el-Hisn
● Hutherib
Athribis

● On
Heliopolis

Western
Desert

30°N

Mit Rahina ○
Memphis

Itjtawy ○
el-Lisht

Illahun ○ ○ Atfih

Ihnasya ○
Herakleopolis
◉ Teudjai
el-Hiba

Permedjed ○
Oxyrhynchus

◎ Cynopolis
Hardai ○

Sinai

Gulf of Suez

Ashmunein ○ Hermopolis
Nefrusy ○

Arabian

Desert

Division of Egypt under the 22nd Dynasty, c. 818 BC

chiefdom of Libu

chiefdoms of Mā

22nd Dynasty

22nd Dynasty princedoms

23rd Dynasty

◉ fortified towns

● local power centres

SHEMA

N

Gesy ◉
Qus

● Wast
Thebes

Perhathor ◉
Gebelein

24°

| 0 | | 200 km |
| 0 | 100 miles | |

30°   34°E

1500
1000
500
200
100
0 m

Kings from Kush

After the withdrawal of the Egyptian administration, Nubia had slowly emerged as a powerful, unified kingdom under the leadership of the royal family of Napata

"The ruler of Herakleopolis, Peftjauawybast, came bearing tribute to the pharaoh ... he threw himself on his belly before him, saying: 'Greetings, O Horus, O King, O bull who subdues the other bulls!'"
The Victory Stela of Piy

The three centuries between the war of Panehsy and the emergence of the Napatan royal house, which would eventually rule in Egypt as the 25th Dynasty, are a notorious dark age. Often we know of Nubia only through Egyptian sources, and after the viceroy had asserted his independence, those sources fell silent. Contemporary texts from Nubia are few, and are generally too obscure to be helpful. Worse still, the archaeology of Nubia in this period is scanty, and scholars have assumed that there was significant depopulation, especially in Wawat, after the withdrawal of Egyptian authority.

What evidence has survived from the 10th to 8th centuries BC probably relates to the emergence of native dynasties competing for pre-eminence after Panehsy's regime was unable or unwilling to maintain a unified realm. These dynasties were based in areas such as Kawa and Semna, that had been crucial to the previous Egyptian administration; they also expressed their authority in Egyptian hieroglyphic inscriptions, and so must surely be recognised as the descendants of the Egyptianized chiefs of New Kingdom Nubia. The best attested group are the rulers of Napata, buried at el-Kurru, and, though little is known of the earliest of their number, clearly it was this group which emerged as the overlords of a united Nubian kingdom. From the reign of Kashta (*c.* 760–747 BC) onwards, they chose to portray themselves as Egyptian-style pharaohs, and their royal culture was founded in the cult of Amun, relying on his oracle at Gebel Barkal to make their most momentous decisions.

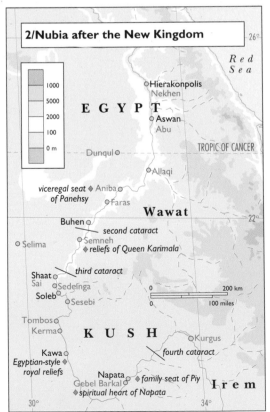

2/Nubia after the New Kingdom

Red Sea

EGYPT

Hierakonpolis
Nekhen

Aswan
Abu

TROPIC OF CANCER

Dunqul

Allaqi

vicereg al seat of Panehsy ♦ Aniba
Faras

Wawat

Buhen
second cataract
Selima
Semneh
♦ *reliefs of Queen Karimala*

Shaat
Sai
third cataract
Sedeinga
Soleb
Sesebi

Tombos
Kerma

KUSH
Kurgus

Kawa
Egyptian-style royal reliefs ♦
fourth cataract

Napata
Gebel Barkal ♦ *family seat of Piy*
♦ *spiritual heart of Napata*
Irem

0   200 km
0   100 miles

The depopulation of Wawat may have provided exactly the buffer between Egypt and Kush which allowed the Napatan regime to flourish and realize the potential of a unified Nubia to dominate the commerce and politics of the Nile, just as the kingdom of Kush had managed briefly in the Second Intermediate Period. The power of the kingdom and its armies allowed Kashta's son and successor, Piy, to dominate the Nile as far north as Hermopolis early in his reign. Piy was the first Napatan ruler to use the full titulary and iconography of a pharaoh, and he was resolute in fulfilling his obligations to Amun. He resolved to celebrate the ancient festival of Opet at Thebes and an army was sent *c.* 728 BC to enforce his authority throughout Egypt. In this Piy may have been further provoked by the expansionism of the powerful chief of Sais, Tefnakht. The Nubian army quickly overpowered the king of Hierakonpolis, Peftjauawybast, and at Hermopolis confronted Tefnakht himself, who was besieged for several weeks. Piy arrived to lead the army in person, the siege was ended, and Tefnakht was obliged to withdraw to the delta. Piy then travelled to Memphis and Heliopolis to worship the ancient gods of Egypt, before receiving homage from the other Egyptian rulers.

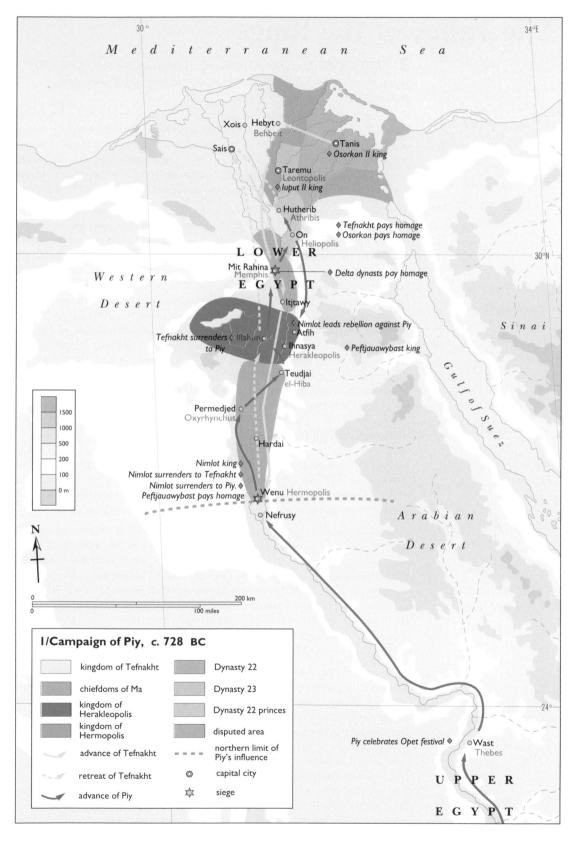

Mediterranean Sea

Xois ○ Hebyt ○
Behbeit

Sais ○
Tanis ○
◇ Osorkon II king

Taremu ○
Leontopolis
◇ Iuput II king

Hutherib ○
Athribis

◇ Tefnakht pays homage
◇ Osorkon pays homage

On ○
Heliopolis

L O W E R

Mit Rahina ☆
Memphis   ◇ Delta dynasts pay homage

E G Y P T

Western   Itjtawy ○
Desert
◇ Nimlot leads rebellion against Piy
Atfih ○

Tefnakht surrenders ◇ Illahun ○
to Piy
◇ Peftjauawybast king
Ihnasya ○
Herakleopolis

Teudjai ○
el-Hiba

Permedjed ○
Oxyrhynchus

Hardai ○

Nimlot king ◇
Nimlot surrenders to Tefnakht ◇
Nimlot surrenders to Piy. ◇
Peftjauawybast pays homage ◇   Wenu ☆ Hermopolis

Nefrusy ○

Sinai

Gulf of Suez

Arabian

Desert

30°N

24°

Piy celebrates Opet festival ◇   Wast ○
Thebes

U P P E R

E G Y P T

	1500
	1000
	500
	200
	100
	0 m

N

0 _____ 200 km
0 _____ 100 miles

I/Campaign of Piy, c. 728 BC

kingdom of Tefnakht	Dynasty 22
chiefdoms of Ma	Dynasty 23
kingdom of Herakleopolis	Dynasty 22 princes
kingdom of Hermopolis	disputed area
advance of Tefnakht	- - - northern limit of Piy's influence
retreat of Tefnakht	◎ capital city
advance of Piy	☆ siege

The Valley of the Kings

The Valley of the Kings served as the royal cemetery for more than 400 years, during which time royal tombs became ever larger and more elaborate.

"In the words of Geb, prince of the gods: O my son, my beloved, my heir upon my throne, Osiris, king Nebkheperura. How excellent is your mummy, how breathtaking is your image, how often uttered in the mouths of worshippers is your name, so that you are fixed in the mouths of the living! Osiris, king Tutankhamun, Ruler of Upper Egypt. On, your desire (remains within) your body for eternity, and will not leave you throughout all time."

The mummy wrappings of Tutankhamun

The death of the king was the spiritual and emotional heart of Ancient Egypt. The resurrected king—Osiris, in mythological terms—was the assurance of eternal afterlife, and so the building of his tomb became a major industry. The builders were free men, with high status, and it is inconceivable that the commitment, skill and emotion which shaped an Egyptian royal tomb could have been forged out of human slavery.

The Theban kings of the 17th Dynasty were buried in pyramids on the lower slopes of their native hills. The tombs of their New Kingdom successors are unknown, until Thutmose I was buried *c.*1481 BC in a plain, undecorated chamber cut deep into a desert wadi (a dry water-course). This seemingly inferior tomb was actually the largest yet seen at Thebes: the wadi sits beneath el-Gurn, the highest crag in the hills, which rises to form a mountainous pyramid upon the royal burial; in addition, a magnificent temple for the worship of the king's spirit was begun amongst the cliffs which border the wadi at Deir el-Bahri. Thutmose I also ordered the building of "the village" at Deir el-Medina in order to provide a permanent home for the masons and artists who would build future royal tombs. Thirty-five years later, the female king Hatshepsut finished her father's temple, and was laid to rest in his tomb, which had been extended to stretch over 200m. through the cliffs. After Hatshepsut, every king was laid to rest in the wadi, which became known simply as "the Great Valley". The burial of Thutmose III became a model for the 18th Dynasty: the plan of the tomb bent sharply, the chambers were painted with texts—detailing the king's journey through dark night to be reborn in a glorious dawn—and the corridors were divided by a well descending into *duat,* "the underworld" (in tombs lower down the valley, the well also protected against flooding). Each tomb was accompanied by a vast mortuary temple built on the edge of the Theban flood-plain.

A break in the development of the Valley occurred when Akhenaten created a royal cemetery near Akhetaten, although the move was short-lived: if the king was ever buried as he intended, his body was apparently later returned to the Great Valley, and laid to rest in the tomb of his mother, Tiy. A decade later his own son, Tutankhamun, was also interred in a small tomb originally intended for a favoured courtier rather than a king; ironically, this untypical tomb has become the most famous of all since it was discovered largely undisturbed in 1922, together with his breathtaking gold funerary equipment. The location of the king's original tomb is unknown.

Shortly after Tutankhamun's death, Deir el-Medina was doubled in size in order to accommodate sufficient men to build royal tombs on a much grander scale than previously, following reforms introduced by Akhenaten. The royal tomb was now built with a straight axis from the entrance to the burial chamber, along which ran twice as many corridors and chambers as before; the once-plain entrances were now spectacular, and every interior wall was decorated, even though simple painting was replaced by delicately sculptured relief that was especially time-consuming on the poor quality limestone of the Valley. Nevertheless, during the 19th–20th Dynasties, the workmen created suitably magnificent homes for the spirits of their immortal rulers; there was perhaps no finer

Entrance to the enigmatic tomb KV 55, cleared in ancient times to protect the corpse of Queen Tiy. However, the workmen left behind the body of a king which had been hastily reburied in a queen's coffin; probably the remains were those of Tiy's controversial son, Akhenaten. The tomb is a few metres from that of his own son, Tutankhamun, whose body was also overlooked in the clearances.

achievement in Ancient Egypt than the tomb of Seti I, cut over 100 metres deep into the rock, and decorated throughout with exquisitely executed scenes based on ancient texts of profound wisdom.

The final 50 years of the Valley were difficult times. A group of ancient texts details a major inquiry into tomb-robbery at Thebes in the reign of Ramesses IX (*c.* 1111 BC), although four days of arrests and interrogations resulted in a qualified vindication of the west bank community. The last king for whom a tomb was prepared in the Valley was Ramesses XI, during whose reign the occupation of Thebes by Panehsy had been a stressful event. As insecurity increased, the villagers abandoned Deir el-Medina for Medinet Habu. Smendes and the 21st Dynasty were buried in the north; Herihor, priest-king of Amun, and his descendants were presumably buried at Thebes, but their tombs have never been found. With the abandonment of the Valley, security arrangements were scaled down, and royal burials seriously put at risk. Consequently, the final chapter in the Valley's story took place *c.* 969 BC, when the priests of Amun removed the bodies of the great rulers of the New Kingdom; some were left in hiding-places around the hills, but most were moved to a secret tomb at Deir el-Bahri, where they lay until discovered by local antiquities smugglers in the early 1870s.

The royal workmen's village at Deir el-Medina viewed from the north on the ancient path leading to the Valley of the Kings. The village itself is enclosed by a wall, and arranged around a single main street. Immediately to the west, the magnificent tombs of the villagers themselves are set in terraces upon the slopes of the Theban hills.

V: The Late Period

A series of invasions from Assyria brought an end to the division of Egypt by allowing Psamtek I of Sais to establish himself as the sole king of a reunified country. So began a revival of the country's fortunes during the 26th Dynasty, which was brutally ended by Persian invaders in 525 BC. For the next two centuries, the rulers of Egypt struggled to maintain her independence.

"When Cambyses chanced to call (Nitetis) by her father's name, she replied: "My lord, do you not realize that Amasis has cheated you? He dressed me in attractive clothes and sent me to you as if I was his own daughter—but I most certainly am not! I am the daughter of Apries, the master he killed when he led the Egyptians in rebellion against him." According to the Persian account, these words—and the issue of the quarrel they exposed—brought upon Egypt the wrath of Cambyses, son of Cyrus."

Herodotos, *The Histories*

The history of Egypt in the years 664–323 BC is essentially the tale of a country attempting to reassert its traditional unity and commercial strength in order to oppose the ambitions of foreign conquerors. In this task the kings of the 26th Dynasty (664–525 BC) were manifestly successful, and the kings of the 30th Dynasty (c. 378–337 BC) somewhat less so; but at other times Egypt found herself submitting to foreign domination, a circumstance she had never previously known. It is also a history which has a distinctly different "flavour" to that of earlier eras because new types of source material are available. The great historian, Herodotos, noted that the influx of Greeks during and after the reign of Psamtek I (664–610 BC) was a watershed in the European understanding of pharaonic Egypt The Egyptians themselves saw the world in terms of their divine pharaoh, his endeavours on behalf of the gods, and in turn their support of him; Greek merchants and mercenaries settled in Egypt, however, traded stories with their kinfolk about kings and queens, treachery, murder and warfare. Therefore, we can elaborate Late Period history with the kind of personality-based gossip so appealing to European minds, but which is simply not available for earlier eras. Moreover, events in the Late Period can be closely compared with the annals of the kings of Assyria and Babylon, the biographical stories of classical Greek authors, and the narratives of the Old Testament, and so can be appreciated from a wider perspective than just that of the Egyptian royal record. As a further benefit, for much of this period dates can be determined to an accuracy of within a year or two on the basis of foreign synchronisms. Since the relevant new sources are from Greece and the Near East—and so are principally about Egypt's relations with Mediterranean and Near Eastern societies—it is not surprising to find that the emphasis in their stories often lies with the Nile delta and with Memphis, the regions nearest both to Palestine and to the Mediterranean, and the regions which were most vulnerable to the invasions of foreign armies.

The Assyrian Invasions

The Kushite king Piy was not a foreign conqueror: he was a traditional pharaoh from the disunited Black Land, who did not force his rivals out of power, nor even seek to deny them the status of king. After successfully prosecuting his war against the delta potentates, he returned to Napata, where he was eventually buried at el-Kurru in an Egyptian-style pyramid, surrounded by favourite horses. He was succeeded at Napata by Shabako (c. 716–702 BC), Shabatka (c. 702–690 BC) and then Taharka (c. 690–664 BC), each of whom similarly imposed themselves on Egypt as recognized overlords without trying to conquer or unite the various regimes which had branched out from the 22nd Dynasty during the early 8th century BC. Looking at this situation from outside, contemporary Assyrian records characterized Egypt as a collection of autonomous kingdoms, and cities whose chiefs were *de facto* kings. Perhaps, the most powerful of these provincial potentates (certainly

Statue from a group in the tomb of Montuemhat, mayor and de facto king at Thebes in the mid–7th Century BC, whose tomb was the largest built in ancient times for non-royal Egyptian.

in the south of the country) was the governor of Upper Egypt, mayor of Thebes, and Fourth Prophet of Amun-Ra, Montuemhat. His Egyptian titles are impressive but still mask the true extent of the authority of the man whom Assurbanipal of Assyria described explicitly as "Mantimanhe, king of Thebes". Montuemhat was typical in this period of a man who inherited high provincial office, both civil and religious, as an hereditary right. He was loyal to his kings, never assuming royal titles or iconography, and during the reign of Taharka, he married a member of the Napatan royal family; but he was also pragmatic, and if necessary prepared to switch his allegiance to whichever king would best serve the interests of the temples and towns of Upper Egypt. Moreover, the kings also recognized his undoubted pre-eminence in a domain stretching from Elephantine to Hermopolis—basically the equivalent of the 17th Dynasty Theban kingdom. Within his domain, Montuemhat commissioned monumental building work on a regal scale, which was often dedicated in his own name as well as those of his royal masters. After his death in *c.* 648 BC, the governor was buried at western Thebes in the largest tomb ever prepared for a non-royal Egyptian in ancient times, and one which was allowed to dominate the entrance to the great rock-bay of Deir el-Bahri, in which were to be seen some of the greatest architectural achievements of earlier Egyptian royalty. It was to be provincial officials like Montuemhat—long-serving, powerful, and pragmatic—who would shape the history of Egypt in the Late Period.

After Shoshenk I, the 22nd Dynasty kings had been unable to repeat the military displays which had traditionally been employed to enforce Egyptian dominance in Syria and Palestine, at a time when the loss of Nubian gold had severely weakened the commercial and military prestige of Egypt. The situation had inevitably been exacerbated by the division of the kingdom in the later dynasty, but the kings of the 25th Dynasty capitalized on their status as overlords—and presumably also on Kushite gold, although they did not exploit the resource as effectively as New Kingdom Egypt had done—in order to commit pharaonic armies once more to the region. This brought the Napatan regime for the first time directly into contact with the armies of Assyria, which during the 8th century BC had overrun Babylonia and areas of the Palestinian coast traditionally allied to Egypt. The situation was loaded

Lifesize portrait of Taharka (c. 690–664 BC) sculpted in black granite. A vigorous and determined king. Taharka ordered building work at several important sites from Napata to Thebes, and the later years of his reign were dominated by his policy of opposing Assyrian expansion in Syria and Palestine. Eventually, however a series of Assyrian invasions led to the collapse of Napatan influence in Egypt.

with potential hostility, but the Napatan kings—presumably fearing the might of the Assyrian military machine—initially maintained a strained diplomatic alliance. However, in *c.* 701 BC Hezekiah of Judah revolted against Assyrian rule and turned to Shabatka as his only possible support. The Napatan king judged the moment to be right to challenge growing Assyrian dominance in the region, and so a combined Egyptian-Nubian army, including the future king Taharka in the rearguard, faced their new rivals in the field at Elteka on the coastal plain of Judah. The king's misgivings were realized when the African army was decisively beaten, but considerable injury was inflicted on the enemy, and Egyptian influence in the region began to grow amongst those chiefs who at least hoped that Assyria could be held in check. Thereafter, various rulers in Egypt, following the lead of the 25th Dynasty, began to foster and support foreign chiefs defying Assyrian domination.

The policy of fostering rebellion was intended to avoid direct military conflict with Assyria, at least on foreign soil, but inevitably it provoked bitter resentment in the Assyrian palace at Nineveh, where Esarhaddon (680–669 BC) finally resolved to destroy opposition to his regime in Palestine at source. Therefore, *c.* 674 BC, in the reign of Taharka, an abortive Assyrian invasion of Egypt took place; undaunted by failure, in 671 BC Esarhaddon himself led an army through Canaan and the coastal plain of Palestine, subduing all of the regions in which pharaonic authority was once more in the ascendant. Egypt was effectively pinned against the ropes, when Esarhaddon's army swept through the eastern delta and occupied the great administrative city of Memphis, leaving Taharka no choice but to flee as far as Nubia. The Assyrian king lacked the desire and resources to conquer and administer a land as distant as Egypt, so he extracted oaths of loyalty from named delta-chiefs who were required to act as vassals, although a small number of Assyrian officials operated amongst them. In this way, Esarhaddon hoped to forestall any Napatan interference in Palestinian politics. Amongst the vassal rulers was Neko, governor of Sais; his son and heir, Psamtek, was taken to Nineveh in order to learn the ways of the Assyrian court, before returning to become prince of Athribis, and presumably the same fate befell the sons of other chiefs. Esarhaddon died in 669 BC, and the Assyrian throne passed to his son, Assurbanipal (669–635 BC); in the meantime, Taharka returned to Egypt, where his authority was unchallenged in the Nile valley, and he

managed to regain control of Memphis. The new Assyrian king was not prepared to allow the 25th Dynasty to rebuild its influence abroad, so in 667 BC
a second Assyrian army entered Memphis, whereupon several delta vassals
who had supported Taharka were executed. Neko of Sais, however, was
appointed to govern Memphis as well as his home town.

Taharka was forced back to Napata, where he died in 664 BC, but his son
Tantamani immediately gathered his forces to march on Memphis, and
defeated an alliance of the delta chiefs who supported Assyrian rule—including Neko of Sais who was killed in the ensuing clashes. However, Tantamani's
triumph was short-lived since he brought upon Egypt the full wrath of the
Assyrian military machine: the north of the country was quickly brought to
heel by the armies of Assurbanipal, which then attacked and plundered the
temples of Thebes. The humiliation of the ancient city sent shock-waves
throughout the ancient world, and was graphically recorded in the Old
Testament. Only the astute diplomacy of Montuemhat and the Theban
authorities prevented the wholesale destruction of the city and its inhabitants. Tantamani retreated to Napata and never returned, although his legit-
imacy as king was still recognized in Thebes until 656 BC. After 664 BC, the
Napatan regime never regained the authority in Egypt which it had held
under Piy and Taharka, and so was never again in any position to influence
the politics of the Near East in a decisive fashion. Kushite soldiers only
returned to Palestinian battlefields as hired troops in Egyptian armies.

The Saite Revival

Out of division, an era of new-found Egyptian unity arose as a positive ideological and political response to the trauma of the Assyrian invasions. The
key figure was Psamtek of Athribis, who took over from his father initially as
prince of Sais and governor of Memphis, but immediately succeeded in having himself recognized as the royal overlord in large tracts of the delta and
the northern Nile valley. It is likely that Psamtek's success was partly sponsored by the Assyrian palace, but he showed his own skills as an accomplished

*View of the palace of Apries
in the northern part of the
sacred area at Memphis. The
Egyptian palace was as a
temple for the living king,
although this particular
example was raised upon a
massive mud-brick platform,
and also served as a powerful
fortress.*

negotiator and soldier, determined to enlarge his domain as a means to the reunification of Egypt. Psamtek also showed great patience, and it was not until 657 BC that he was finally able to coax the loyalty of the chiefs of the Ma and the Libu in the delta; for pre-eminence in the south of the country he waited until the death of Tantamani in the following year, at which point he was recognized as overlord at Thebes. Thereafter, however, as Theban officials died or left office, they were replaced by a member of Psamtek's own court, so that his formal acceptance as overlord in the south of the country was gradually translated into genuine power. He was astute enough, though, to maintain key figures in office, such as Montuemhat of Thebes. Moreover, there is no reason to suppose that Psamtek I coveted Nubia as part of his own kingdom, nor that he made any attempt to depose the 25th Dynasty at Napata. At his death, Psamtek was able to bequeath the unified kingdom of Egypt to his son, Neko II (610–595 BC), without any apparent resistance, and so establish the Saite regime, which was remembered in a subsequent tradition as a renaissance.

It is not known how the kings of Assyria felt about the developing career of their erstwhile subject, Psamtek I; their system of government via vassals never permitted any strict control of Egyptian politics short of military intervention, and it is apparent that the Assyrian armies had left Upper Egypt in the care of governor Montuemhat as early as 662 BC. By 630 BC, Psamtek's armies occupied Ashdod in order to reassert Egypt's traditional involvement in Philistia—an assertion of Egyptian confidence hardly likely to have been welcomed by Nineveh. Nevertheless, by this time Assyria was distracted on its eastern border by the aggression of the Chaldaean regime in Babylon, and so Psamtek I was able to maintain a formal alliance with Assyria in spite of his own ambitions. In 616 BC an Egyptian army actually campaigned in Syria against growing Babylonian influence, in territory untrodden by an Egyptian army since the 19th Dynasty. Neko II, also recognized that there were commercial interests in Palestine best served by Egypto-Assyrian co-operation to maintain the political *status quo*, exemplified when armies from the two countries came together to defeat the kingdom of Judah—formerly Egypt's ally—in battle at the historic trading town of Megiddo. His armies continued to campaign in Syria, until in 605 BC a large force was decisively routed at Carchemish by Babylonian troops under the command of the crown prince Nebuchadrezzar; the retreating army was caught and once more put to the sword at Hamath.

The relationship between Egypt and Babylon was decisively recast after the encounters at Carchemish and Hamath. Egypt was left in no doubt that opposition to Babylon was not an option intended to prop up the embattled Assyrian regime: it was a necessary course of action in defence of her political and commercial interests. However, Nebuchadrezzar was a determinedly aggressive general, who became king in that same year, and already knew the satisfaction of inflicting two humiliating defeats on the African kingdom. The destruction of pharaonic influence in Syria and Palestine promised Babylonian domination of the Near East, and so invasions of Egypt were launched in 601 BC, during the reign of Neko, and again in 581 BC, during the reign of Apries (589–570 BC). Saite Egypt, however, was to prove a more than capable match for Chaldaean Babylon: both invasions were quickly and decisively repelled, and Apries began sponsoring foreign dissent against Babylon in a manner which recalled Taharka's policy towards Assyria. He committed his support to the Judaean revolt in 589 BC, and then between 574–570 BC used his armies to occupy the ports of Tyre, Sidon, and (briefly) Cyprus in order to build a co-ordinated economic and military base in Egypt

Detail from a pillar in the temple of Sobk and Horus at Kom Ombo. From the beginning of history, the king of Egypt led the nation in worshipping the gods, and acted as high priest in every temple. This ritual scene, from the Ptolemaic era, conforms to a pharaonic design created over two thousand years earlier.

and the Levant from which to oppose Chaldaean ambitions. In 570 BC, however, the king was deposed in favour of the general, Amasis.

Nebuchadrezzar hoped to destabilize Egypt by supporting the deposed king; three years later, Apries returned to Egypt at the head of a Babylonian army, which was defeated *en route* by troops under the leadership of Amasis himself. Amasis (Ahmose II) as king was as shrewd as he had been skilful as a general, and he was implacably opposed to the ambitions of Nebuchadrezzar. He devoted much of his energy to fostering goodwill towards Egypt in the international community by making generous donations to foreign shrines, especially in Greece, and he forged strategic alliances—occasionally cemented by royal marriages—with anti-Babylonian states. Of course he also appreciated the value of decisive military action, and made his most decisive gain by occupying the seaports of Cyprus in 560 BC.

Persian Imperialism

By 560 BC Amasis had been entirely successful in asserting Egypt's political and commercial domination of Syria and Palestine in the face of Babylonian aggression. However, his later years were preoccupied with the emergence of another expansionist regime which sought to displace Egyptian authority in the region, Persia. The kingdom of Persia, probably located south of Lake Urmia in modern Iran, was first mentioned in Assyrian texts of the 9th century BC, but had grown quickly during the reign of Cyrus II in the mid-6th century BC, so that it stretched from the Indus region in the east to Turkey in the west. In 546 BC, Persian armies defeated Lydia, an ally of both Amasis and Babylon; in 545 BC, Egyptian-held Cyprus was conquered; and in 538 BC Babylon itself fell to the new military superpower. Amasis was obviously obliged to focus his international diplomacy towards alleviating this new threat, principally by fostering alliances with the Greek city-states which were aggressively opposed to Persia. His personal standing in the Near East, allied to internal difficulties within the Achaemenid dynasty of Persia after the death of Cyrus, allowed Egypt to buy time in the face of the seemingly inevitable onslaught. However, the death of Amasis in 526 BC was inopportune since within months a Persian army attacked and defeated his kingdom. Amasis'

Detail from the temple at Amun-Ra at Luxor depicting Alexander the Great in the presence of Horus. In Egypt, Alexander generally adopted the dress, religion and conduct expected of pharaoh in order to bolster his claim to rule this ancient kingdom. The same policy had been successful for his Persian predecessors, Cambyses and Darius, and would in turn be adopted by the Ptolemies and the Roman emperors.

son and successor, Psamtek III, was deposed, and Persian *satraps* (governors) were appointed to administer Egypt as a Persian province.

Unlike her Assyrian conquerors, the kings of Persia administered Egypt directly, and maintained a personal presence within the country. Cambyses (525–521 BC) and his successor Darius (521–485 BC), were frequently represented within Egypt in traditional pharaonic iconography, and they maintained their ancient governmental practice of personally dispensing gifts to loyal officials. In this way, they were able to gain widespread acceptance amongst the ruling élite of Egypt, many of whom were reconciled to accepting respectful foreigners as legitimate kings. Nevertheless, the reigns of Cambyses and Darius were a honeymoon which had to end: when the kings themselves were not present in the country, many officials and provincial chiefs were unwilling to accept the domination of the *satrap* and his staff, who found themselves stranded too far from their own court to govern such an enormous kingdom effectively. Moreover, the cultural and diplomatic ties formed between Egypt and Greece during the Saite monarchy—including the presence of Greek soldiers settled in land donated by pharaoh—were still strong, and so the Egyptian élite was unable to remain disinterested in the fierce Greek resistance to Persia, which culminated in the ignominious defeat of Darius' armies at the battle of Marathon in 490 BC. In Egypt, the defeat provoked frequent rebellions led by Egyptian chiefs throughout the 5th century BC. The Persian regime responded with a degree of cruelty and brutality towards the country, especially during the reign of Xerxes (485–464 BC), which inevitably destroyed any goodwill which might have been between the two sides. The city of Athens—the leading proponent of anti-Persian sentiment in Greece—recognized that the might of Persia was extremely vulnerable in Egypt, and began to provide economic and military aid to the rebels: in *c.* 459 BC, an Athenian fleet, diverted from Cyprus in support of the rebellion of a shadowy figure called Inaros, sailed along the Nile to lay siege to Memphis itself. The rebellion of Inaros was brutally suppressed, but the resolution of the Egyptian rulers was not, and in 414 BC the ruling house of Sais emerged as the champions of Egyptian independence. The now-despised Persian administration was finally driven out of the country in 404 BC.

The six decades of Egyptian independence during the 4th century BC, principally under the kings of the 30th Dynasty, were constantly overshadowed by the spectre of further Persian invasions, which became reality in the years 374 BC, during the reign of Nektanebo I (*c.* 378–360 BC), and 351 BC, during the reign of Nektanebo II (*c.* 358–342 BC). The first of these campaigns probably only failed because dissent broke out between the Persian *satrap*, leading the campaign, Pharnabazes, and his officers, who were mainly Greeks. By the time the second invasion was repelled by an Egyptian army, the prohibitive cost of constantly financing war preparations had undermined the effectiveness and prestige of the Egyptian administration at home and abroad. The country could therefore offer little genuine resistance to an invasion by the armies of Artaxerxes III in 343 BC, characterized by the desecration of sacred sites and the slaughter of many of the sacred animals whose cults had been specifically patronized by the kings of the Late Period. Nektanebo II probably retained some authority in the south of Egypt, and was briefly succeeded by an enigmatic king called Khababash, but the independence of Egypt was no longer in the hands of her own people. Deliverance from the hated Persians came in the form of another conqueror, Alexander the Great, whose Macedonian armies swept into Egypt a decade later. The rivalries and misrule of Alexander's agents condemned Egypt to twenty more years of abusive government, but eventually the accession of general Ptolemy as king in 305 BC restored royal authority. The Ptolemaic dynasty rebuilt Egyptian hegemony out of Alexander's fractured empire, and fostered pharaonic rule for nearly 300 years, until finally it was overrun by the juggernaut of Roman imperialism.

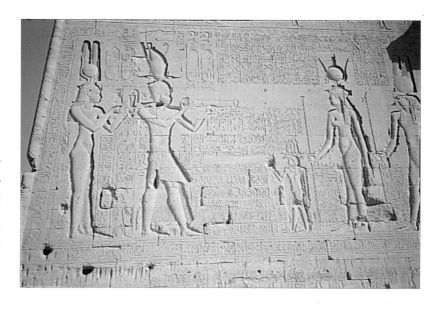

Detail from the walls of the temple of Hathor at Dendera, depicting Ptolemy XV and Cleopatra VII offering to the gods. Ptolemy is known to European history as Caesarion, the queen's son by Julius Caesar; although only a child, he was briefly king, and in this scene is conventionally represented as an adult.

The Sack of Thebes

The 25th Dynasty reasserted pharaonic involvement in Palestine, but fell foul of the kings of Assyria, who inflicted a series of humiliations on Egyptian soil.

"Are you better than Thebes? ... Kush and Egypt were her strength, Punt and Libya were among her allies. Yet she was taken captive and went into exile; her infants were dashed to pieces at head of every street; lots were cast for her nobles, and all her great men were put in chains."

Nahum 3,8—10

A relief from the palace of Assurbanipal at Nineveh depicts the siege and surrender of a fortified Egyptian town. The captured defenders include Nubian mercenaries as well as local conscripts.

Whilst the potentates of Egypt squabbled amongst themselves, the kings of Assyria had broken the power of Babylon and gained widespread influence in the Near East. As the 8th century ended, King Sennacherib, in his majestic new palace at Nineveh, could claim control over much of the Palestinian coast and many traditional allies of Egypt, including Byblos. By contrast, 22nd Dynasty policy towards Palestine had been less assertive since the reign of Shoshenk I, and its response to the presence of Assyria was limited to diplomacy; it was by now apparent that the loss of Nubian gold had severely undermined the commercial and military prestige of Egypt. Moreover Piy did not depose his rivals in Egypt, nor seek to deny them the status of king: his successors similarly imposed themselves as overlords without trying to unite the now disparate regimes. Contemporary Assyrian records characterize Egypt as a collection of autonomous states, whose chiefs and mayors were *de facto* kings. However, the kings of the 25th Dynasty did use their armies once again to intervene directly in the politics of Palestine, and in this area at least were able to establish a unity of purpose in Egypt and Nubia.

Initially the Napatan kings maintained a strained alliance with Assyria, but around 701 BC, after Hezekiah of Judah had defied Sennacherib and turned to Egypt for support, an Assyrian army engaged a coalition including Egyptian and Nubian troops at the battleof Elteka. Although the African army was decisively beaten, sufficient injury was inflicted on Assyria for Egypt to begin to hatch dissent against Nineveh amongst the cities of Palestine. Taharka (*c.* 690–664 BC) was so aggressive in this policy that he earned the eternal emnity of king Esarhaddon (680–669 BC). In 674 BC an Assyrian army invaded Egypt and was roundly defeated, but in 671 BC Esarhaddon himself led an army against Tyre, Egypt's strongest ally, and then subdued Egypt as far as Memphis. This event marked the first successful invasion of the Nile valley by a foreign army, and Taharka fled to Nubia. Assyrian officials were appointed to head the Egyptian administration, ushering in a decade during which control of Egypt fluctuated between the armies of Napata and Nineveh. Taharka returned to Memphis but was again driven out in 667 BC, and the new Assyrian king, Assurbanipal (669–635 BC), deposed the local rulers who had supported the Nubians. Neko of Sais, however, represented a body of opinion which now preferred a distant Assyrian overlord to Taharka's presence in Egypt. Subsequently, by excluding Nubian armies from Palestine, many rulers in the delta were able to win the support and trust of Assurbanipal, although only Neko consented formally to be his servant.

In 664 BC, Taharka died at Napata, and his son, Tantamani, immediately defeated near Memphis an alliance of Egyptian forces which supported Assyrian rule. The true result, however, was a heavy price, decisive intervention by Assurbanipal's armies, and the traumatic plundering of the sacred city of Thebes. Ancient religious monuments were removed to Nineveh, and widespread destruction was only avoided by a humiliating political accommodation between the authorities at Thebes and her conquerors.

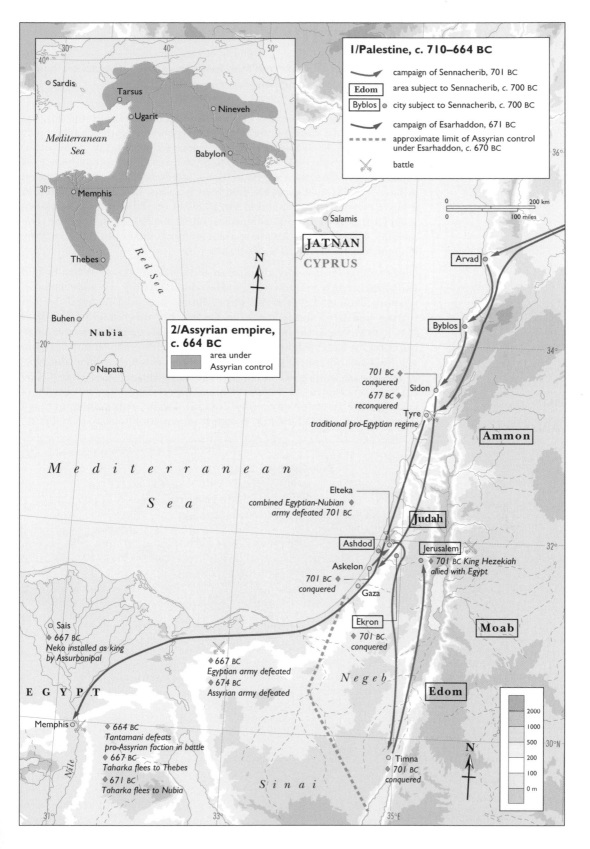

1/Palestine, c. 710–664 BC

campaign of Sennacherib, 701 BC

Edom   area subject to Sennacherib, c. 700 BC

Byblos ⊙   city subject to Sennacherib, c. 700 BC

campaign of Esarhaddon, 671 BC

approximate limit of Assyrian control
under Esarhaddon, c. 670 BC

✕   battle

Sardis

Tarsus

Ugarit

Nineveh

*Mediterranean
Sea*

Babylon

Memphis

Thebes

Red Sea

N

Buhen

N u b i a

**2/Assyrian empire,
c. 664 BC**

   area under
Assyrian control

Napata

Salamis

JATNAN
CYPRUS

Arvad

0   200 km
0   100 miles

Byblos

701 BC ◆
conquered

677 BC ◆
reconquered

Sidon

Tyre ✕

traditional pro-Egyptian regime

Ammon

M e d i t e r r a n e a n

S e a

Elteka

combined Egyptian-Nubian ◆
army defeated 701 BC

Judah

Ashdod

Jerusalem ✕

◆ 701 BC King Hezekiah
allied with Egypt

Askelon

701 BC ◆
conquered

Gaza

Ekron

◆ 701 BC
conquered

Moab

N e g e b

Sais
◆ 667 BC
*Neko installed as king
by Assurbanipal*

✕ ◆ 667 BC
Egyptian army defeated
◆ 674 BC
Assyrian army defeated

Edom

E G Y P T

Memphis ✕

◆ 664 BC
*Tantamani defeats
pro-Assyrian faction in battle*
◆ 667 BC
Taharka flees to Thebes
◆ 671 BC
Taharka flees to Nubia

Nile

Timna

◆ 701 BC
conquered

S i n a i

N

2000
1000
500
200
100
0 m

The Saite Monarchy

Psamtek I reunified Egypt and freed her from Assyrian domination, with military and economic support from Greece.

"It is said that the reign of Amasis was a time of exceptional material prosperity for Egypt: the river gave its wealth to the land, and the land to the people."
Herodotos, *The Histories*

In spite of the servility of Neko of Sais, his son, Psamtek I (664–610 BC), was to be the king of a powerful, unified and independent Egypt. Spending part of his youth in a divided country (ruling from *c.* 671 BC as prince at Athribis), and part at Nineveh, he learned how to be by turns astute and diplomatic or ruthlessly aggressive in enlarging his dominion: by 656 BC he was recognized as king throughout Egypt; his daughter, Nitokris, had been accepted as future God's Wife of Amun; and the chiefs of the Libu and Ma had been assimilated into the formal administration of the reunified kingdom. The attitude of the kings of Assyria to these events is unknown, but by 639 BC Psamtek had apparently shaken off their yoke.

Greek tradition maintained that Ionian and Carian mercenaries had helped Psamtek to victory, and, according to Herodotos, his reign was a watershed in relations between Egypt and Europe. Hitherto contact between the two regions had been indirect via the Levant, but now Greeks, as well as Phoenicians, were instrumental in generating military and commercial superiority for the Saites within Egypt. Sais became the commercial hub of Egypt, and Naukratis became its port. There is evidence of Greek commercial activity at Naukratis as early as *c.* 615 BC and during the reign of Amasis (570–526 BC) it was officially instated as the centre of Graeco-Egyptian trade (partly, of course, to keep it within direct royal control). Other Greek communities settled at Memphis and elsewhere, alongside immigrant Phoenicians and Jews.

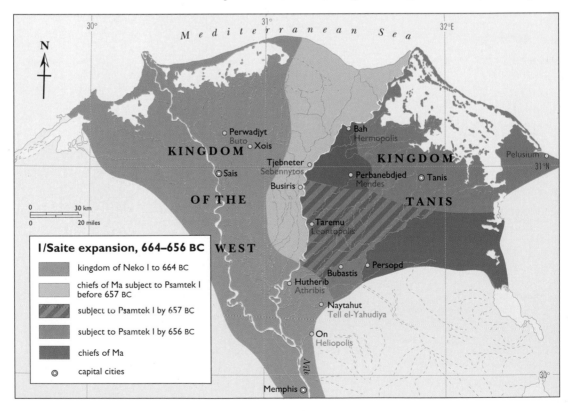

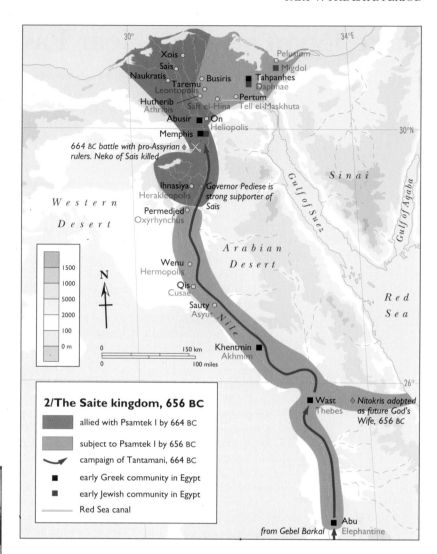

Map labels:
Xois, Sais, Naukratis, Taremu, Leontopolis, Busiris, Pelusium, Migdol, Tahpanhes, Daphnae, Hutherib, Athribis, Saft el-Hina, Pertum, Tell el-Maskhuta, Abusir, On, Heliopolis, Memphis

664 BC battle with pro-Assyrian rulers. Neko of Sais killed

Ihnasiya, Herakleopolis, Governor Pediese is strong supporter of Sais

Permedjed, Oxyrhynchus

Western Desert

Gulf of Suez, Sinai, Gulf of Aqaba

Wenu, Hermopolis

Arabian Desert

Qis, Cusae

Sauty, Asyut

Nile

Red Sea

Khentmin, Akhmim

Wast, Thebes

◇ Nitokris adopted as future God's Wife, 656 BC

N

Scale:
1500
1000
5000
2000
100
0 m

0 — 150 km
0 — 100 miles

2/The Saite kingdom, 656 BC
- allied with Psamtek I by 664 BC
- subject to Psamtek I by 656 BC
- campaign of Tantamani, 664 BC
- early Greek community in Egypt
- early Jewish community in Egypt
- Red Sea canal

Abu, Elephantine
from Gebel Barkal

In order to recreate great pharaonic traditions, the kings of the 26th Dynasty looked for inspiration to the art and architecture of the Old Kingdom. This entrance is the beginning of a shaft cut into the south face of the Step Pyramid of Djoser during the 26th Dynasty in order to examine the interior of a majestic monument which was already 2,000 years old at that time.

The Saite kings were as determined to re-establish the traditions of pharaonic authority as they were to exploit a new order. The prestige of kingship had been unaffected by Assyrian domination, as since the Egyptians would not blame their king for such a trauma; instead they looked to him to restore the elemental order. In response the Saites, especially Psamtek and Amasis, became prodigious builders, and their craftsmen drew upon Old Kingdom archetypes for inspiration in architecture and iconography. Provincial authority was often retained by families with hereditary claims to their offices, but they were careful to recognize the king as the guarantor of those rights. Moreover, most cultivated land was in the hands of the temples and 'warriors' (including foreign mercenaries) as the gift of pharaoh. Traditional patterns of commerce were also endorsed, as evidenced by new expeditions to Byblos and Punt; an ambitious scheme was even initiated in the reign of Neko II (610–595 BC) to link the Nile to the Red Sea by canal. Silver coins, circulating amongst foreign traders, were separated from the non-monetary economy of Egypt, and so acknowledged outside Naukratis only as bullion. The success of Saite rule in balancing the best of the old and the new was recognized in later tradition, which remembered a period of peace and prosperity.

Saite Egypt and the Near East

The Saite kings defended Egypt's commercial interests from the threat of the empires of Assyria and Chaldaean Babylon with a vigorous blend of traditional policies and tactical innovations.

"While Josiah was king, pharaoh Neko, king of Egypt, went up to help the king of Assyria by way of the Euphrates river. King Josiah marched out to meet him in battle, but Neko faced him and killed him at Megiddo ... Jehoahaz was twenty-three years old when he became king ... Pharaoh Neko put him in chains ... and he imposed on Judah a levy of a hundred talents of silver and a talent of gold. Pharaoh Neko made Eliakim, son of Josiah king in place of his father Josiah, and changed Eliakim's name to Jehoiakim ... Jehoiakim paid pharaoh Neko the gold and silver he demanded."

II Kings 23

Having opposed his original sponsor to reunify Egypt, Psamtek I eventually came to support Assyria against the expansionism of the Chaldaean kings of Babylon from 616 BC until his death in 610 BC. In alliance with Nineveh, his son Neko II, met and defeated the army of Josiah of Judah in battle at Megiddo; the location itself suggests that Egypt was once again prepared to defend her commercial connections. As early as 630, Psamtek had occupied Ashdod and so begun to reassert Egypt's influence in Philistia, and to recreate a strategic distance between Palestine and Egypt. If such strategies were familiar from history, there were also calculated innovations in policy during these two reigns: alliances were formed with Greek city-states (after the battle at Megiddo, Neko had sent his battle clothing to a shrine in Greece, a precedent followed by several dynasty kings); cavalry became a new and crucial element in the army; and powerful fighting fleets of Greek-built triremes were assembled in the Red Sea and Mediterranean. In effect, a commitment was made as never before to integrate the commercial and military potential of the country, so that each was harnessed to meet the needs of the other.

Beyond Palestine, Egypt at this time claimed considerable influence in Syria as far as the River Euphrates, where an army of Psamtek I had campaigned against Babylon in 616 BC, and Neko II had conducted three campaigns in the period 610–605 BC. But then, in 605 BC, a large Egyptian army was roundly defeated at Carchemish and again at Hamath by Babylonian armies under Nebuchadrezzar. The reinvigorated policies of the Saites were wrong-footed but not floored: a Babylonian invasion of Egypt itself was swiftly repulsed in 601 BC (and again twenty years later), and in 592 BC Psamtek II (595–589 BC) reinstated the traditional pharaonic tour through Philistia. Apries (589–570 BC) committed Egypt to support of the Judaean revolt against Babylon, and in 589 BC relieved the siege of Jerusalem, albeit briefly. Between 574–570 BC the king's armies occupied Tyre and Sidon and attacked Cyprus, in order to create a co-ordinated economic and military base in Egypt and the Levant from which to oppose Chaldaean ambitions.

In 570 BC Apries also sent an army to help king Adrikan of Kyrene, who was trying to limit the expansion of Greek settlement in that region. This army was badly defeated and the king's misjudgment subsequently cost his throne—he was deposed in favour of the general, Amasis. The turn of events allowed Babylon to meddle with the internal politics of Egypt: Apries was received at Nebuchadrezzar's court, and returned to Egypt with the support of a Babylonian army—although Amasis himself led the summary defeat of the invaders, and Apries was killed. Egypt was now set on a path intended to be as staunchly anti-Babylonian as it was in her own self-interest, and ties with Greek city-states (ironically, especially Kyrene) were increased and strengthened. Following the death of Nebuchadrezzar in 562 BC, and the occupation of Cyprus in 560 BC, Amasis could finally claim to be the dominant power in Palestine and the Levant.

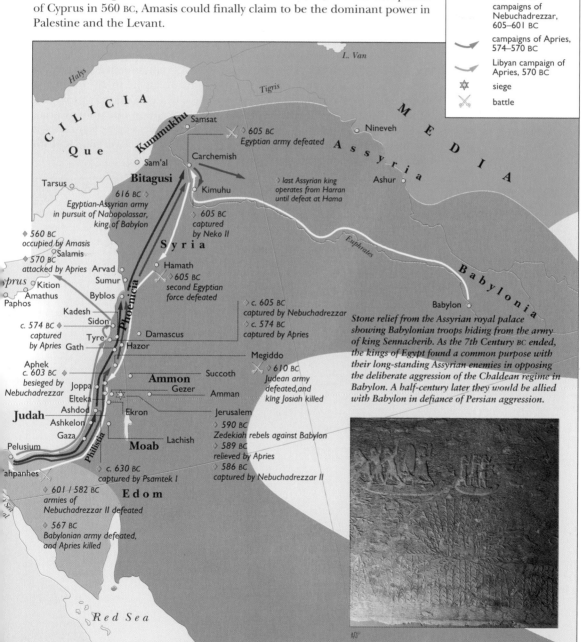

Egypt and the Near East, 630–560 BC

Neo-Babylonian empire

Median empire

area of Egyptian control

area of Egyptian dominance

campaigns of Psamtek I, 616 BC

campaigns of Neko II, 610–605 BC

campaigns of Nebuchadrezzar, 605–601 BC

campaigns of Apries, 574–570 BC

Libyan campaign of Apries, 570 BC

siege

battle

L. Van

Halys

Tigris

C I L I C I A

Que

Kummukhu

Samsat

Ninveh

M E D I A

Carchemish

› 605 BC
Egyptian army defeated

A s s y r i a

Ashur

Tarsus

Sam'al

Bitagusi

Kimuhu

› last Assyrian king
operates from Harran
until defeat at Hama

616 BC ›
Egyptian-Assyrian army
in pursuit of Nabopolassar,
king of Babylon

› 605 BC
captured
by Neko II

S y r i a

B a b y l o n i a

Euphrates

◆ 560 BC
occupied by Amasis
Salamis

◆ 570 BC
attacked by Apries   Arvad

yprus   Kition   Sumur

Amathus   Byblos

Paphos

Hamath
✗ › 605 BC
second Egyptian
force defeated

› c. 605 BC
captured by Nebuchadrezzar
› c. 574 BC
captured by Apries

Babylon

Kadesh

Sidon

P
h
o
e
n
i
c
i
a

c. 574 BC ◆
captured
by Apries   Gath

Tyre

Hazor

Damascus

Megiddo
✗ › 610 BC
Judean army
defeated, and
king Josiah killed

Stone relief from the Assyrian royal palace showing Babylonian troops hiding from the army of king Sennacherib. As the 7th Century BC ended, the kings of Egypt found a common purpose with their long-standing Assyrian enemies in opposing the deliberate aggression of the Chaldean regime in Babylon. A half-century later they would be allied with Babylon in defiance of Persian aggression.

Aphek
c. 603 BC ◆
besieged by
Nebuchadrezzar   Joppa

Ammon   Succoth

Gezer

Elteka   Amman

Judah   Ashdod   Ekron

Ashkelon   Jerusalem

Gaza   › 590 BC
Zedekiah rebels against Babylon
› 589 BC
relieved by Apries
› 586 BC
captured by Nebuchadrezzar II

Pelusium   Lachish

ahpanhes ✗   **Moab**

P
h
i
l
i
s
t
i
a

› c. 630 BC
captured by Psamtek I

◆ 601 / 582 BC
armies of
Nebuchadrezzar II defeated   **E d o m**

◆ 567 BC
Babylonian army defeated,
and Apries killed

R e d   S e a

40°

The Nubian Legacy of the 25th Dynasty

The Napatan kings maintained the tradition of pharaonic rule in Nubia, from which emerged the powerful kingdom of Meroë.

"South of Elephantine the country is inhabited by Ethiopians ... After forty days' journey on land, there is another boat journey of twelve days to reach a great city named Meroë, said to be the capital city of the Ethiopians. The people there worship only Zeus and Dionysus amongst the gods, but hold them in the highest honour. There is an oracle of Zeus there, and they go to war' following its decrees, learning from it both the time and the purpose of their various expeditions."
Herodotos, *The Histories*

After the disasters of 664 BC, Tantamani retreated to Napata and never set foot in Egypt again, although his authority was still recognized in Thebes until the Saite monarchy finally prevailed in 656 BC. There is no evidence that Psamtek I considered Nubia part of his own kingdom, nor that he made any attempt to displace the 25th Dynasty line, although Apries later appointed his own viceroy of Kush, Neshor, who claims to have defeated rebels consorting with Napata. The essential character of the Nubian regime was unaltered, and there is only slight evidence of any residual animosity between the two monarchies arising from this period. At the beginning of the 6th century, however, the Nubian king Anlamani (623–593 BC) assembled an army in Wawat, which was understood by the king of Egypt to be hostile: at Anlamani's death, and the succession of Aspelta (593–568 BC), Psamtek II despatched his own army into Nubia. This expedition, including Carian, Greek and Jewish mercenaries, apparently penetrated as far as Napata itself, perhaps beyond, and its intentions are unknown, and it certainly did not lead to any lasting Egyptian domination of Nubia.

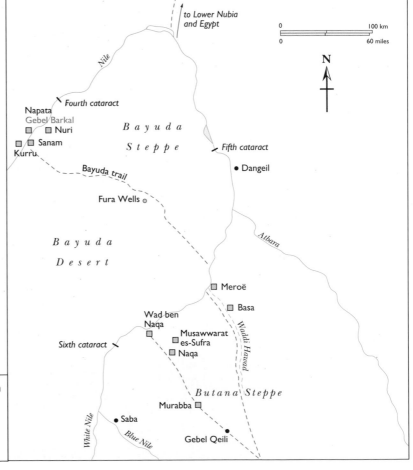

2/The Meroitic kingdom in the 6th century BC

- - - - - trade routes
- □ settlement
- • inscription site

The pyramids at Meroë, decorated inside with pharaonic images and hieroglyphic texts, are obviously a local adaptation of the royal funerary traditions of Egypt.

Taharka moved the royal cemetery of Napata from el-Kurru to Nuri, where there are burials of perhaps twenty kings following Aspelta. Many of these kings are known only from their burials, generally in pyramid-tombs, which exhibit the iconography of pharaonic kingship. Funeral inscriptions suggest that these kings campaigned in pharaonic style against various (largely unknown) African peoples; there is no clear reference to involvement with Egypt. King Nastasen (*c*.335–310 BC) did campaign against a northern enemy who has been identified as Cambyses, but this identification, if accepted, would create enormous chronological difficulties: his enemy could just as easily be an otherwise unknown African chief. Nevertheless, Nastasen is one of a group of kings in succession to Amunneteyerike (*c*.431–405 BC) whose reigns are again part of history: they resided not at Napata but at Meroë, the great southern city of the Nubian kings, known as early as the reign of Aspelta. However, these kings still journeyed to Napata for their coronations, and were probably appointed by the oracle of Amun at Gebel Barkal, just as their 25th Dynasty predecessors had been. Meroë itself stood at the far end of the Bayuda trail from Napata, and its monarchy flourished until the 4th century AD. Nastasen was the last Nubian monarch buried at Nuri, and thereafter even the royal cemetery was moved to the southern city. Although the kings of Meroë stood in direct line of succession from the 25th Dynasty, the increasing physical distance between the power centres of Egypt and those of Nubia was proof of the divergence of the two nations.

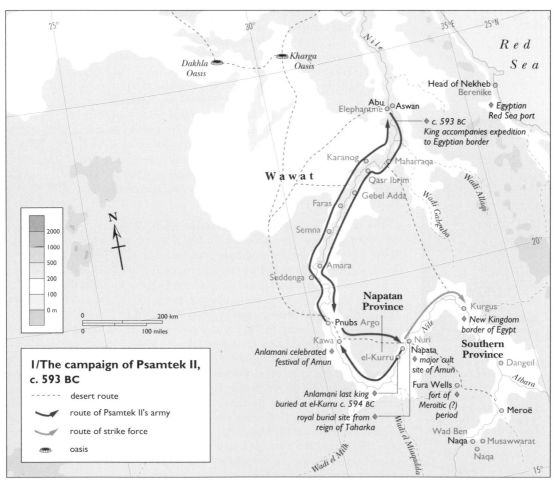

Persia and Egyptian Independence

For two centuries, beginning in 545 BC, the political and economic life of Egypt was dominated by Persian aggression.

"The dual king, Cambyses, came to Sais, and went in person to the temple of Neith. He bowed low before her image as every king has ever done."
Statue inscription of Wadjhorresnet

Amasis' control of Cyprus was ended in 545 BC by the armies of Persia; in the previous year, he had seen Lydia fall to the same armies despite a treaty of mutual protection agreed between pharaoh, the king of Babylon, and Kroisos, king of Lydia; then in 538 BC Babylon also succumbed. Only domestic problems afflicting the Achaemenid dynasty of Persia offered Egypt any respite from this aggression, but Amasis did not doubt that its rulers had made meticulous plans for breaking the power of Egypt as well. Amasis therefore devoted his attention, and the resources of his country, to fostering alliances with Greek city-states opposed to Persian aggrandizement. However, within months of his death in 526 BC, an Egyptian army finally encountered a Persian army, near Pelusium, and was comprehensively defeated. The new pharaoh, Psamtek III, was deposed and later executed for plotting against the Persian king Cambyses; *satraps* (governors) were appointed to administer Egypt as a province of Cambyses' empire.

Cambyses (525–521 BC) and his successor, Darius (521–485 BC), were tolerant and respectful rulers of Egypt despite the brutality of the initial Persian occupation. Cambyses, it was widely rumoured, was the son of an Egyptian princess, and Darius was inclined to spend as much time as possible in the country. Both chose to have themselves represented as pharaohs in time-honoured fashion, rewarding loyal officials and building extensively in traditional Egyptian styles. Even the annual tribute levied from Egypt could be met without undue hardship. Nevertheless, Egypt was a proud kingdom far away from the power base of the Persian kings, and many of her officials and local potentates were unwilling to accept foreign domination. Inspired by fierce Greek resistance to Persia, the Egyptian nobility responded with revolts which blazed frequently throughout the 5th century. Inevitably this provoked harsh repression from the Persian regime, and the reign of Xerxes (485–464 BC) especially was remembered as one of cruel oppression.

In 404 BC after a decade of rebellion, the ruling house of Sais, led by Amyrtaeus, once again established a native monarchy in Egypt. Nevertheless, the following sixty years of wilful independence were overshadowed by the spectre of further Persian invasions. Even the industrious and determined kings of the 30th Dynasty had only limited scope in dealing with foreign issues, and faced enormous domestic problems arising directly from the need to finance war preparations almost constantly: in 374 BC, and then again in 351 BC, an invasion was repelled in the delta itself. However, Takos (*c.* 360–*c.*358 BC) was vilified for the extreme character of his anti-Persian policy, which entailed the impiety of stripping the economic assets of the temples. Takos, therefore, was deposed in favour of Nektanebo II (*c.* 358–342 BC), who acted more cautiously—and more in accordance with tradition—but was consequently unable to finance any effective resistance to an invasion by the armies of Artaxerxes III in 343 BC. Thereafter, for twenty years Egypt, and Kyrene also, were reduced to the status of a satrapy, and the humiliation wrought by this second era of Persian rule would later be remembered with bitterness as an abuse of all that was humane and decent.

Darius the Great is portrayed in a stone relief from the Persian capital at Persepolis. A ruler of considerable wit and ability in administering his vast realm, Darius often adopted traditional pharaonic style when in Egypt, and so won the support, if not the hearts, of the Egyptian court and provinces.

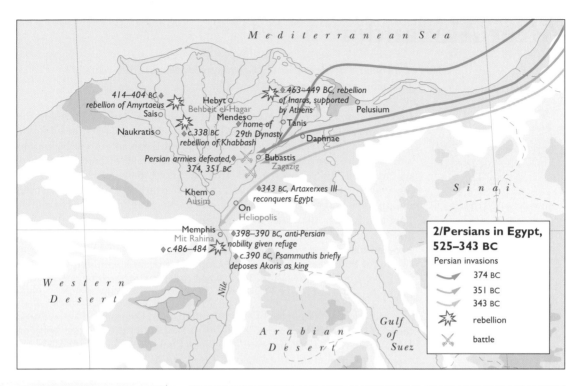

414–404 BC,
rebellion of Amyrtaeus
Sais

Hebyt
Behbeit el-Hagar
Mendes

Naukratis

*c.338 BC
rebellion of Khabbash*

*home of
29th Dynasty*

*463–449 BC, rebellion
of Inaros, supported
by Athens*

Tanis
Daphnae

Pelusium

*Persian armies defeated,
374, 351 BC*

Bubastis
Zagazig

Sinai

Khem
Ausim

*343 BC, Artaxerxes III
reconquers Egypt*

On
Heliopolis

Memphis
Mit Rahina

c.486–484

*398–390 BC, anti-Persian
nobility given refuge*

*c.390 BC, Psammuthis briefly
deposes Akoris as king*

*Western
Desert*

Nile

*Arabian
Desert*

*Gulf
of
Suez*

Mediterranean Sea

2/Persians in Egypt, 525–343 BC

Persian invasions

374 BC
351 BC
343 BC

rebellion

battle

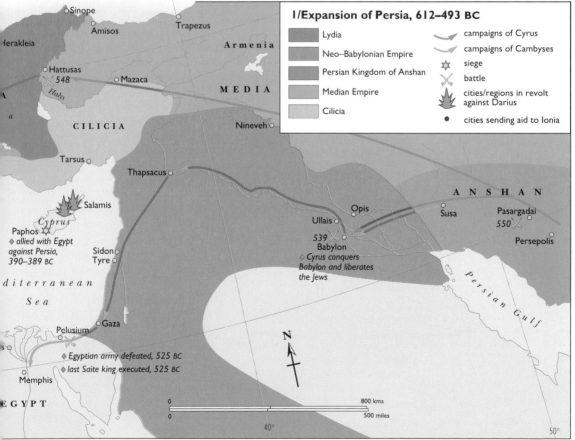

Sinope
Amisos
Trapezus

Herakleia

Armenia

Hattusas
548
Halys

Mazaca

MEDIA

CILICIA

Tarsus

Nineveh

Thapsacus

Salamis
Cyprus

Paphos

*allied with Egypt
against Persia,
390–389 BC*

Sidon
Tyre

Opis

Ullais

539
Babylon
*Cyrus conquers
Babylon and liberates
the Jews*

ANSHAN

Susa

Pasargadai
550

Persepolis

Persian Gulf

*Mediterranean
Sea*

Pelusium
Gaza

Egyptian army defeated, 525 BC

last Saite king executed, 525 BC

Memphis

EGYPT

N

1/Expansion of Persia, 612–493 BC

Lydia

Neo–Babylonian Empire

Persian Kingdom of Anshan

Median Empire

Cilicia

campaigns of Cyrus

campaigns of Cambyses

siege

battle

cities/regions in revolt
against Darius

cities sending aid to Ionia

0   800 kms
0   500 miles

40°   50°

After Alexander

The armies of Alexander the Great heralded nearly 300 years of Ptolemaic rule in Egypt.

"The great horn was broken, and instead of it there came up four conspicuous horns."
The Book of Daniel, 8:8

In 332 BC, the clash of Macedonia with the empire of Darius III brought the armies of Alexander the Great to Egypt. Alexander presented himself to the native population as a liberator: he worshipped Egyptian gods at Heliopolis and Memphis, and approached the celebrated oracle of Siwa, which pronounced him the son of the god Ammon. Like Cambyses before him, the Macedonian warlord was recognized as Egypt's legitimate king; folklore even maintained that he had been fathered by Nectanebo II, the last native pharaoh. In fact, Alexander was destined to be yet another undistinguished absentee ruler of Egypt, but the post-mortem division of his conquests between his warring marshals, empowered Ptolemy, son of Lagus, initially as regent for Philip Arrhidaeus and Alexander II, then as king himself from 305 BC. It fell to this self-styled Ptolemy Soter (saviour) to restore a stable, resident monarchy to Egypt.

The Macedonian kings sought to reinvent Egypt in the political and cultural ferment of the Hellenistic world. Centuries of cultural exchange between Egypt and Greece were distorted into the deliberate Hellenization of crucial aspects of Egyptian life: in particular, Greek-speakers gained the upperhand in government, and the incorporation of European values into Egyptian law would eventually reduce the status of women. Many Egyptians repudiated the jewel in the Ptolemies' crown, the great Hellenistic city of Alexandria, as a symbol of this process, and wilfully referred to it as *Rakote*, the original name of the site in their own language. Nevertheless, by embracing the ancient iconography and formal responsibilities of Egyptian kingship, the new dynasty found widespread acceptance amongst the people and attained some kind of continuity with the past. If Egypt's view of the world became increasingly coloured by Hellenistic politics, her Red Sea fleet and treaties negotiated with the kings of Meroë were tangible proof of continuing political and economic involvement in Africa. Traditional building activities were vigorously pursued: new temples were founded, and others refurbished or

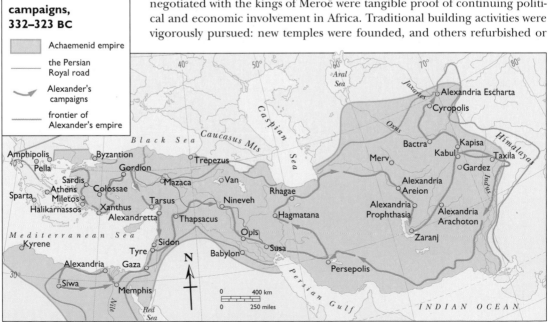

2/Alexander's campaigns, 332–323 BC

Achaemenid empire

the Persian Royal road

Alexander's campaigns

frontier of Alexander's empire

rebuilt with workmanship comparable in quality to the best of the New Kingdom. Amongst their Hellenistic subjects, the Ptolemies sponsored the hybrid Graeco-Egyptian cult of Serapis ahead of traditional Greek gods, whilst the older native cults were imbued with such vitality that they survived long after Egypt was absorbed into the Roman Empire, following the death, after the battle of Actium in 30 BC, of the last Egyptian-speaking ruler, the legendary Cleopatra VII.

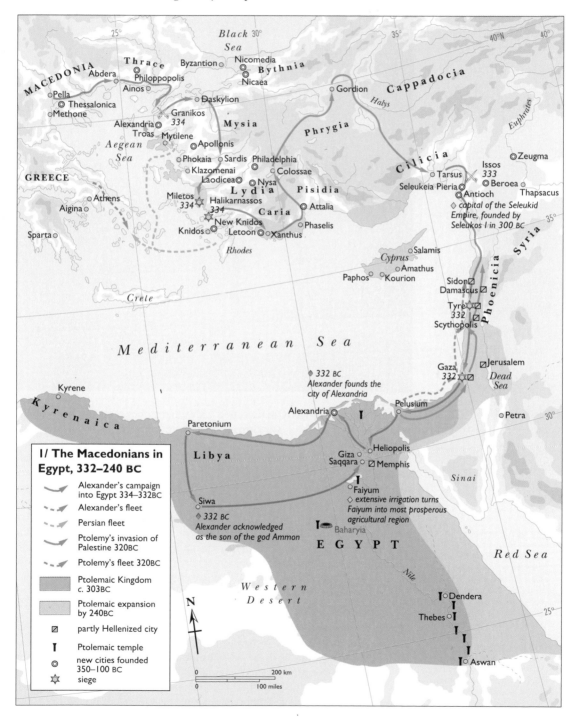

1/ The Macedonians in Egypt, 332–240 BC

- Alexander's campaign into Egypt 334–332 BC
- Alexander's fleet
- Persian fleet
- Ptolemy's invasion of Palestine 320 BC
- Ptolemy's fleet 320 BC
- Ptolemaic Kingdom c. 303 BC
- Ptolemaic expansion by 240 BC
- partly Hellenized city
- Ptolemaic temple
- new cities founded 350–100 BC
- siege

332 BC Alexander founds the city of Alexandria

capital of the Seleukid Empire, founded by Seleukos I in 300 BC

332 BC Alexander acknowledged as the son of the god Ammon

extensive irrigation turns Faiyum into most prosperous agricultural region

0   200 km
0   100 miles

Women in Egypt

Dynastic Egypt was a society in which the structures of government were in the hands of men. Women of high status were enabled by convention to be powerful members of their communities, but still reliant on male support.

"The overseer of the army of pharaoh to the chief lady of the harîm of Amun-Ra, king of the gods, the noble lady, Nodjmet, in life prosperity and health, and in the favour of Amun-Ra, king of the gods. I ask every god and goddess I pass by to give you life and give you health, and to let me see you when I return, and fill my eyes with the sight of you each and every day."
Letter to Thebes from General Piankh in Nubia

Above right: *Limestone pair of the vizîr Rahotep, son of king Khufu, and his wife Nofret. These beautiful statues from their joint tomb at Meidum preserve the details of Nofret's exclusive clothes, collar and wig. The image of a man and woman as equal partners was presented as the ideal basis for adult life in Egyptian society. However, Nofret, although high-born, never held an official career, and depended for her wealth and status on her husband.*

Ancient Egyptian society maintained a distinction between the roles of the sexes. Certain female occupations in wealthy households—such as musician, beautician or hairdresser—may have been considered professions rather than menial tasks. Women might rise to become "overseers" of female servants (but not of men), or attain high-ranking employment in the palace or temple. The wife of a high-ranking official would organize his domestic servants in her capacity as *nebet per*, "lady of the estate". Women were never appointed to administrative office, but they could represent their husband in an official capacity. Wills could be made in their favour, and they had the right to own property or servants; an exceptional few were able to live independently after being well provided for by a wealthy family. Nevertheless, such circumstances were untypical in a society in which unmarried women and widows were considered amongst its most vulnerable members, and in which the lives of most women were dictated by marriage.

Marriage was conducted without ceremony as a simple agreement between the couple. Despite this informality, it was governed by conventions of reasonable behaviour, and the responsiblities of both partners were taken seriously by the couple and their community. Violence or infidelity on either part were generally unacceptable. Divorce could be achieved through agreement or on the basis of blame for reasons such as infidelity or infertility.

In the Late Period—perhaps earlier—women could initiate divorce, and had legal protection regarding the division of property. In addition a prenuptial agreement was sometimes negotiated, in which a woman could list her own possessions on entering marriage, in order to retain them exclusively in a subsequent divorce.

Divorce and death ensured that many married Egyptians became single again at a productive age and so serial monogamy was common. There is also evidence that multiple marriages were tolerated, at least for men, although this probably entailed maintaining wives in separate homes. According to other indications, the head of a household might have sex with servants or other women in the household (provided the relationship was not incestuous); possibly wives with children of their own tolerated such liaisons, which could add children to the household whilst reducing their own risk of pregnancy, with its attendant dangers.

A family with several children was presented as the ideal; children were commended as "the staff of old age", and a typical household supported widowed parents and unmarried siblings. Several families in Deir el-Medina adopted children, but this seems to have been less desirable than pregnancy. Medical papyri include many tests for pregnancy—sensibly based on observations of the skin and breasts of the mother, or urine tests—as well as treatments for infertility. Women usually gave birth squatting in a temporary shelter, in which they might be kept screened for several days afterwards in a period of "purification". This purification may relate to recuperation rather than any pollution taboo; the first room of the house, the most public room adjoining the street, contained a brick altar for the worship of ancestral spirits, and it has been suggested that the birth shelter was sometimes erected here, thus according pride of place in the household to the newly-delivered mother. Certainly, the altar was decorated with images of gods who protected mothers, such as the group of demons known as *Bes*. Children were conventionally nursed for up to three years, and many married women would undergo several pregnancies—with a consequent impact upon their health.

Below: A typical house at Deir el-Medina. The house consisted of two main rooms, with a kitchen, a room perhaps for sleeping, and cellars for storage; the roof and outdoor yards were also used for eating and sleeping, although there are indications of multi-storey buildings in urban areas.

A married woman's life was centred on the maintenance of the home and most of her time was taken up with childcare, cooking and weaving textiles. These activities were socially respectable, and certainly not dismissed as mere "women's work", since they were usually undertaken by male servants on the estates of high-ranking officials. A woman might also support the family by working alongside men in the fields or by taking occasional employment as a servant in another household, whilst tomb-scenes show women at the roadside selling textiles or cakes surplus to their own domestic needs. Few households were self-sufficient, and it must have fallen to women to procure necessary provisions through various forms of economic exchange.

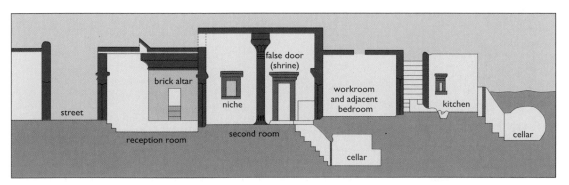

Egyptian Kings and Rulers, 2900–323 BC

Scholars organize the kings of ancient Egypt into thirty dynasties, and then into three "kingdoms" – normally with only one king in Egypt – and 'Intermediate Periods' when the kingship was often divided (the two systems are used together although they are not always compatible). Neither system, however, was employed in Egyptian sources: they listed kings in a continuous sequence beginning with the reign on earth of the sun-god. Nor did the ancient Egyptians employ a system of absolute dating: instead events were dated to one year in the reign of a particular king (regnal dating). Since our information about reigns is far from complete, the dating of Egyptian history is not certain. In this volume reference is often made to regnal dates and dynasties: absolute dates, where given, are the lowest conventionally accepted. For the 1st millenium BC, however, dates derived from reliable Assyrian and Greek sources are often available, and these have been used in the later chapters.

† indicates female king

1ST DYNASTY C. 2900– C. 2770

Narmer
Aha
Djer
Djet
Den
Anedjib
Semerkhet
Qaa

2ND DYNASTY C. 2770– C. 2650

Hetepsekhemwy
Raneb
Nynetjer
Weneg
Sened
Peribsen
Khasekhem(wy)

3RD DYNASTY C. 2650– C. 2575

c. 2650–c. 2630	Zanakht
c. 2630–c. 2610	Netjerykhet (Djoser)
c. 2610–c. 2603	Sekhemkhet
c. 2603–c. 2600	Khaba
c. 2600–c. 2575	Huni

4TH DYNASTY C. 2575– C. 2465

c. 2575–c. 2551	Snofru
c. 2551–c. 2528	Khufu
c. 2528–c. 2520	Djedefra
c. 2520–c. 2494	Khaefra
c. 2490–c. 2472	Menkaura
c. 2472–c. 2465	Shepseskaf

5TH DYNASTY C. 2465– C. 2323

c. 2465–c. 2458	Userkaf
c. 2458–c. 2446	Sahura
c. 2446–c. 2426	Neferirkara
c. 2426–c. 2419	Shepseskara
c. 2419–c. 2416	Neferefra
c. 2416–c. 2392	Nyuserra
c. 2396–c. 2388	Menkauhor
c. 2388–c. 2356	Djedkara Izezi
c. 2356–c. 2323	Unis

6TH DYNASTY c. 2323–c. 2150

c. 2323–c. 2291	Teti
c. 2289–c. 2255	Pepi I
c. 2255–c. 2246	Merenra
c. 2246–c. 2152	Pepy II

8TH DYNASTY c. 2150–c. 2135

c. 2150–c. 2135	*18+ kings, details uncertain*

9TH–10TH DYNASTY c. 2135–c. 1986

c. 2135–c. 1986	*18+ kings at Herakleopolis*

11TH DYNASTY c. 2080–c. 1937

c. 2080–c. 2074	Montjuhotep I
c. 2074–c. 2064	Inyotef I
c. 2064–c. 2015	Inyotef II
c. 2015–c. 2007	Inyotef III
c. 2007–c. 1956	Montjuhotep II
c. 1956–c. 1944	Montjuhotep III
c. 1944–c. 1937	Montjuhotep IV

12TH DYNASTY c. 1937–c. 1759

c. 1937–c. 1908	Amenemhat I
c. 1917–c. 1872	Senusret I
c. 1875–c. 1840	Amenemhat II
c. 1842–c. 1836	Senusret II
c. 1836–c. 1817	Senusret III
c. 1817–c. 1772	Amenemhat III

c. 1772–c. 1763	Amenemhat IV
c. 1763–c. 1759	†Sobknefru

13TH DYNASTY c. 1759–c. 1641

c. 1759–c. 1641	*33+ kings at Memphis*

14TH DYNASTY c. 1641–c. 1606

c. 1641–c. 1606	*76+ kings, details uncertain*

15TH DYNASTY c. 1636–c. 1528

c. 1636–c. 1528	*6 kings at Avaris*

16TH DYNASTY

dates uncertain	*32+ kings, details uncertain*

17TH DYNASTY c. 1641–c. 1539

c. 1641–c. 1539	*15+ kings at Thebes*
Senakhtenra Taa	
c. 1541–c.1539	Kamose

18TH DYNASTY c. 1539–c. 1295

c. 1539–c. 1514	Ahmose
c. 1514–c. 1493	Amenhotep I

c. 1493–c. 1481	Thutmose I
c. 1481–c. 1479	Thutmose II
c. 1479–c. 1425	Thutmose III
c. 1473–c. 1458	†Hatshepsut
c. 1427–c. 1392	Amenhotep II
c. 1392–c. 1382	Thutmose IV
c. 1382–c. 1344	Amenhotep III
c. 1344–c. 1328	Amenhotep IV (Akhenaten)
c. 1330–c. 1327	†Nefernefruaten (Smenkhkara)
c. 1327-c. 1318	Tutankhamun
c. 1318-c. 1315	Itnetjer-Ay
c. 1315–c. 1295	Horemheb

19TH DYNASTY C. 1295–C. 1186

c. 1295–c. 1294	Ramesses I
c. 1294–c. 1279	Seti I
c. 1279–c. 1213	Ramesses II
c. 1213–c. 1203	Merenptah
c. 1203–c. 1200	Amenmesse
c. 1200–c. 1194	Seti II
c. 1194–c. 1188	Siptah
c. 1188–c. 1186	†Tausret

20TH DYNASTY C. 1186–C. 1069

c. 1186–c. 1184	Sethnakht
c. 1184-c. 1153	Ramesses III
c. 1153–c. 1147	Ramesses IV
c. 1147–c. 1143	Ramesses V
c. 1143–c. 1136	Ramesses VI
c. 1136–c. 1129	Ramesses VII
c. 1129–c. 1126	Ramesses VIII
c. 1126–c. 1108	Ramesses IX
c. 1108–c. 1099	Ramesses X
c. 1099–c. 1069	Ramesses XI

21ST DYNASTY C. 1069–C. 945

c. 1069–c. 1043	Smendes
c. 1043–c. 1039	Amenemnesu
c. 1039–c. 991	Psusennes I
c. 993–c. 984	Amenemipet
c. 984–c. 978	Osorkon (the Elder)
c. 978–c. 959	Siamun
c. 959–c. 945	Har-Psusennes II

22ND DYNASTY C. 945–C. 715

Kings at Tanis

c. 945–c. 924	Shoshenk I
c. 924–c. 889	Osorkon I
c. 890–c. 889	Shoshenk II
c. 889–c. 874	Takelot I
c. 874–c. 850	Osorkon II
c. 870–c. 860	Harsiese
c. 850–c. 825	Takelot II
c. 825–c. 773	Shoshenk III
c. 773–c. 767	Pimay
c. 767–c. 730	Shoshenk V
c. 730–c. 715	Osorkon IV

23RD DYNASTY C. 818–C. 715

Kings at Leontopolis

c. 818–c. 793	Pedubast I
c. 804–c. 803	Iuput I
c. 793–c. 787	Shoshenk IV
c. 787–c. 759	Osorkon III
c. 764–c. 757	Takelot III
c. 757–c. 754	Rudamun
c. 754–c. 720	Iuput II
c. 720–c. 715	Shoshenk VI

24TH DYNASTY C. 727–C. 715

Kings at Sais

c. 727–c. 720	Tefnakht
c. 720–c. 715	Bakenrenef

25TH DYNASTY C. 780–656

Kings at Napata

c. 780–c. 760	Alara
c. 760–c.747	Kashta
c. 747–c.716	Piy
c. 716–c.702	Shabako
c. 702–c.690	Shabatka
c. 690–664	Taharka
664–656	Tantamani

26TH DYNASTY C. 672–525

c. 672–664	Neko I
664–610	Psamtek I
610–595	Neko II
595–589	Psamtek II
589–570	Apries
570–526	Amasis
526–525	Psamtek III

27TH DYNASTY 525–404

Persian rulers of Egypt

525–521	Cambyses
521–485	Darius I
485–464	Xerxes
464–423	Artaxerxes
423–404	Darius II

28TH DYNASTY C. 404–C. 397

c. 404–c. 397	Amyrtaeus

29TH DYNASTY C. 397–C. 378

c. 397–c. 391	Nepherites I
c. 391–c. 378	Akoris
c. 390	Psammuthis
c. 378	Nepherites II

30TH DYNASTY C. 378–337

c. 378–c. 360	Nectanebo I
c. 360–c. 358	Takos
358–342	Nectanebo II
342–337	Ochus

31ST DYNASTY 340–323

Persian rulers of Egypt

340–337	Artaxerxes III
337–335	Arses
335–332	Darius III
332–323	Alexander of Macedon

Further Reading

ANCIENT WRITERS

Herodotus, *The Histories*, tr. A. de Sélincourt (rev. ed.), Penguin Classics, 1972

Waddell, W.G., *Manetho*, Loeb Classical Library, 1940

Useful selections of ancient texts and translations can be found in the following:

Lichtheim, M.A., *Ancient Egyptian Literature, A Book of Readings*, (3 vol.), California University Press, 1973—1980

— *Ancient Egypt Autobiographies, Chiefly of the Old and Middle Kingdoms*, Orbis Biblicus et Orientalis 84, 1988

Parkinson, R., *Voices from Ancient Egypt*, Thames and Hudson, 1991

Pritchard, J.B., (ed), *Ancient Near Eastern Texts Relating to the Old Testament*, (rev. ed.) Princeton University Press, 1974

Wente, E.F., *Late Ramesside Letters*, Studies in Ancient Oriental Civilisation 33, 1967

MODERN SOURCES

The general reader is not well served by books on Ancient Egypt: many current volumes are simply out-of-copyright reprints, whilst others rehash the standard, but often outdated views set out in *The Cambridge Ancient History*. The situation is, however, improving and the following is a selective list of books and articles which should be readily available; those marked * are dated but still useful. Other references, including regional studies, can be found in the bibliographies of these works.

*Adams, W.Y., *Nubia, Corridor to Africa*, Allen Lane, 1977

Baines, J.R., & Malek, J., *Atlas of Ancient Egypt*, Phaidon, 1980

Bierbrier, M., *Tomb–Builders of the Pharaohs*, Colonnade, 1982

Butzer, K.W., *Early Hydraulic Civilisation in Egypt, A Study in Cultural Ecology*, Chicago University Press, 1976

Davies, W.V., *Egyptian Hieroglyphs*, British Museum Press, 1987

Davies, W.V., (ed), *Egypt and Africa, Nubia from Prehistory to Islam*, British Museum Press, 1991

Dodson, A.M., *Monarchs of the Nile*, Rubicon, 1995

* Edwards, I.E.S., *The Pyramids of Egypt*, (rev. ed.), Penguin, 1993

Ellis, W.M., *Ptolemy of Egypt*, Routledge 1994

Gurney, O.R., *The Hittites*, (rev. ed.), Penguin, 1990

Hoffman, M.A., *Egypt Before the Pharaohs, The Prehistoric Foundations of Egyptian Civilisation*, Routledge & Kegan Paul 1979

Hornung, E., *Valley of the Kings*, Timken 1990

* Kees, H., *Ancient Egypt, A Cultural Topography*, Chicago University Press, 1961

Kemp, B.J., *Ancient Egypt, Anatomy of a Civilization*, Routledge, 1991

Kitchen, K.A., *Pharaoh Triumphant, The Life and Times of Ramesses II King of Egypt*, Aris & Phillips, 1982

— *The Third Intermediate Period in Egypt (1100—650 BC)*, (rev. ed), Aris & Phillips, 1986

Leahy, M.A. (ed.), *Libya and Egypt c.1300—750 BC*, School of Oriental & African Studies, 1990

Moran, W.L., *The Amarna Letters*, Cambridge University Press, 1992

O'Connor, D., "The Toponyms of Nubia and Contiguous Regions in the New Kingdom", in *Cambridge History of Africa*, 1982, pp. 925—940

— "The Location of Irem", in *Journal of Egyptian Archaeology 73*, 1987, pp. 99—136

Quirke, S.J., & Spencer, A.J., *The British Museum Book of Ancient Egypt*, British Museum Press, 1992

Redford, D.B., *Egypt, Canaan and Israel in Ancient Times*, Princeton University Press 1992

Robins, G., *Women in Ancient Egypt*, British Museum Press, 1994

Romer, J., *Valley of the Kings*, Michael O'Mara, 1981

— *Ancient Lives*, Weidenfeld & Nicholson, 1984

Sandars, N., *The Sea Peoples, Warriors of the Eastern Mediterranean*, (rev. ed.), Thames & Hudson, 1985

Shaw, I.M.E., *Egyptian Warfare and Weapons*, Shire, 1991

Shaw, I.M.E., & Nicholson, P.T., *British Museum Dictionary of Ancient Egypt*, British Museum Press, 1995

Spencer, A.J., *Early Egypt, The Rise of Civilisation in the Nile Valley*, British Museum Press 1993

Taylor, J.H., *Egypt and Nubia*, British Museum Press, 1991

Trigger, B.G., *Nubia Under the Pharaohs*, Thames & Hudson, 1976

—*Early Civilisations, Ancient Egypt in Context*, American University in Cairo Press, 1993

Trigger, B.G., Kemp, B.G., O'Connor, D., & Lloyd, A.B., *Ancient Egypt, A Social History*, Cambridge University Press, 1983

Uphill, E.P., *Egyptian Towns and Cities*, Shire, 1988

Index

R
911.32
M279

108877

Acknowledgements

Picture Credits

LINCOLN CHRISTIAN COLLEGE AND SEMINARY

Front Cover

(clockwise from top left)

Werner Forman Archive, (The Egyptian Museum, Cairo): Statues of Prince Rahotep and his wife Nofret

Werner Forman Archive: The Giza Sphinx with the pyramid of Khufu in the background

Werner Forman Archive, (Egyptian Museum, Berlin): The crowned head of Nefertiti

Werner Forman Archive, The Egyptian Museum, Cairo): Wooden statue of Ka–Aper

Werner Forman Archive: The sacred lake at Karnak

Werner Forman Archive, (Dr. E. Strouhal): A detail of a painting on stucco in the tomb of Sennedjem

Werner Forman Archive: The colossal statue of the god Horus at the entrance to the temple of Horus, Edfu

Werner Forman Archive: A detail of a wall painting in the tomb of Queen Nefertari

Internal

Author's Collection: 32, 35, 36, 37, 60, 61, 62, 85, 86, 88, 91, 94, 109t, 115, 116, 117, 121

Michael Holford: 28, 57, 74, 78, 80

Robert Morkot: 26, 38, 39, 41, 42, 44, 46, 53, 66, 77, 96,

David Rohl: 55, 104, 109b, 111, 112, 113

Sonia Halliday Photographs: 82 (Hassia); 70 (Laura Lushington); 18, 126 (T.C. Rising);

Werner Forman Archive: 13b, 15, 65, 82, 89, 125; 13t (Ashmolean Museum, Oxford); 21, 118, 123 (British Museum, London); 17 (Cheops Barque Museum); 23, 59, 130 (The Egyptian Museum, Cairo); 25 (The Louvre Museum, Paris)

FOR SWANSTON PUBLISHING LIMITED

Concept:
Malcolm Swanston

Editorial and Map Research:
Stephen Haddelsey
Elizabeth Wyse

Illustration:
Ralph Orme

Cartography:
Andrea Fairbrass
Peter Gamble
Elsa Gibert
Kevin Panton

Typesetting:
Andrea Fairbrass
Charlotte Taylor

Picture Research:
Stephen Haddelsey
Charlotte Taylor

Production:
Andrea Fairbrass
Barry Haslam

Separations:
Central Systems, Nottingham.

Index:
Jean Cox
Barry Haslam